SEARCHING FOR A CORPORATE SAVIOR

Searching for a Corporate Savior

The Irrational Quest for Charismatic CEOs

Rakesh Khurana

PRINCETON UNIVERSITY PRESS

PRINCETON AND OXFORD

Copyright © 2002 by Princeton University Press

Published by Princeton University Press, 41 William Street, Princeton, New Jersey 08540

In the United Kingdom: Princeton University Press, 3 Market Place, Woodstock, Oxfordshire OX20 1SY

All Rights Reserved

Library of Congress Cataloging-in-Publication Data

Khurana, Rakesh, 1967–

Searching for a corporate savior : the irrational quest for charismatic CEOs / Rakesh Khurana.

p. cm.

Includes bibliographical references and index.

ISBN 0-691-07437-2 (alk. paper)

1. Executives—Recruiting.   2. Chief executive officers.   3. Executive succession.   I. Title.

HF5549.5.R44 K48   2002

658.4'07111 — dc21   2002070379

British Library Cataloging-in-Publication Data available

This book has been composed in Goudy Typefaces

Printed on acid free paper. ⊗

www.pupress.princeton.edu

Printed in the United States of America

10 9 8 7 6 5 4 3 2 1

For Stephanie

CONTENTS

PREFACE

THIS BOOK is about the basic mechanics of the CEO labor market, how it has changed in the past twenty years, how it differs from prevailing economic and sociological accounts of it, and whether it is successful in placing the best candidates in the available jobs. It pays particular attention to the growing tendency of boards of directors to ignore candidates inside their own firms and to hire CEOs from outside. I argue that this trend has emerged not because of the intrinsic merits of the "external market" or its efficacy in identifying better matches for the CEO position, but rather because of the rise of investor capitalism and changing cultural conceptions of the role of the CEO. Drawing on a combination of fieldwork and quantitative evidence, I attempt to demonstrate how the interplay of various structural and cultural factors at work in the external CEO market closes it off from genuine competition, to the detriment of large American corporations and their many constituents.

The choice of organizational leaders for large, publicly traded corporations has significant impact, direct and indirect, on the lives of millions of Americans. From the stock market, where our college and retirement funds are invested in the firms these executives control, to the office cubicle or factory floor, where ordinary citizens earn their livelihoods day by day, we are all in some way affected by the health and future prospects of corporations. And because the choice of corporate leaders, particularly at the level of CEO, can have a significant impact on both the real and the perceived prospects of firms (often, as I argue, more on the perceived than on the real, although in our current system of investor capitalism perceptions easily and quickly become dollar-

and-cents realities), the processes and structures governing CEO selection deserve serious study.

Many corporate decision-making processes, especially at the level of the board of directors, are shrouded in mystery for observers both inside and outside the corporation. Insiders are often in the dark because their own individual positions in the hierarchy provide only a local perspective, rarely allowing an unobstructed view of the totality of forces affecting senior management's or the board of directors' decisions. Outsiders, for their part, see only the outcomes of these decisions and therefore must often rely on speculations and ex-post rationalizations in their attempts to understand them. The selection of a new CEO—a process sometimes described as only slightly less mysterious than the election of a new pope—certainly falls into the category of corporate decisions made well outside the view of most interested parties. (Even my fellow organizational scholars, owing to the difficulty of gaining access to business elites, have produced surprisingly little research on this topic.) The opacity of such decision-making processes, in turn, raises questions about both the efficacy and, equally important, the legitimacy of the decisions to which they lead.

The questions that I raise about the efficacy of the external CEO selection process revolve around both its closed nature—that is, its way of restricting competition for the CEO position to a handful of individuals who are valued for their social attributes rather than for their possession of relevant skills and experience—and its tendency to select a certain kind of individual for the job. Because external CEO searches are generally undertaken by companies in the throes of real or perceived crisis, boards of directors and various corporate constituents hope that the outsider CEO will be their savior. Because single-handedly saving a troubled corporation is no ordinary job, boards of directors bent on finding a corporate messiah are not much interested in ordinary qualifications (e.g., knowledge of their company or relevant industry or functional background). Rather, the kind of candidate considered qualified for the role of corporate savior is one who is thought to possess "charisma."

Enron Corporation was not seen as a troubled company when its board of directors hired Jeffrey Skilling in December 2000 to be the company's new CEO. Nor was Skilling, by this point, any longer an outsider, having left the prestigious consulting firm McKinsey & Co. in

1990 for the first of several management posts at Enron. Yet because Skilling's style of "leadership" was completely typical of what boards of directors at struggling companies seek in an outsider CEO today, his brief career as a CEO offers not merely a dramatic but also an instructive illustration of the perils of charismatic corporate leadership.

As we now know, Jeffrey Skilling's skills as a New Economy strategist were considerably overrated, and his ability—or willingness—to impose discipline and accountability on himself and his organization, nonexistent. What Skilling clearly excelled at was motivating subordinates to take risks and "think outside the box," and turning stock market analysts and investors into devotees of the cult of Enron. In the conception of the CEO's role that lies at the heart of the external CEO market today, the ability to inspire and motivate employees and instill confidence in analysts and investors is paramount. Strategic, political, and other merely managerial skills are discounted as pedestrian and boring, or simply ignored as irrelevant. Until he became a pariah less than a year after the Enron board hired him, Jeffrey Skilling was a paragon. Today we stand at a crossroads where, it would seem, many corporations would do well to reconsider their models of leadership and ways of choosing leaders.

Obviously, the crisis that the Enron debacle and the many less spectacular, though no less important corporate scandals of recent times are now posing for American capitalism has to do with much more than just conceptions of leadership and the character (or sometimes lack thereof) of today's CEOs. Yet to the extent that the hidden nature of the external CEO selection process raises questions not just about its efficacy but also about its legitimacy, shining a light into this obscure corner of the American corporate system can help address some of the larger questions that now demand answers.

At the dawn of the twenty-first century, there is no question that corporations and markets have generally contributed to the well-being of our society. Not since the Great Depression of the 1930s, however, has the legitimacy of the corporation and of markets come under greater scrutiny than it is facing in America today. After the champagne days of the 1990s, phenomena such as the bursting of the dot-com bubble, skyrocketing pay and special benefits for CEOs, the implosion of Enron, and the compromising behavior of many of those we have counted on to safeguard the integrity of our economic system—directors, analysts, bankers, regulators, accountants, lawyers—are now raising legitimate questions about whether the modern corporation is an institution constructed to contribute to the greater good or, instead, an elaborate structure for enabling a handful of well-connected insiders to benefit at the expense of the average person. As we now have no reason not to understand, any corporate process—especially one as important as that by which corporations choose their leaders—that creates even a slight impression of an insiders' game ultimately weakens our entire system. Unfortunately, this is exactly the picture that emerges from a close examination of the closed process of external CEO succession.

My account of the emergence and functioning of the external CEO market can be summarized as follows. In the past twenty years, institutional investors have become far more likely to intervene in companies' management, in part because they now own so many shares that they find it difficult to sell them when a company underperforms. They have pressured boards of directors to make CEOs more accountable, thereby disrupting the historically cozy relationship between CEOs and boards. When a company performs badly, institutional investors are likely to demand that the CEO resign and be replaced by someone who is from outside the firm and thus more likely, they believe, to be unencumbered by organizational history. Boards wish to find a new CEO with as much star power as possible because a high-profile, high-status appointment is almost certain to inspire public confidence in the company and immediately boost share prices. The external CEO search process that ensues is characterized by unusual secrecy; anxious attention to the expectations of outsiders such as analysts, investors, and the business press; a focus on an extremely small number of candidates (people who are already high-profile leaders); and an emphasis on the elusive, culturally based qualities of "leadership" and "charisma" at the expense of concrete knowledge of a firm and its problems. This process not only frequently fails to hire the best people available for the jobs at hand but also tends to produce leaders with almost identical social, cultural, and demographic characteristics.

Furthermore, because investors put so much faith in the ability of a "star" CEO to solve a firm's problems, boards pay such CEOs exorbitantly to entice them to take the job while also saddling them with unrealistic expectations. These expectations are formed, in part, by a fervent though erroneous belief that the quality of the CEO is the primary determinant of firm performance—and therefore that it is realistic to hope that a high-powered CEO can be a corporate savior. When CEOs fail to meet such extravagant expectations, boards are quick to remove them and to start anew the same sort of search. Recourse to the external CEO market, in short, too often undermines a firm's stability, emphasizes short-term share-price increases at the expense of long-term strategy, and undermines the loyalty of the senior managers who are the most promising internal candidates. It also raises valid questions, as I have just suggested, about the legitimacy of corporate leadership and decision-making from the point of view of American society as a whole.

The means by which I present and analyze the external CEO market in this book can be summarized as follows: First, I examine the structural character of this market, the cultural context within which it operates, and the interaction between the two. I then describe the behaviors and beliefs of the three main sets of actors in the market—buyers, sellers, and intermediaries—and how these differ from those of actors in the more conventional kind of market that the external CEO labor market is often (erroneously) assumed to be. Along the way, I reconsider and challenge many of the assumptions that undergird, rationalize, justify, and reproduce the contemporary external CEO succession process.

Outline of the Book

Owing to the secrecy surrounding the external CEO search process, relatively few readers of this book will be familiar with it, while those who are may experience a salutary shock of recognition from seeing it laid out in concrete detail from start to finish. Thus I begin the book, in chapter 1, with a case study of a recent CEO succession at a large financial services firm. Assembled through a combination of first-hand interviews, previous cases about the organization, and secondary materials such as press accounts, the case introduces the basic process of external CEO succession, its principal protagonists, and the factors driving their behavior and decision-making processes. Not every external CEO succession exactly resembles this particular case, for every episode is in many ways unique. Yet besides furnishing a concrete enactment of the underlying dynamics of most external successions, the case provides a factual anchor for the theoretical arguments and conceptual frameworks that I offer in the remainder of the book, and particularly in chapters 2 and 3.

In chapter 2, I examine the structural characteristics of the external CEO market and find it to be characterized by three defining features: small numbers of buyers and sellers, high risk to both, and concern on the part of both these participants in the market and various onlookers as to its very legitimacy. These structural features, I argue, both distinguish the external CEO market from other executive labor markets and define it as a *closed* market. In this chapter, I also introduce my basic theoretical framework for studying the external CEO market, which is the concept of this market as a socially constructed institution.

Having outlined the fundamental structural characteristics of the external CEO market, I then turn in chapter 3 to an account of the basic cultural factors that interact with the structural ones to give rise to this market and determine its workings. I do this by means of an historical account of the transition (beginning in the early 1980s) from the system of managerial capitalism to our present system of investor capitalism, and of the implications that this fundamental change had for conceptions of the CEO and his role. In short, I argue that it was this historic shift in the relationship between owners and managers in American capitalism (accompanied by, among other things, a new quasi-religious conception of business, an historic expansion of the number of Americans investing in the stock market, and the resulting emergence of the contemporary business press) that gave rise to the figure of the charismatic CEO, brought into the company from the outside, who now dominates the external CEO market.

Chapters 1 through 3 thus form the background to the more detailed examination of the external CEO search process itself that I undertake in chapters 4 through 6. In these later chapters, I consider, in turn, the role of the board of directors in external CEO search, the role of the executive search firm, and the nature of the interaction between directors and candidates that results in the selection of the new CEO. In every one of these cases, I challenge prevailing views that conceive the external CEO market in the way that mainstream economists look at all markets—that is, as systems of exchange in which autonomous individuals act rationally in pursuit of their own interests, without any relation to social and cultural institutions and beliefs. On the contrary, I argue, what are often the apparently *irrational* roles and behavior of these actors in the external CEO market can be accounted for only by understanding its social and cultural dimensions.

In chapters 4 and 6 (focusing on boards of directors and the late-stage interactions between directors and candidates, respectively), I show how the initial narrowing of the candidate pool, and then the selection of the winning contestant, both depend on processes that put socially defined attributes ahead of particular skills and experience. In chapter 5, I show how the essential function of the executive search firm is not to bring buyers and sellers together in the manner of a market broker, but rather to facilitate the social dimensions of the external CEO search process while simultaneously helping to disguise them—thus helping the search to achieve legitimacy in the eyes of interested observers. Chapter 6 also details how the charismatic succession process that external CEO search becomes, concludes with the handing of extraordinary rewards and power, along with equally extraordinary expectations, to the winning candidate, thus setting the stage for future instability and disappointment.

Finally, in chapter 7, I consider the implications of the external CEO search and succession process, with all of its manifest flaws, both for corporations themselves and for American society in general. After detailing the many harmful effects of this process for all concerned, I conclude the chapter and the book by offering ideas about how a rethinking of our society's prevailing ideas about two of the major subjects I have treated in this book—the nature of leadership and the nature of markets—could help pry open the closed market in which external CEO search now takes place, to the benefit of both corporations and society.

Methodology and Acknowledgments

This project began as my 1998 dissertation, *The Changing of the Guard: Causes, Process, and Consequences of CEO Turnover*. In the dissertation I was concerned with the antecedents, process, and consequences of CEO turnover in large corporations. Some unexpected findings in this thesis led me to the larger problem of understanding the CEO labor market as a general phenomenon. Following my graduation I expanded the field research and enlarged the entire project into a broad look at the CEO labor market.

The foundation of this project was a database of all the CEO turnovers in the 850 largest American corporations from 1978–96 (since expanded to 1999 for some sub-samples). The dataset led to many important insights, and several unanticipated findings signaled that both the current literature and my own understanding of the topic were still limited. The findings predicted by the economic perspectives of agency theory, the efficient-market hypothesis, and transaction-cost theory, and by the sociological perspective on managerial capitalism that informed much of my analyses of the data, were not always evident. There were too many anomalies. I then expanded the project to include a significant field research component. My time in the field with directors, executive search firms, and CEOs forced me toward a theory that could reconcile the statistical evidence with the day-to-day discontinuities of the reality of the CEO labor market. The subjects of these interviews, most of which were conducted between 1997 and early 2001, included people who served as directors, search consultants, and CEOs. I also spent a great deal of time at the executive search firms' offices, having an opportunity to observe actual searches in progress and get a feel for the people. I am grateful to Sally Laroche, Kate Bryant, John Hawkins, and Judy Smith for helping me in gaining access to some very busy people. Most of my interviewees have asked that certain quotes remain unattributed or that their firms remain disguised. They know who they are, and I thank them for their candid assessments as well as their time (and patience) in explaining a complex process to a novice. Because the CEO labor market is rapidly evolving, I should note, some of the people I interviewed have changed affiliations or retired. In keeping with convention, when I do identify interviewees I use the titles and affiliations of these individuals at the time they were interviewed. The methodology and description used to collect both the field and quantitative data are described in greater detail in the appendix.

Since many of the themes of the book emerged from my field data and observations, my first debts are to those who got me into the field. Peter Marsden and Jay Lorsch pushed me to get out and talk to the people actually making the CEO succession decisions. Despite my howls and protests that this was going to set me back at least six months from my plan to finish the Ph.D. program, both of them were unyielding. They pushed, shoved, and cajoled me to do something other than report some statistics (albeit, they conceded, some interesting statistics) and really open the black box of CEO succession. Once I was in the field, Nitin Nohria and Aage Sørensen (now deceased) pushed me into collecting additional statistical data to test what I was finding there. Again despite my howling and moaning that I didn't have the financial resources to collect the data and that this would set me back another six months, I am (in hindsight) very grateful for their advice. While on sabbatical, Nitin gave me unfettered access to his research assistants, Qian Sun and Chris Allen, to assist me in the data collection effort. Aage gave me unfettered access to his ideas on which models to run.

Beyond these general debts, I have some specific ones for certain ideas presented in the book. These ideas are not mine, but were revealed to me in hours of conversation and numerous e-mails with my colleagues and dissertation committee members. I am sure I will forget to acknowledge some important people and I wish to apologize to them in advance.

I owe most to Aage Sørensen, who passed away in the early spring of 2001. As my dissertation chair, my intellectual mentor, and a renowned labor market sociologist, he never ceased to amaze me. His rigorous criticism and intellectual honesty—sometimes frustrating to me, but always well intended—gave form to the theory described in the book. Aage also first encouraged me to publish the dissertation research as a book rather than a series of articles. Coming from a person whose own career was built on a series of journal articles, this suggestion was surprising and much appreciated. Aage stressed the relevance of social closure for my research. He also pushed me to read both volumes of Weber's *Economy and Society*, saying that I should read this work as a religious zealot would read the Bible. I will always be grateful for this advice, and I return to the text continuously. While I have qualms about some of Weber's ideas, his contributions to my understanding of society, comparative methods, charisma, bureaucracy, and the differences between status, class, and party, are etched in my mind and continuously shape my thinking. *Economy and Society* inspired more ideas in this book than any other past sociological work and I have borrowed extensively from it.

In addition to Weber, there are several important thinkers whose writings inspired many of the ideas in this book. First, Georg Simmel, who early in the twentieth century originated what is still some of the best theory available on how social groups work. In particular, Simmel's essays on the social roles of third parties, secret societies, and the stranger have been critical to my interpretations of the role of executive search firms and outsider CEOs. Mark Granovetter's seminal work on weak ties, social embeddedness, and the social construction of markets is one of the two pillars upon which the theory presented in chapter 2 rests. Viviana Zelizer's on the relationship between culture and markets is the second. In particular, Zelizer's work on how social values shape the strategies of market participants, and her concept of legitimate markets, inspired me to think about how role expectations of CEOs influence the trajectory of the CEO labor market and the succession process. The influence of Ronald Burt's incisive work on structural holes, especially his ideas about information flow and social networks, is evident in my description of the CEO labor market. Robert Merton's comments about the effects of marginal status on individual behavior and social roles inspired my discussion of executive search firms.

After Aage Sørensen passed away, Nitin Nohria (Harvard) and Misiek Piskorski (Stanford) picked up the conversation and helped me continue to elaborate on the core idea of social closure. Peter Marsden inspired me to think about networks in terms of theory, not method. His detailed comments on a paper written for his class on network methodology inspired the distinction between general and fine-grained information. Peter also suggested using alternative centrality measures as a way to measure how different types of information flow through strong-versus weak-tie networks—a conceptual and methodological break-through for me on how to write papers that combined my field research with the statistical data.

My discussion of boards of directors was strongly influenced by discussions with Michael Useem, Rosabeth Moss Kanter, and Ezra Zuckerman. Mike's books *The Inner Circle* and *Executive Defense* were instrumental in helping me think through the ideas of chapter 3. My discussions with Rosabeth and her own interest in the topics of corporate structures and culture inspired me to think through how external forces affect the processes of cohesion. Ezra Zuckerman's comments and suggestions on the social matching process and its similarities to and differences from categorical assignment were also critical.

Although the study of third parties and intermediaries is a fashionable trend in sociology today, my thoughts on intermediaries were deeply influenced by discussions with Joel Podolny and Ezra Zuckerman—two individuals who I think are and have been at the forefront of this important topic.

A number of people have read the book manuscript or pieces of it. Over the years, colleagues at both Harvard and MIT as well as some outside of Cambridge have commented on this work: Tom Kochan, Paul Osterman, John Van Mannen, Eleanor Westney, Rick Locke, Lotte Bailyn, Deborah Ancona, Bob Gibbons, Roberto Fernandez, Jesper Sørensen, Scott Stern, Scott Shane, Fiona Murray, Mark Mizruchi, Gerald David, Olav Sorenson, Richard Tedlow, Chris Winship, Misiek Piskorski, Linda Hill, Herminia Ibarra, Jack Gabarro, Mike Beer, Monica Higgins, Leslie Perlow, Robin Ely, Tiziana Casciaro, Joshua Margolis, David Thomas, Brian Hall, George Baker, Michael Jensen, Orlando Patterson, Jose Luis Alvarez, Damon Phillips, Jeff Sonnenfeld, Don Hambrick, Heather Haveman, John Kotter, Sandy Green, Michael Beers, Brooke Harrington, Diego Gambetta, Scott Snook, Jim Baron, Charles Smith, Warren Bennis, Hugo Utherhoven, Tom Piper, Krishna Palepu, Mike Tushman, William Ocasio, Ranjay Gulati, Brian Uzzi, and Julio Rotemberg all provided suggestions, advice, and encouragement.

I appreciate the patience, thoughtfulness, and comments of all my friends in Harvard's sociology department who have heard me present several papers related to this research. I also thank business school colleagues at the University of Chicago, Wharton, Yale University, MIT, and Stanford, and the sociology departments at Harvard and Columbia for allowing me to present material.

Special thanks go to Harvard Business School (where I finished the manuscript) and MIT's Sloan School of Management (where I began it). Dean Kim Clark of Harvard and Dean Richard Schmalansee of Sloan were very supportive of this project, providing both financial support and encouragement.

I would like to thank the staff of Princeton University Press. Ian Malcolm has been a superb individual to work with in every capacity. Had it not been for his initiative, this book would not exist. During the entire process of turning the book from proposal to finished product, Ian called me regularly, took trips up to Cambridge, and gave me invaluable guidance. Tim Sullivan skillfully copyedited the manuscript, and Maura Roessner adroitly coordinated the production process.

Daniel Penrice provided multifaceted help during the project. In addition to being one of the most decent human beings I have ever known, Dan worked closely with me as an editor, interlocutor, adviser, sometime therapist, and friend. His ability to probe ideas for soft spots, identify gaps in the logic, keep me focused on the overall shape and direction of the argument, and turn occasionally foggy abstractions into clear prose (meanwhile helping me constructively channel my frustrations with the revision process) contributed greatly to the coherence and readability of the book. I am so grateful to him.

I would like to thank my family: my parents, Ram and Anjana Khurana, for their daily phone calls and unconditional love; my brothers, Pradeep and Hareesh, for being sources of comic relief whose constant reminders of my childhood and teenage antics are a check on my ego; and my extended family, Trent, Rita, and Marisa, for their emotional and babysitting support.

And, finally, my dearest ones—Stephanie, Sonia, Nalini, and Jai. My wife Stephanie, a CEO (albeit of a smaller company that has beat the dot-com odds), never failed to provide a reality check on what I was saying. She is a constant source of inspiration and insight. My children, Sonia, Nalini, and Jai make everything worthwhile. Everything I do, I do for all of you.

SEARCHING FOR A CORPORATE SAVIOR

CHAPTER 1

"EVERYONE KNEW HE WAS BRILLIANT":
THE WOOING OF JAMIE DIMON

In 1999, Chicago's Bank One Corporation was headed for trouble. Many investors and board members believed that they knew the precise source of the problem: Bank One's CEO, John McCoy.

Although Bank One could trace its roots back to 1868, it was under McCoy's stewardship that it had grown into a modern colossus. Appointed CEO in 1984, McCoy was one of the first bankers to take advantage of loosening restrictions on interstate banking. Beginning in 1986, Bank One purchased banks throughout the Midwest and Southwest. Within a decade, it had made over one hundred acquisitions, propelling it from the thirty-seventh largest bank in the nation to the fourth. Over the same period, Bank One's stock price had increased 500 percent and John McCoy had become one of the nation's most profiled bankers.[1]

In 1999, however, after completing its purchase of First Chicago NBD—its largest acquisition to date—Bank One began to falter; its stock price started a steep descent in an environment in which most financial stocks were booming. The First Chicago acquisition was not supposed to have turned out this way. The $19 billion merger had been intended to create an earnings powerhouse with branches stretching across Florida, the Midwest, and the Southwest, and total assets exceeding $260 billion.[2] Integrating First Chicago, however, had turned out to be more difficult than anyone at Bank One had expected. Operationally, there were a number of overlapping services that needed to

I

be eliminated and disparate information systems that needed to be integrated. Culturally, Bank One's decentralized, entrepreneurial culture clashed with First Chicago's more conservative style. Politically, jockeying for position was endemic and old loyalties not easily disentangled.

Meanwhile, in the opinions of many investors and board members, John McCoy seemed to have lost interest in running Bank One. This view may have simply represented a new interpretation of a management style for which McCoy had long been known and even celebrated. Once one of the country's most highly regarded banking executives, McCoy had a leadership style that had been immortalized in a case taught in the Harvard Business School's required General Management course.[3] His trademark as a leader was his trust in people. In particular, McCoy exhibited this characteristic when integrating acquisitions, trusting managers at the banks he acquired to run their businesses effectively in what Bank One referred to as its "Uncommon Partnership" philosophy. Moreover, McCoy was known for his ability to win the trust of others—a talent he exercised while on the road as often as three days out of five, meeting with employees and customers.

Only as Bank One began to stumble in the wake of the First Chicago acquisition did these features of McCoy's management style begin to be labeled as a problem. As the company's performance deteriorated through 1999, investors and directors began to characterize the CEO's behavior as indifferent and aloof.[4] Many of the company's problems were caused by Bank One's credit card operation, which was experiencing severe pricing and customer-retention problems that seemed to have materialized out of nowhere. Yet even as the national press chronicled an active customer revolt against Bank One's poor customer service that summer, McCoy appeared unconcerned. He drew criticism when he refused to cancel a European vacation after delivering a surprise earnings warning to investors in August. When he traveled to Dallas in mid-September for the Senior PGA Tour—which Bank One was sponsoring, and which several Bank One customers were attending—the Chicago press had a field day, and First Chicago veterans groused.[5] Donald P. Jacobs, dean of Northwestern's Kellogg School of Management and a former First Chicago director, remarked censoriously, "A good banker goes to where the emergency is, hunkers down, and goes to work."[6]

Such comments began to be uttered more and more often, and that fall a full-scale revolt against McCoy started gathering steam. Former First Chicago directors were bombarded with faxes, e-mails, and phone calls arguing that McCoy was not taking the bank's problems seriously. Many analysts began telling Bank One board members that they felt they could no longer trust him.[7] The CEO's informal style and supposed inattention to detail earned him the nickname—one that he despised—of "Fly-by McCoy."[8] Part of the problem seemed to be that many of the former First Chicago executives and board members simply didn't take to McCoy's folksy ways. Another was the blow to civic pride that Chicago had sustained when a bank from Columbus, Ohio, took over a venerable local institution.[9] The Chicago newspapers seemed to have a direct line into Bank One via the First Chicago connection, and articles on Bank One regularly cited sources from the board room or "a former First Chicago executive." These articles often ridiculed McCoy, making him the object of suspicion.[10] Routine events became news, and people in Chicago started whispering about matters that would have gone unnoticed before but that became grist for the anti-McCoy coalition's mill. For example, not only the CEO's vacation plans but even the number of weekly managerial meetings he held were regularly reported on.

Finding himself in a political snake pit unlike anything he had ever faced in Columbus, McCoy reportedly remarked to his wife, "Get me out of this trap. This is not fun. I don't like playing these games."[11] But others were, by now, preparing to extricate him from the situation. During one board meeting that fall, a group of former First Chicago directors brought up the CEO's frequent absences from the office. As soon as this occurred, the endgame was inevitable: John McCoy would have to step down. (An office pool sponsored by former First Chicago executives was actually taking bets as to the day that the board would ask for his resignation.) After the announcement of another earnings shortfall in November, the Bank One directors lowered the boom. In a November 1999 meeting with his few remaining friends on the Bank One board, McCoy—four years shy, at 56, of his planned retirement age—negotiated a separation agreement that included a $10.3 million cash payment on top of $7.5 million in "special recognition" awards for 1997 and 1998, plus a pension of $3 million a year beginning in 2001.[12] With 1.87 million shares, McCoy also remained a major Bank One shareholder.

When in early December the board announced McCoy's departure and the appointments of former First Chicago executive Verne Istock as interim CEO and outside directors John Hall and James Crown as interim co-chairmen, Bank One's stock jumped 11 percent.[13] When the board also announced the formation of a search committee consisting of six outside directors—three from Bank One and three from the former First Chicago—the business press and retired First Chicago employees deluged Russell Reynolds Associates, the search firm that the board had engaged, with phone calls. The retired employees wanted the search consultants to know that they had most of their retirement savings in Bank One stock. The business press was interested in the human drama of the high-profile search. As December progressed, Bank One's stock price became increasingly volatile, shifting dramatically with every rumor of a possible successor. The stock price swings, heightened media and analyst attention, and employee and investor anxiety[14] combined to create a sense of urgency among the directors.

From the start of the search, the head of the search committee, John Hall, made it clear that Verne Istock would be considered as a finalist against any outsider. Istock, often described as a staid, conventional banker, had run First Chicago before the merger with Bank One and was now actively working to heal the wounds from McCoy's departure. The former First Chicago board members on the search committee actually favored, and pushed for, awarding Istock the CEO job permanently. The non–First Chicago board members on the committee, however, were lukewarm to the idea. While considering Istock an excellent manager, they felt he lacked the stature that Wall Street analysts and the business press demanded. These committee members argued that a full-blown external search was needed. "We viewed our task as no less than to find the best person in the United States to lead us back to the top," said Hall.[15] As Charles Tribbett III and Andrea Redmond of Russell Reynolds tell it, the old Bank One directors on the committee felt that the company needed a high-profile outsider, someone with a financial services reputation big enough to restore Bank One's prominence in the eyes of the outside world. While every committee member ranked financial services experience and branding as important,

---

<u>CHAIRMAN AND EXECUTIVE OFFICER</u>   01F074-NA

Company Description

Our client, Bank One, is the nation's fourth largest bank holding company with assets of more than $260 billion. Bank One offers a full range of financial services to commercial and business customers, and consumers. Bank One is the nation's second largest credit card issuer as ranked by the Sept. '99 issue of *American Banker* and also the third largest bank lender to small businesses, one of the top 25 managers of mutual funds and a major national automotive lender. It operates more than 1,900 banking centers and a nationwide network of ATMs. It is a major commercial bank in the United States and in select international markets.

The Corporation operates national lines of business, which include the retail, commercial banking, investment management and trust, finance company and card organizations. Other line and support areas also operate on national platforms.

Bank One's philosophy is to hold the number one, two or three market positions in the major markets it serves. The Corporation continues to expand its market share by offering a range of innovative, high-quality products to its diverse customer base.

Executive Responsibilities

Reporting directly to the Board of Directors, the Chairman and Chief Executive Officer will be the organizational leader with regard to the development and leadership of corporate strategy, the implementation of business plans, the management and integration of operations and will provide division and motivation for the Bank client's employee population. The Chief Executive Officer will be the key communicator with external constituencies and will be responsible for setting and managing expectations with regard to growth and profitability. The Chief Executive will be responsible for the overall financial management of the organization and will be the key driver in integrating the substantial operations as a result of previous mergers. The Chief Executive Officer will also lead and manage a talented executive team who in turn manage large and geographically disperse workforces. Clearly, the successful candidate will be charged with the positioning this high profile financial institution for future profitability and success.

Qualifications

The Chairman and Chief Executive Officer must have demonstrated an unquestionable track record of outstanding leadership within the banking industry. Background in wholesale banking and retail banking is important and experience in the credit card industry will be an added advantage coupled with a solid track record of successfully managing large, complex and highly matrixed environments. The next Chief Executive at Bank One must have impeccable integrity and should have demonstrated the fundamental qualities of being decisive and trustworthy by external and internal constituencies. Proven success in the development and implementation of strategy, the integration of technical and service organizations and

PAGE TWO

---

outstanding risk management judgement will be critical to the success of the Chief Executive Officer. The ability to motivate and inspire executive teams will be critical as well as the ability to communicate effectively with analysts, investor groups and importantly, the employee populations. The successful candidate should have demonstrated the ability to refocus troubled operations and built profitable enterprises within the highly competitive marketplace of financial services.

Compensation

Clearly, the successful candidate will be compensated commensurate with the responsibility of this position and as such, a highly attractive base salary, a variety of incentive plans and stock plans will be included.

EXHIBIT 1.1 Specification Sheet for Bank One CEO Search. *Source*: Russell Reynolds Associates (retyped by author)

many members also sought the prestige that a celebrity CEO would bring to the company. According to Redmond, "Most important was to find a CEO who could reinvigorate and revitalize the company. Someone who could harness the energy of its employees and inspire them to excellence." The overriding principle guiding the search, Redmond adds, was "leadership, leadership, leadership."[16]

Once the search committee and the search firm began putting together its list of names, it wasn't long before the directors became captivated with one particular individual: James (Jamie) Dimon, one of the most successful financial services executives in the world, recently ousted as president of Citigroup by his former mentor and longtime partner Sanford (Sandy) Weill. Ordinarily, a firing would have disqualified a figure such as Dimon from being considered as CEO at a major corporation. Yet because it was well known that his dismissal had resulted from internal corporate politics, not performance, Dimon's star had continued to shine. Indeed, his entire career to date had already made him a legendary, even mythic, figure in the world of finance.[17]

Jamie Dimon had been all of forty-two years old when he became president of Citigroup, the company created by the merger of Citibank and Travelers in 1998, now the largest integrated financial services firm in the United States; he also served as chairman and co-CEO of Citigroup's subsidiary investment bank, Salomon Smith Barney. At the time of his firing, Dimon had been viewed both inside and outside Citigroup as the leading candidate to be the next chairman of the financial services giant. Dimon's professional career had begun in 1982, almost at the start of the investor revolution of junk bonds, takeovers, and mergers that was about to forever change the world of Fortune 500 companies. A graduate of Harvard Business School, he began his career near the top. Dimon's first job out of business school was at American Express Company, where he became assistant to the president, Sandy Weill, with whom he formed a close relationship that would last sixteen years.

The Weill and Dimon families had been close for several years, and Dimon had actually written his undergraduate thesis on Shearson Lehman, the company Weill had built during the 1970s and sold to American Express in 1981.[18] At American Express, Weill and Dimon were known for their ability to rapidly restructure poorly performing American Express subsidiaries such as its Fireman's Fund Insurance division. Eventually, with his path to the CEO position blocked by the master corporate chess player James Robinson III, Weill quit American Express.[19] Surprisingly, Jamie Dimon—only three years into his job, and presumably with a successful and secure career at American Express to look forward to—decided to follow his boss into unemployment. The two rented an office in Manhattan, where they formed perhaps one of the most successful ventures in modern financial history.

Weill and Dimon began by buying Commercial Credit Corporation, a privately held, struggling Baltimore loan company whose primary business was lending money to working-class families from a network of four hundred field offices.[20] While most financial executives would have seen no future for this business, Weill and Dimon viewed it as a base from which to begin building a large, integrated financial services company.[21] Both commuted during the week to Baltimore and worked weekends at Weill's home in Greenwich, Connecticut.[22] Through a combination of cost cutting and investment in sales and marketing, the partners dramatically improved the firm's performance. During this period, Dimon began to acquire a reputation as a smart but arrogant executive whose angry outbursts were calculated to intimidate critics—a mode of behavior very much like that of his mentor. Dimon and Weill's screaming matches were legion, but their argumentative style, by all accounts, resulted in a greater mutual respect and sharpened both men's business skills.

The turnaround of Commercial Credit and its subsequent successful initial public offering provided the capital for Weill and Dimon to begin expanding their company. In 1988, Commercial Credit acquired Primerica Corporation and adopted its name. Primerica, a conglomerate that had fallen on hard times, owned the well-known brand of the brokerage Smith Barney.[23] In 1993, Weill and Dimon extended their reach to the insurance company Travelers and again adopted their acquisition's name. Travelers, which was struggling owing to the recession and poorly performing investments in the real estate market, was ripe for Weill and Dimon's type of surgery. Then in 1997, the two made one final move that put them in the big leagues on Wall Street. After several failed attempts to acquire the famed investment bank J.P. Morgan,

Weill and Dimon landed the trading house Salomon Brothers. Like their previous two acquisitions, Salomon had run into financial problems but also had a valuable brand—this time, one known around the world. The Salomon acquisition gave Travelers the global presence it needed to push its way into Wall Street's upper tier of financial services companies.[24]

Since his early days on Wall Street, Weill had spoken about "competing on a 24-hour cycle."[25] Even in his days at American Express, he had envisioned the creation of a global financial supermarket—a world in which "Chilean teachers and Polish miners will each be buying annuities from Travelers and term insurance from Primerica."[26] With the financial supermarket he and Dimon had built since their purchase of Commercial Credit, Weill was closer than ever to realizing this dream. Yet the Salomon acquisition also focused greater attention on Jamie Dimon. With each acquisition in Weill's expanding financial empire, Dimon's responsibilities and visibility had increased. As president and chief operating officer of the renamed Travelers and as president of the newly created Salomon Smith Barney, Weill's protégé increasingly received as much notice in the business press as did Weill himself. Stories began to circulate about how Dimon had labored, almost single-handedly and in Weill's shadow, to build Travelers' financial empire.[27] His singular focus, standard eighty-hour work weeks, and willingness to leave a family vacation in a remote coastal town in Turkey to solve an important business problem became the stuff of legend, even in the workaholic realm of high finance. The loyalty of Dimon's staff was extraordinary in a world in which political expedience usually trumped a person's word. The business press sought him for his views about the investment banking and brokerage industries. Analysts responded positively to his straightforward manner and his energy. And both journalists and analysts openly speculated that Dimon was the heir apparent to the financial empire that he and Weill had built. Several analysts described him as one of the best executives in the financial services industry.

Meanwhile, the acquisition of Travelers and the creation of their vast financial empire in such a brief span had begun to take a toll on Weill and Dimon's relationship. Although the fighting between the two had been legendary, they were likened by both insiders and outsiders to an old married couple that always made up.[28] Yet despite his tremendous success, Weill was a notoriously insecure individual who wanted to be involved in, or aware of, every business decision.[29] Dimon, now president of Salomon Smith Barney, had begun to exert increased independence, believing that unless Weill was willing to decentralize decision-making, it would be difficult to grow the firm. Relations between Dimon and Weill were further strained when Weill's daughter, Jessica Bibliowicz—a successful financial manager in her own right at Smith Barney—announced that she would be leaving the firm to become a principal of a private-equity firm specializing in financial services acquisitions. The private speculation was that Weill blamed Dimon for Bibliowicz's resignation.[30] The two men were, however, still able to join forces in planning what remains to this day one of the most audacious mergers of its kind ever attempted.[31]

Citicorp is perhaps the best known name in global banking. In 1997 it had $23 billion in adjusted revenues and the biggest credit card, retail banking, and corporate banking operations in the world. After two decades at the top, John Reed, the celebrated CEO of Citicorp, was searching for a way to reenergize the company.[32] Reed had long been regarded as the most visionary banker of his generation. He was most famous for seeing the central role that information technology would play in banking, investing heavily in computerizing Citibank's operations, developing detailed databases on its credit card customers, and rolling out ATMs while most banks were still debating whether people would ever trust a machine. Reed shared Weill's vision of the world of global finance as operating on a twenty-four-hour cycle.[33] Weill, for his part, made a personal appeal to Reed, telling him that Travelers would be the ideal partner for Citicorp. With $37 billion in revenues, Travelers offered Citicorp a new distribution channel through its 10,600 brokers, 11,800 insurance agents, and 28,000 Primerica financial service representatives.[34] Travelers's culture also appealed to Reed. Whereas Citicorp was hierarchical and top-heavy, Travelers was organized like an investment bank—informal and entrepreneurial, with a lean staff. The merger would also be the first of its kind since Depression-era laws had prohibited banks from underwriting insurance. Momentum had been growing in Congress to modify the Glass-Steagall Act, which prohibited such a merger, and Reed and Weill believed that the announced merger would force Congress to pass the legislation quickly.[35] The two agreed to a merger of equals and a power-sharing agreement in which they would be co-CEOs and co-chairmen of the new entity.

While Reed and Weill had a common vision of where the world of global finance was heading, their management styles could not have been more different. Reed, professorial and reserved, was the antithesis of Weill, who was at his best backslapping insurance agents at sales parties and high-fiving brokers on the trading floor.[36] Reed preferred communicating and receiving information through memos.[37] Weill preferred the gossip network. Their relationship was a delicate balancing act, and its maintenance, some came to believe, would eventually require Reed to acquiesce in the sacrificing of Jamie Dimon.

When the merger of Travelers and Citicorp went into effect in 1998, Dimon was appointed president of the new entity. In addition to running day-to-day operations, Dimon was responsible for mediating between Reed and Weill. He also continued to serve as co-chairman of Salomon Smith Barney (a position to which he had been elevated after Travelers's acquisition of Salomon). As had happened after Travelers acquired Salomon Brothers, Dimon's appointment was applauded by Wall Street analysts and the business press. Both Reed and Weill were expected to retire in less than five years, and Dimon was the logical heir apparent. Yet things did not work out as smoothly as planned. The tension between Weill and Dimon began to rise and was chronicled in the New York papers. Mention of Dimon's name in the press was usually accompanied by some variation of the phrase "expected to become CEO of Citigroup"—which did not sit well with the insecure Weill. While Reed had expected Dimon to become Citigroup's next CEO, Weill began publicly stating that no such decision had been made or would be made in the near future. There were hints that Weill wanted to stay in his position longer than he had given the impression he would at the time of the merger.

On a Sunday in November 1998, Dimon was asked to come to a meeting at Citigroup's executive retreat in Armonk, New York.[38] The stated purpose of the meeting was to discuss continuing difficulties in particular aspects of the merger. Dimon knew that there had been several cultural clashes and recognized that several executives would have to be moved. He never thought that he would be one of them. Presented with a fait accompli and asked for his resignation, Dimon replied stoically, "OK." Weill, suddenly overcome with emotion, reached out to embrace him. "No hugs, please," Dimon reportedly responded.[39]

Suddenly, one of the most well-regarded executives in the financial services industry found himself without a job. The story, which was splashed across the front page of the *Wall Street Journal*, had all the ingredients of myth. Dimon had been ousted by his onetime mentor, a man the press had portrayed as his symbolic father.[40] Yet despite their falling out, Dimon was said to be following in Weill's footsteps, setting out on his own much as Weill had done after leaving American Express. Press accounts described the factors leading to Dimon's firing in Shakespearean terms, and portrayed Citigroup as a hotbed of Machiavellian intrigue. Dimon's abrupt departure also shook up Wall Street and raised questions about Citigroup's plans for merging its far-flung businesses.[41] Dimon, who had many fans on Wall Street, openly questioned whether the company would be able to cope with his loss.[42] Reed himself wished the ouster hadn't happened, and the business press speculated that Reed felt obliged to acquiesce to preserve his relationship with Weill.

Like most fired senior executives, Dimon had no financial worries. In addition to his annual salary of $650,000, Dimon received a $30 million separation package from Citigroup.[43] He had also done well during the years he spent building Travelers, and his net worth was estimated at over $100 million. After almost two decades of eighty-plus-hour weeks, Dimon took some much-needed time off, vacationing with his family and starting a vigorous exercise program.[44] He toyed with the idea of just spending the rest of his life enjoying time with his family— after all, at forty-two he was financially set for life. But a person such as Jamie Dimon does not sit still for long, and besides, the calls from the executive search firms started coming in almost immediately.

Many of the phone calls were intriguing. In all, it was a job seeker's dream. There was no combing the want ads or making awkward calls to friends and acquaintances about potential openings. Barclays PLC, the British bank, called, as did George Soros. Dimon was reportedly considered a possible CEO of Home Depot, the hardware retail superstore.[45] Amazon.com's Jeff Bezos invited him to Seattle to visit the company, but Dimon, although he admitted to being impressed with the e-commerce operation, said that he didn't really understand the financial model.[46] As he remarked, "I saw lots of different businesses and met with very interesting people. However, I realized after kicking around a lot of different ideas, including buying a business, that financial services is my craft. . . . It's what I learned to do . . . and I learned it from one of the best and toughest in the business [Weill]."[47] Dimon finally decided that he wanted a job in the industry he knew best. He also vowed that he would not put himself in a position where what had happened to him at Citigroup could happen again. In his next job, he wanted to control his destiny.

Meanwhile, Charles Tribbett and Andrea Redmond of Russell Reynolds had called Dimon to ask if he would be interested in talking about an opportunity at a large bank. Dimon was not surprised by the call. Given his high status in the financial services industry, he had expected to be contacted about the Bank One job, and replied that he was willing to listen.[48] After completing an interview with a candidate in California, Tribbett and Redmond took the red-eye to New York to meet with Dimon the next morning. At the late January 2000 meeting, Dimon interviewed Tribbett and Redmond about Bank One. He made it clear that he was not in a rush to find a new job, and that he was unwilling to risk repeating his experience at Citigroup. He wanted to know what Bank One's culture was like, what the business lines were, and what the company's strengths and weaknesses were. He wanted to know how much free rein he would have in making critical decisions.

Tribbett and Redmond, for their part, had already placed Dimon near the top of their potential candidate list. Now, on the basis of this preliminary interview, they were captivated by him. Tribbett's impression of Dimon during the interview was that "he was an infectious leader who shows mentorship and shows tremendous allegiance to people."[49] Dimon's knowledge of the financial services industry, his reputation among analysts and investors, and his straight-talking New York style were, they believed, just what the Bank One board was looking for. When Tribbett and Redmond reported back to the search committee Dimon's interest in being considered for the position, the directors were elated. One major question in their minds, however, was whether Dimon would really move to Chicago. A decade earlier, First Chicago had hired a CEO, Barry Sullivan, who had promised to move to Chicago but never did.[50] The directors from the former First Chicago board did not want another commuting CEO. Redmond and Tribbett assured the committee members that Dimon could be persuaded to move to Chicago. Based on the search consultants' experience, anyone was movable if properly motivated.

Tribbett and Redmond went to work on Dimon right away. They knew that it would be difficult to convince the native New Yorker, with three school-age children and a wife who served on several New York–based nonprofit boards, to move to the Midwest. They also knew that they could not rely on money as a lure. Dimon was already rich. They had to appeal to his ego. They told Dimon that in the United States there are only five banks that drive the economy. "That means there are only five individuals who will have an opportunity to effect the entire world," Tribbett outlined the situation for the candidate. "You will not have an opportunity, at least for the foreseeable future, to affect the world in such a consequential way if you do a start-up or wait around for another position." Dimon ran through in his head the list of the top five banks and the estimated age of their CEOs: Tribbett and Redmond were right. A CEO position at a top five bank would not likely open up again in the next few years. Tribbett continued with the sales pitch: "At your age, wouldn't it be nice to take your career to the pinnacle by being the real number one? If you don't explore this, you will always wake up in the middle of the night for the rest of your life wondering: 'Should I have at least have explored it?' Only if you explore it, can you know." Tribbett and Redmond were successful. Dimon told the search consultants to include him in the final list and to tell the Bank One search committee that he would move to Chicago if given the position.

Soon the Bank One search committee had a short list of five candidates, with Dimon the clear favorite among the directors who had worked for Bank One before the merger with First Chicago. On paper, the candidates were difficult to tell apart: each had rated high on the matrix of weighted skills developed by the committee and the search consultants. Except for Dimon, each of the reported candidates for the position was actively employed as either the CEO or the chairman of a major financial institution. This made it all the more important for the search committee members to gather information on the candidates that was unavailable on a résumé. As it happened, all four of the external candidates were from firms at which Bank One board members had both direct and indirect personal connections, either through employment with these companies or via service on other corporate boards. Board members Jim Crown and John Hall, in particular, made use of their extensive connections throughout corporate America and Wall Street. Thus the committee was able to talk with five or six people who had worked with each of the external candidates as well as with First Chicago executives who had worked with Istock, still the leading internal candidate. Committee members inquired after Dimon's personal qualities as a leader and his decision-making style. While references on four of the five finalists were mixed, Dimon received nothing but accolades. "His references were outstanding. No negatives," Hall reported. "People raved about his ability. He really was admired and almost everyone who had ever worked for him said they would do so again in a heartbeat."

Having received this all-important testimony from trusted sources about each of the candidates, the directors now would meet them face-to-face. At this point, the search committee and its consultants believed, it was a matter of chemistry. "When you are this far along into the process," Redmond says, "it comes down to executive presence and the confidence directors have in the individual." She and Tribbett also thought they knew which candidate had "executive presence"—Jamie Dimon. "He was not your classic bank executive. His energy was palpable. He was the sort of person who, when he walks into a room, every eye is upon him," Redmond explains.

In late February, Dimon flew into Chicago to deliver a two-hour presentation to the Bank One search committee. By this time, he had decided that he wanted the job. Dimon's presentation seemed to leave his audience breathless.[51] He talked about his philosophy of management, covering such topics as his leadership style and the importance of clearly articulating to people their roles and responsibilities.[52] He also spoke about the importance of instituting a more extensive stock-option plan to better align the incentives of the executives with those of the shareholders. Dimon's bluntness and self-confidence impressed the committee. "It was clear from the interview," one individual involved with the search reported, "that here was a guy who wasn't afraid to lead. I could see it right a way. He said all the right things. He had a plan. How he would bite the bullet on costs, how he would make the tough decisions that others wouldn't make. It was exactly what we wanted to hear." According to committee chairman Hall, Dimon "described how he felt that it was important to expect a lot from people, while helping them understand their duties and treating them kindly. He also said that it was important to maintain a strong financial position, but not let the balance sheet lie to investors." Overall, as Hall summarized the reaction to Dimon, "Everyone knew he was brilliant, but the presentation showed just how brilliant he was. In the two-hour presentation, he had answered all our questions: 'Is he going to embrace Chicago, or is he coming for a short time?' 'Is he mature enough for the job?'" In short, in one relatively brief appearance that Dimon himself largely orchestrated, he appeared to have met Bank One's high (if somewhat nebulous) standards of leadership.

Dimon, for his part, describes his Bank One interview by saying, "I told them how I think a company should be run. I went through a number of issues, including how I thought my first 100 days as CEO would play out. I thought it was very important that we all understood what needed to be done and how it would get done."[53] He also said, "I thought it was important that they [the board] see me for who I am. . . . It's kind of like getting married." (The marriage metaphor was a good one, for Dimon would actually end up bringing a dowry of sorts: as an act of good will, he would acquire two million shares of Bank One for nearly $60 million just before he was hired, a symbolic and substantive gesture that greatly impressed the board.)

The search committee, meanwhile, was ready to tie the knot. It voted unanimously that very afternoon to recommend Dimon to the full board as Bank One's next chairman and CEO. Yet things were not completely settled. A small contingent of former First Chicago directors stood their ground and continued to advocate for Istock's appointment as the new CEO. They talked about the merits of an inside successor versus an outside one. Given the infighting between the Bank One and former First Chicago executives, the former First Chicago directors felt that an insider was more likely to be sensitive to the concerns of both camps. Others, arguing for Dimon, felt that an outsider would be able to restore stability and begin healing the divisions within the company and even within the board itself. Still others felt that Dimon's hiring would stop the negative press about Bank One, which was causing all of the directors distress (even though some of them had actually fueled the feeding frenzy). Hiring a star like Dimon would create a new halo for the bank, they believed.

Istock, himself a member of the board, protested Dimon's appointment. But it was too late. The merits of Istock's case were discounted. The search committee made a point of again highlighting Dimon's celebrity and the sea change that his appointment would represent. It would be like starting anew. Despite a final maneuver to delay the selection, Istock's supporters finally conceded, and Hall was authorized to have the bank's attorneys begin negotiating a contract with Dimon.

Dimon's and Bank One's attorneys began a marathon, five-day negotiation. Dimon had hired Joseph Bachelder, a New York lawyer known for negotiating generous and airtight contracts for CEOs.[54] There were no major issues. All the important points had been worked out in the mating dance coordinated by Bank One's search consultants. Dimon even agreed to a clause in his employment contract that required the relocation of his primary residence to the Chicago area.[55] His five-year employment agreement stipulated a $1 million base salary, plus a $2.5 million bonus in his first year and future cash bonuses that could range from zero to $4 million depending on the price of Bank One's stock. He also received 35,242 shares of restricted stock, ten-year options on 3.24 million common shares, and a guarantee that he would not receive any less than $7 million in annual stock grants. This pay was similar to that of other CEOs in the industry. Dimon did, however, receive a kicker in the form of a two-for-one pension maturation: he would receive two years' credit toward his pension for every one year worked. It was also agreed that Dimon, if terminated, would receive a cash payment two-and-a-half times his base salary and any prorated bonus for that year, plus $2.5 million. He would also be credited, in that event, with two-and-a-half years of additional service for purposes of his pension (five years if the termination occurred after a change of ownership).[56] All of his stock options would immediately vest if Bank One were sold.

Dimon's appointment was greeted with much rejoicing when it was announced on March 27, 2000. Conditions at Bank One had continued to deteriorate during the search, and board members had become

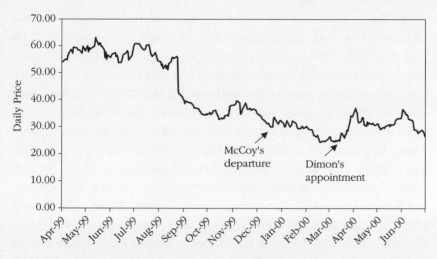

FIGURE 1.1 Daily Closing Stock Price of Bank One, April 1, 1999–June 30, 2000. *Source*: CRSP

increasingly aware that the company's problems went beyond the credit card division. Bank One's portfolio of non-performing loans was growing, making it clear that it would have to increase its loan-loss reserves. Yet within a week of the announcement of Dimon's selection, shares of Bank One—which had fallen by more than half since their peak in May 1999—soared 30 percent.

In the coming days and weeks, stock market analysts and investment professionals would hail Dimon's appointment, describing it as a chance for him to prove that he could lead a company to greatness and apply all that he had learned from Sandy Weill. One mutual fund manager, who had added to his Bank One position following the announcement of Dimon's hiring, told a reporter that an investment in Bank One was "a play on [Dimon's] ability to steer a bunch of underperforming assets."[57] Credit Suisse First Boston bank analyst Michael Mayo, although continuing to rate Bank One a "sell," nevertheless said, "Bank One got a home-run hitter in getting Jamie Dimon. . . . That's a real coup for the company." The headline of the article that quoted Mayo summed up the reaction well: "Bank One Gains Wall Street Credibility with Citigroup Veteran as CEO."[58] Another bank analyst remarked enthusiastically that Dimon was a "strong charismatic leader" and a "winner."[59] Meanwhile, during his first public meeting with shareholders and the press, Dimon had his audience laughing and applauding as he described his plans for Bank One's future. Several analysts commented on his energy and "walking away with a good feeling." "In the mind of investors, it's clear sailing ahead because the dirt has been scraped off the boat," said Joan Goodman, an analyst with the investment bank DLJ.[60]

Yet only two months after the announcement of Dimon's appointment, Bank One's stock had settled closer to its earlier levels. Although some analysts continued to profess faith in Dimon, others were becoming more skeptical about his chances for success. At least a few investors and business reporters had begun having doubts almost immediately after his appointment about Dimon's suitability for the job. "Jamie Dimon: The Wrong Man for the Bank One Job?" asked the title of an April 18 article in *Business Week,* quoting a "notable dissenter" in the investment community who said of Dimon, "A dealmaker is a different personality than a leader."[61] That summer, *Barron's*—while proclaiming itself inclined, on the whole, to bet on Dimon—wrote about "Wall Street's disenchantment with Bank One" along with "a growing recognition that the Dimon makeover will take many quarters to pull off."[62] The industry press, for its part, soon became critical of the speed with which Dimon had removed several Bank One executives, downsized the board, and filled key management slots with former investment banking colleagues from Citigroup.[63] *US Banker* magazine wondered whether "Dimon had free reign to do whatever he pleases," and asked, "Is anyone monitoring Jamie Dimon?"[64]

By April 2001, just over a year after Dimon's arrival at Bank One, the new CEO had cut costs, increased loan-loss reserves, and taken other measures to clean up the balance sheet; he had even negotiated an acquisition (of Wachovia's $8 billion credit card operation) that would put the bank in contention for the number two spot among the nation's credit card issuers. Bank One's stock price had also bounced back to a few dollars below the level it had reached in the euphoric days just following the announcement of Dimon's appointment. Yet it was clear, considering the breadth and depth of its problems, that the company's turnaround effort still had a long way to go. One of the skeptics this time was a stock market analyst who observed of Bank One's attempt to right itself, "You can't get there simply by cutting costs. They don't have any growth plans. They're losing market share every day, morale is bad, and personnel turnover is up." This same analyst proclaimed, "Bank One has become a cult stock without the track record." A financial reporter quoting this remark was clear about her view: at the center of this cult stood Jamie Dimon.[65]

CHAPTER 2

A DIFFERENT KIND OF MARKET

THE SUCCESSION PROCESS that resulted in Jamie Dimon's hiring as the CEO of Bank One followed an increasingly familiar script. A company's performance declines, and the board responds by forcing out the incumbent CEO, who is blamed for its troubles. An external search is initiated with an extraordinary emphasis on hiring a candidate with demonstrable "leadership" and "charismatic" qualities. Much less emphasis is placed on the company's strategic situation and how appropriate the background of the candidate is in light of this. The entire search process is orchestrated to produce a corporate "savior," to find a new CEO whom investors and the business media regard as a star. The standard profile of this savior is of an individual who has served as a CEO or president at a high-performing and well-regarded company. Only a few candidates make it through this filtering process. Using the elusive concept of leadership to distinguish among the candidates, directors come to focus their attention on a single individual. Next comes the effort of convincing this person to accept the position. To rationalize the organizational and monetary resources that go into recruiting the favored candidate, boards convince themselves that the person they have identified through the search process is, in fact, worth the effort and expense—that he (or, more rarely, she) really is a better candidate than any available inside the firm. Not only is the new executive now expected to be the solution to the company's problems, but his very presence is interpreted by the financial markets and the business media as a vote of confidence by the directors that these problems can and will be quickly solved. Everyone's expectations run high.

This storyline, however, often has a dubious ending from the point of view of those whose long-term interests directors are supposedly representing (i.e., shareholders). In the effort to convince the candidate to join the firm, directors yield control of the process to the demands of the recruit, who is in an unusually strong position to bargain with the board about subsequent power and compensation arrangements. If the new CEO is unable to deliver results relatively quickly, the wisdom of the selection is questioned. In some instances, boards find themselves trapped in an infinite loop of dashed expectations and CEO churn.

The extraordinary focus on the CEO as the source of a company's problems, and the blind faith that directors show in the charismatic CEO's powers to heal what ails the firm, introduce the first strain of irrationality into what—considering what companies believe to be at stake in the choice of a new CEO—one might expect to be a rational, carefully considered process. The widespread, firmly held belief in the overriding importance of the CEO is all the more noteworthy considering that there is no conclusive evidence linking leadership to organizational performance. In fact, most academic research that has sought to measure the impact of the CEO on firm performance confirms Warren Buffett's observation that when good management is brought into a bad business, it is the reputation of the business that remains intact. Because so much of this research is so much at odds with the conventional wisdom, it is worth summarizing it briefly here.

Two schools of thought dominate the literature on CEOs and firm performance. The "leadership" school suggests that CEOs play a critical role in affecting firm performance. Because CEOs are at the top of the organizational hierarchy, leadership scholars argue, they can and do affect firm performance by means of the decisions that they make about the company's mission, strategy, structure, and culture. Most of the support for this perspective comes from detailed comparative field studies and individual firm case studies that document the links between executive qualities, organizational decisions, and subsequent firm performance. While their methods have been persistently questioned by a small number of other researchers, the leadership scholars have convincingly made the case that CEOs can indeed affect firm performance in particular instances.[1]

On the other side of the debate, "constraint" researchers (in fields such as, for example, population ecology, resource dependency, and new institutional theory) argue that CEOs are so constrained that they have little impact on company performance.[2] The most careful research on this topic strongly suggests that a variety of internal and external constraints inhibit CEOs' ability to affect firm performance; these constraints include internal politics, previous investments in fixed assets and particular markets, organizational norms, and external forces such as competitive pressures and barriers to exit and entry.[3] Glenn Carroll and Michael Hannan, who have been at the forefront of an effort to study the life-course of organizations (using samples consisting of thousands of firms from scores of industries), have found convincing evidence to support this perspective. By studying the rates of organizational foundings and dissolutions over several decades, and by keeping track of attempts at major organizational change, the authors conclude that CEOs and other top executives have no statistically significant impact on firm performance, even when they make major decisions about strategy or structure. They write:

> The common, but distorted, view of organizational change as easy and beneficial likely arises from the unsound way many observers collect data on corporations. Frequently, analysts and popular management authors collect information on a set of organizations currently performing very well and then look at the evolution of their strategies and structures. This selective, retrospective view of firms often shows that successful firms went through one or several previous transformations that led to later good performance. It is tempting—and many analysts succumb—to infer from this information that, had other organizations attempted the same changes, they too would have experienced success. Unfortunately, this inference comes from considering data that are heavily biased toward the successful firms. The information available does not justify an inference of cause-and-effect with respect to the changes. Nor does it provide the basis of generalization to other firms. Such a sample cannot support dependable analyses of the consequences of change.[4]

Given the divergence between the conclusions reached by these two schools of thought on CEOs and firm performance, some scholars have recently suggested that both the leadership and the constraint researchers have been asking the wrong question. This third group of scholars contends that the appropriate question to be asking is not "*Does* leadership matter" but rather "*When* does leadership matter." The emerging answer to this question is that the impact of a leader on a firm is highly case-sensitive, varying according to individual situations, industries, companies, and CEOs. And while the CEO does indeed affect firm performance in particular situations, even then the overall CEO effect is swamped by contextual factors such as industry and macroeconomic conditions.[5]

Yet despite the overall evidence now pointing to at best a contingent and relatively minor cause-and-effect relationship between CEOs and firm performance, the cultural context within which contemporary CEO succession is conducted gives little consideration to this contingent perspective and instead operates on the assumption that a more precise and definitive relationship exists than scholars have been able to demonstrate. What then accounts for the persistence of the popular belief? As several scholars have noted, strong social, cultural, and psychological forces lead people to believe in cause-and-effect relationships such as that between corporate leadership and corporate performance. In the United States, the cultural bias towards individualism largely discounts the influence of social, economic, and political forces in human affairs so that accounts of complicated events such as wars and economic cycles reduce the forces behind them to personifications (as when people attribute the performance of the economy to the actions of Alan Greenspan)[6]. This process of exaggerating the ability of individuals to influence immensely complex events is strongly abetted by the media, which fixate the public's attention on the personal characteristics of leaders at the expense of serious analysis of events. More generally, in their study of what they call performance-cue effects, social psychologists have found that the construction of leader images is a process of matching leaders' characteristics with performance outcomes: outcomes, whether positive or negative, are attributed to leaders, and then determine whether these leaders are viewed in a positive or negative light.[7]

Such social-psychological forces exert a powerful pull on all of a society's members, elites as well as ordinary people. Their power over corporate directors becomes evident when overestimation of the CEO's importance turns the external CEO search into a quest for a charismatic corporate savior. Recall the Bank One directors gushing about Jamie Dimon's intelligence, and their resultant high expectations as to how analysts and the media would react to the appointment of such a star— as opposed to the negative reaction, it was presumed, with which Verne Istock's appointment as permanent CEO would have met. All this attention to Dimon's charisma is all the more extraordinary when one considers how little the Bank One board's search for a new CEO seems to have been geared to evaluating candidates in light of specific, demonstrable needs of the organization. For example, while Dimon did have tremendous clout on Wall Street, he did not have much experience with retail banking or credit card operations—two of Bank One's largest businesses, and the latter the source of many of its operational problems at the time of the search.

Furthermore, given the distinct culture of commercial and retail banking, Dimon was a somewhat odd choice. After all, he had spent virtually his entire career as a dealmaker and on the investment banking side of financial services, a world described by Roger Brunswick and Gary Hayes as focused on the "here and now" and the art of the deal.[8] In their book *Doing Deals*, a study of the management of investment banks, Robert G. Eccles and Dwight B. Crane find that individuals who excel at investment banking typically have extraordinary financial acumen, impressive sales skills, indefatigable energy, keenly developed intuitive skills, and oversized egos.[9] By contrast, commercial and retail banking are predicated on analytically and objectively calculating and assessing long-term trends and risks. Banking cultures such as those of Bank One and First Chicago value recognizable facts that can be discussed and debated beyond the influences of personality and emotions. The individuals in this industry tend to be methodical and focused on the long term, for effective coordination across their enterprises has traditionally depended on the predictable behavior of executives. This being the case, an inability or unwillingness to control one's temper— qualities for which both Dimon and Sandy Weill had become known— would have been considered in an earlier era a prima facie disqualification for the CEO position in a commercial or retail bank (as they would have been in virtually any professionally managed organization).

Yet one other difference between commercial and retail banking, on the one hand, and investment banking, on the other, does help to explain Bank One's choice of Dimon. In terms of organizational practices, commercial and retail banks have always paid far more attention than their investment banking counterparts to promotion from within and have traditionally invested heavily in human resource systems to support managerial recruitment and training.[10] Investment banks and brokerages have largely relied on a star system for recruiting.[11] It is therefore not too surprising that few U.S. bankers displayed Dimon's energy and seemingly unique persona, and even less surprising that Bank One's board was so taken with Dimon, given the importance that it had attached to the criterion of charisma.

As the Bank One story also illustrates, however, it is not only the criteria directors use in choosing a new CEO that call into question the efficiency and overall rationality of the external CEO market. So do many other features of the search process itself. For example, while it is often assumed that CEO searches are wide and extensive, the Bank One story illustrates that the external search is actually a very closed process: in this case, all four external finalists were known, directly or indirectly, to members of the Bank One board before the search even began. Moreover, much of the information about the candidates was gathered through the contacts of two board members, John Hall and Jim Crown. While being closed in this way, the external CEO search process is at the same time surprisingly porous in being influenced by the views of outside actors such as shareholders, analysts, the press, and others who are not direct parties to the transaction. Interactions between the searching firm and the candidates, moreover, are facilitated by another set of outsiders, the executive search consultants, whose role in the process—again as illustrated by the Bank One case—appears more like that of a master of ceremonies or diplomat than that of a broker facilitating connections among atomized buyers and sellers (the latter being the commonly held view of their function).

Finally and, in some ways, most tellingly, the external CEO search often ends with an outcome that seems less than efficient from an economic point of view. Like other new CEOs hired as the result of external searches, Jamie Dimon exercised his extraordinary bargaining power to strike a highly favorable compensation scheme. While the initial stock run-up following his appointment suggested that Dimon was worth the price, several studies examining the long-term consequences of outsider CEOs on firm performance find that such initial bounces in stock prices are usually short lived. Most of the long-term studies find no effect on firm performance from hiring an outsider CEO. And in some circumstances, the arrival of an outsider results in a decline in long-term performance.[12]

In the case of Bank One, not only did the initial boost to the company's stock price following the announcement of Dimon's hiring prove to be very short lived, but outsiders also quickly began to question whether the board was exercising any control over its new CEO. The question was apt. CEOs have traditionally wielded enormous clout relative to the boards that are, legally as well as in theory, their bosses, and Dimon, newly installed as Bank One's CEO, looked well set to follow in this tradition. The Bank One board invested Dimon with a great deal of power when, for instance, it returned to the practice of combining the CEO and chairman positions, which had been separated following McCoy's departure.[13] Then in August 2000, five months into his tenure, Dimon announced that Verne Istock and five other directors had "volunteered" to retire from the board, which would thus be shrunk from nineteen to thirteen members. Unbeknownst to shareholders, moreover, the search committee had agreed in advance to the cut during its negotiation with Dimon. Dimon had concluded that a smaller board "would be more nimble" and effective for Bank One shareholders; he probably also recognized, as do many CEOs, that a smaller board would be easier for him to control.[14] Two months later Dimon also convinced the board to appoint two of his earlier acquaintances as board members: Heidi Miller, the former CFO of Citigroup, and David Novak, the CEO of the restaurant conglomerate Tricon, on whose board Dimon himself sat. Finally, in a move that was criticized by several industry observers, Dimon dismissed a number of Bank One executives and replaced them with trusted former Citigroup and Travelers colleagues.[15] In all, as part of the price for obtaining the charismatic CEO that it so fervently desired, the Bank One board had handed Dimon the kind of extraordinary power and privilege that charismatic leaders, in all times and places, are accustomed to command. Whether the benefits the board thus hoped to gain for shareholders would materialize at all—let alone prove to be worth the price the directors had agreed to pay in anticipation of them—would, of course, remain an open question for an unforeseeable length of time.

How are we to account for these remarkable, ultimately disquieting features of the external CEO search: the overestimation of the CEO's role and the fixation on charisma; the somewhat Byzantine nature of the search process itself, simultaneously closed to many presumably qualified candidates and open to the influence of many external actors; and the questionable outcomes that this process often produces? This book is an attempt to answer this very question. For the time being, any clear-eyed analysis of the external CEO search process must begin with one central fact: the external CEO labor market is not a "market" in the ordinary sense. It is not even like the market for other executive positions. Scenarios such as Bank One's wooing and winning of Jamie Dimon unfold against the background of several conditions that make the external CEO labor market a truly different kind of market. Its uniqueness arises from a combination of three features: small numbers of buyers and sellers, high risk to participants, and concerns about legitimacy.

Small Numbers of Buyers and Sellers

Rather than being what economists call a "perfect" market, with large numbers of buyers and sellers engaged in relatively anonymous exchange, the external CEO labor market is one in which buyers and sellers—or at least those considered *qualified* sellers—are relatively few. The number of buyers is a function of how many (or rather how few) companies are looking for a new CEO at any given time. Indeed, most potential candidates are aware of which companies are conducting a CEO search, particularly when poor performance has led to the decision to change CEOs. (Recall that, in the case of Bank One, Dimon himself felt that he would likely be considered for the CEO position, and therefore had expected a call from the search firm.) The small number of "sellers" in the external CEO market (for reasons that will become apparent momentarily, "sellers" has to be used in a very restricted sense in this context) can be illustrated by the lists of candidates that the Bank One search committee considered at various points in its CEO search. Drawing on both the directors' and the search consultants' knowledge of the banking industry, the Bank One search committee and its consultants produced an initial list of the leading lights of finance, one that contained thirty names. After a week of fact checking, the search consultants reduced this first list but also added some women and minorities whose names had not originally appeared. They then gave the search committee a booklet with profiles of each of the remaining candidates. The names of almost all of these candidates were familiar to the directors since the pared-down list was a virtual dream team for banking and finance. Some of the directors even knew several of the candidates personally.

A situation such as that in which the Bank One directors were aware of the candidates, and the candidates of the vacant CEO position at Bank One, is not unusual in CEO searches by large, publicly held firms. Relatively few CEO positions open up each year in comparison to other positions. Table 2.1 presents the number of outsider CEO searches undertaken by the firms in the sample in comparison to searches for vice presidents of marketing by these same firms. Firms conduct only one-sixth as many CEO searches as they do VP-marketing searches. Moreover, search firms receive no unsolicited resumes from individuals looking for CEO jobs. One search consultant cogently summarizes both consultants' and directors' common perception by stating that "unlike [with] other positions, the CEO market is not simply a problem of a person looking for a job, but a job looking for a person."

Table 2.1 also quantitatively represents the most commonly held perception of directors, executive search firms, and CEO candidates about this market—that the supply of qualified candidates for the CEO position in large corporations is thin. When contrasting the search for a CEO with that for other executives, one search consultant whom I interviewed commented that "the number of people who can run a 50,000-person organization is small, and most of us know them off the top of our head." Directors, too, lament the presumed shortage of CEO talent.

Ideally, of course, one would want lots of organizations and lots of ex-

TABLE 2.1
Search Firm Statistics Contrasting CEO Search with VP Marketing Search

	CEO		VP Marketing	
	Firm A	Firm B	Firm A	Firm B
Number of Outside Searches	31	45	190	221
Initial Set of Candidates Collected	30	36	310	380
Candidates Contacted by ESF	18	19	92	80
Candidates Interviewed by ESF	5	7	17	14
Candidates Interviewed by Client	3	3	6	6
Average Days Search is Open	187	173	36	29
Number of Unsolicited Resumes	0	0	2500	~3000*

Data reported are rounded averages for CEO searches conducted between 1990 and 1998.
*Firm B did not differentiate in its database between Senior VP and VP positions, thus an approximation was made using the 1998 proportion of senior VP to VP of marketing searches.

ecutives looking at one another to ensure a good match over the long run between executives and open CEO positions. Most firms, however, rarely realize these conditions in their external CEO searches. Yet while describing the condition of small numbers of buyers and sellers in the external CEO market, it is important to note that this scarcity is exacerbated, if not actually created, by the participants themselves.

The shortage of qualified sellers is at its core a misperception largely driven by the fact that boards employ extremely limiting criteria to define the pool of eligible candidates. These criteria, which are loosely (if at all) coupled to the specific strategic challenges facing the firm, are adopted largely with the intention of producing a candidate who will be seen as legitimate by external constituents, namely, financial analysts and the business media. The application of these criteria focuses the board's attention on a small number of candidates. As a result, the perceived shortage of qualified CEO candidates is exactly that—more social fiction than empirical reality. Bank One's directors, for example, insisted on a candidate who would restore the credibility of the company with Wall Street and financial analysts. This translated into a candidate pool in which the final external candidates were either CEOs or presidents of major financial institutions that had performed relatively well and were recognized as being of high quality and status. (Additional support for this interpretation is found in Table 2.1, which shows that the number of candidates perceived to be qualified for the position in the initial stages of a CEO search averages only thirty. On average, only five of these candidates are formally interviewed by the directors.) For their part, most of these candidates shared Dimon's view that there were "likely only one or two other firms I would ever be happy at."[16]

How does the "thinness" of the external CEO market affect its functioning? The number of buyers and sellers in a market is both an indication of the number of alternative relationships available to actors and a critical element in their definition of the market itself. For competitive markets to exist, economists have argued, the number of buyers and sellers must be so large that the ordinary transactions of any single one of them do not appreciably affect the conditions under which other transactions are made. Conversely, the smaller the number of sellers in a given market, the greater the effect of the transactions of any one seller on the fortunes of the others. In the external CEO market, the initial, totally artificial reduction of the size of the candidate pool is generally followed by a similar market-distorting maneuver during the negotiation of compensation. Both Derek Bok and Graef Crystal have argued that the reason CEO pay continues to ratchet upward—even during periods of declining firm performance—is that it is usually anchored to a median calculated from a ranking of a small number of other CEOs.[17] Because the comparison group is small and most boards have adopted a convention to pay their CEOs above the median of their comparison group, an increase in pay for one CEO will result in raising the pay of others.[18] The ratcheting is further exacerbated by CEOs' exertion of influence on the comparison group, via their chosen compensation consultants, by "eliminating certain companies and adding others."[19]

Small or thin markets also reduce competition by limiting the set of other actors with whom a focal actor may contract in efforts to conduct transactions, and by making the search for these trading partners more problematic. For example, buyers and sellers in disconnected or sparse networks may not be aware of the full range of trading partners or opportunities for exchange. Even actors in the same social networks may not be aware of each other's complementary interests if the actors constituting that network are differentiated with regard to activities or interests or beliefs about what is discussable, so that direct interchange between such actors is muted.[20] For example, two members of a golf club or university club may not be aware of how they could benefit each other if talking business at the club is discouraged. This suggests that two actors will be accessible to each other for exchange only if their interests become known and are tolerably consistent. This creates a problem in CEO search because both candidates and boards of directors lack the information necessary to make informed decisions. Aside from the small number of companies known to be searching for a new CEO, a potential CEO candidate will not know what opportunities exist in the market. Similarly, directors will not know if there are qualified people who would be willing to take on the position for less pay than the small number they have already identified as candidates presumably would.

Another analysis of the significance of small numbers of buyers and sellers in a market has been proposed by the sociologist Wayne Baker, who studied the Chicago commodities markets to demonstrate the implications of the numbers of buyers and sellers for a market.[21] Baker found that in contrast to the competitive markets typically described by economists, in which no set of buyers or sellers can dominate the market, many commodities markets were specialized and esoteric, and only a handful of dealers in the world knew how to buy and sell the goods in them. Baker found that to work, these markets needed extensive coordination between buyers and sellers to create the market in the first place. That is, the formal market structure of thinly traded commodities was supplemented and occasionally subverted by an informal social structure of roles, relationships, and collective action. People would often repeatedly trade with the same people. At other times, traders would avoid taking opportunistic advantage of another trader whose financial exposure was too great. One consequence of this small number of participants is that these markets did not display the processes of equilibrium so often assumed in standard economic analysis. Instead, there were large price discrepancies and evidence that the participants' behavior resembled that in a village store, with concerns about interpersonal relationships, reciprocity, and trust—rather than the relentless pursuit of profits—undergirding the behavior of the traders.[22]

Elements such as reciprocity and trust, in turn, become important in the external CEO labor market owing to a second fundamental condition of this market: the risks faced by both buyers and sellers.

High Risk

Previous researchers have not explicitly considered the problem of identifying the potential pool of candidates in the external CEO market. Since most candidates in the CEO labor market are already employed, those seeking to employ them do not have a clear view of whether any of these individuals would be willing to leave their current positions or whether they would be interested in a particular firm that has an opening. The basic condition of a passive CEO labor market creates a high-risk situation for both firms and potential candidates.

The risk to both the candidates (sellers) and the firm (buyer) in this market is reflected in much of the behavior that we observed in considering Bank One's CEO search. In the Bank One case, once the search committee had whittled its list of thirty candidates down to five finalists, the Russell Reynolds consultants arranged the interviews to ensure the utmost confidentiality and even secrecy. One reason for the secrecy was that, with the exception of Dimon, the external final candidates were actively employed as CEOs or presidents at other firms. The *Chicago Tribune* and the *Chicago Sun-Times* published rumors about the identities of the candidates almost daily, and if it could be confirmed that any of the finalists other than Istock and Dimon had interviewed for the position, it would not bode well for these executives at their current firms. Since all of the finalists except for Istock were from outside Chicago, the consultants were careful to schedule interviews in Chicago for days when board meetings were also being held, so as not to arouse suspicion among Bank One executives should any of them run into an out-of-town director. They also took pains to schedule the candidates' flights to eliminate any possibility of their seeing one another at the airport. The interviews were held at Russell Reynolds' downtown Chicago offices, where Redmond and Tribbett carefully choreographed arrivals, departures, and the use of rooms to ensure, again, that there would be no possibility of the candidates' catching so much as a glimpse of one another.

Meanwhile, even though Jamie Dimon was not actively employed at the time of the Bank One search—and therefore not at risk himself— even his name had to be kept under wraps for the sake of Bank One. Tribbett points out that if it had become public that Dimon was being considered, and then that he was not interested in the position or had actually refused it, any CEO who was eventually appointed, no matter how good he might be, would find it difficult to succeed. "If employees and analysts think the selected CEO is the 'second-best' person to run the firm, he has no shot," says Tribbett. (As confirmation of this, consider the example of AT&T's 1997 CEO search, which will be discussed in greater detail in chapter 4. John Walter was clearly the second choice of the AT&T board when C. Michael Armstrong refused the position, and AT&T's image was dealt a severe blow.) Moreover, not wanting to be regarded as the second choice, the remaining strong candidates often withdraw themselves from consideration in circumstances where this danger exists, thereby often forcing the search to start all over again.[23]

Confidentiality also becomes an issue when obtaining information about a candidate's skills or capabilities, since such information cannot be obtained directly from his or her current employer. As one consultant comments, "You can't exactly go to the guy's boss and let him know you are thinking of hiring his CEO." Although general information about a candidate's educational background or work history can be collected easily from public sources, the firm searching for a CEO must rely on other, more private sources to gain particular knowledge about a candidate's capabilities, temperament, character, and skills. Economists describe this need for detailed information as linked to the problem of adverse selection, a process by which the least desirable objects from any observationally similar group enter a market in which information is poorly distributed between buyers and sellers.[24] Although on the surface they may appear alike, outside candidates cannot be presumed equal. Some outsiders have deceptive career patterns and are available in the market because they continue to fail upward. Legal requirements and privacy protections make it hard to find detailed information about a candidate's history. In other words, if a board relied simply on the information produced by the conventional market process, it would know little other than what the résumé and the candidate offered. In an example of the pitfalls of such an approach, consider the CEO search at Sunbeam that resulted in the hiring of Al Dunlap, a case in which the search firm was unaware that the candidate it had placed had been dismissed from a previous job for overseeing an accounting fraud that had culminated in the firm's bankruptcy. While I will return to this point in chapters 4, 5, and 6, for now keep in mind that much of the particular information required to minimize risks to the hiring firm is gathered not by the search firm but by the directors. To obtain such information, directors rely on their prominence and strong ties to individuals who have had direct experience with the persons under consideration.

While some degree of adverse selection is always inherent in transactions in which information about an individual's past behavior is incomplete, the problem is aggravated by a second type of risk specific to information about present and future behavior. This second type is now commonly described as an agency problem. Whenever one individual depends on the action of another, an agency relationship arises; for example, a lawyer is an agent for his or her client, and a CEO is an agent for the shareholders. An agency problem arises when participants in an exchange have divergent objectives, and information about how they are behaving and will behave in the future is imperfect or unavailable.[25]

In the relationships that exist between CEOs and their companies, agency costs can be quite high.[26] Michael Jensen and others have offered examples of cases in which self-interested decisions by CEOs at the expense of shareholders have led to multibillion-dollar losses.[27] Moreover, even when information comes to light about irresponsible actions on the part of a CEO, it is often difficult to remove him. A CEO cannot be dismissed as easily as other members of the organization. CEOs, in fact—despite the increase in CEO dismissals over the last decade—have several tools at their disposal to make themselves both difficult and costly to replace, including controlling the agenda of board meetings and the ability to appoint board members.[28] Under such risky conditions, directors would not likely participate in the exchange that external CEO search represents without a means for reducing the information uncertainty associated with adverse selection and agency relationships.[29]

Returning again to the case of Bank One, neither Bank One's directors nor Dimon had the information required to engage in fully informed decision-making. Let us consider the situation from Dimon's point of view first. While the Bank One directors were somewhat forthcoming with their leading candidate regarding the problems facing the bank, they also wanted him to take the job and so tried not to make these problems look insurmountable. In any event, most had only limited understanding of the firm's situation by virtue of being directors rather than full-time executives. (Most of the information that Bank One's external directors relied on for assessing the firm's condition came from the external environment and from former First Chicago executives—agents whose motivations potentially diverged from those of the directors themselves.) While Dimon, in the meantime, contacted financial analysts to better understand Bank One's problems, he recognized that analysts rely primarily on financial indicators to analyze the company. One ironic consequence of this particular information asymmetry was that Dimon was able to negotiate a relatively high salary and guaranteed bonus as a type of insurance in the event that the problems at Bank One proved to be more severe than he had understood. Thus the apparent risk to Dimon turned out to increase the risk to the directors.[30]

For their part, in an effort to gain specific and detailed information about Dimon, Bank One's directors relied on trusted social connections, particularly with other directors who had known or worked with Dimon in the past. Yet even after gathering as much information of this kind as possible, the directors found it impossible to know ex ante whether they had made an intrinsically sound choice. By picking a candidate who was highly regarded (given Dimon's performance as president of one of the most highly regarded financial institutions in the world, Citigroup), they hoped at least to be able to justify their decision to others. In its manifest concern for the opinions of others, their strategy for dealing with risk points to the third key feature of the external CEO market.

Concerns about Legitimacy

The third important feature of the external CEO labor market is the way in which it is driven by concerns about legitimacy. According to the sociologist Richard Scott, the legitimacy of an action "is determined by the amount of consensus within the relevant sector or field regarding the appropriateness of the means selected to achieve the desired ends."[31] Because the directors and candidates involved in external CEO search are embedded in a community of overlapping business and social relationships, they are particularly sensitive to maintaining the appearance of propriety in the conduct of the search among their peers. Moreover, because the opinions of external actors such as analysts and the business media are so important to ensuring the eventual acceptance of the candidate, that the process be perceived by these outsiders as both objective and proper is critical.

In the Bank One search, the directors faced enormous pressure from shareholders, analysts, and the business press first to fire McCoy and then to act quickly to find a successor. This successor was also going to have to be someone whose appointment would signal to this external audience that Bank One was serious about solving its problems, and that it still enjoyed sufficient prestige to achieve outside director John Hall's stated goal of finding "the best person in the United States to lead us back to the top"—which would require mounting what outsiders would accept as a wide-ranging, objective search. (The very real link between the external CEO search process and the maintenance of a firm's standing in the eyes of external constituents is reflected in the stock market's response first to the news of McCoy's departure, then to Dimon's appointment, and eventually to the doubts that were quickly raised about the latter's ability to perform as expected. The idea that the CEO's performance determines a company's fortunes may be a myth, but that does not make it any less powerful.) Finally, the search had to be pursued in the midst of more-or-less open strife between two opposing factions on the board. The highly politicized context that this conflict created made it all the more imperative that the Bank One directors and their candidates appear to have conducted themselves appropriately.

The importance of concerns about legitimacy in the external CEO search process is highlighted by one aspect of the role of the executive search firm: the part that search consultants play in overcoming the reservations both parties may feel about their own participation in the market. Although a key part of the search firm's role, this function is easily obscured by other issues that arise between firms in the market for a CEO and CEO candidates.

The high stakes and high risks for both directors and candidates in external CEO searches greatly increase the possibility of heightened emotions among the actors: for example, the hiring firm can easily become frustrated with a candidate who seems to take too long to make a decision, or who is perceived as making extraordinary demands regarding compensation, perquisites, or employment contracts. Much as in international diplomacy, such complex, emotionally fraught negotiations usually require the participation of a third party to resolve not only substantive issues such as compensation but also human issues such as frustration or anger—factors that can easily poison a working relationship between a board and its desired candidate. One consultant, describing his job as "part recruiter, part messenger, and mostly marriage counselor," recounts a particularly intense negotiation in which the firm had become frustrated with the "seemingly endless demands the candidate was making on compensation-related issues":

> [Steve] kept making a longer and longer list of what he thought should be covered in order to "make him whole" as a consequence of the move. Meanwhile, the board was getting pretty annoyed at looking at the detailed requests about unexercised options, initiation fees at new country clubs, and deferred compensation, etc. I saw what was happening with respect to the frustration level. . . . I stepped in and said, "Why don't we just put all of this into a one-time signing bonus? In that way, [Steve] doesn't have to go through accounting for every little cost he was going to incur and the board didn't have to review and approve every one of these . . . expenses." . . . [T]hey [quickly] came to agreement on an amount that was perceived fair by both sides. I think it was twenty percent of the first year's cash compensation.[32]

When search consultants are asked to explain why candidates and directors—often portrayed as the kinds of people who are rational, cool, and in control of their emotions—become so sensitive and easily frustrated during such negotiations, they almost always seem irritated by a

CHAPTER TWO

question about what to them is an obvious point. In two-person inter-actions, they point out, directly negotiating a salary or other sensitive matters can provoke intense emotions. The use of an intermediary, however, dampens the feelings that normally arise in such negotiations and represents one party's demands or responses to the other in a more conciliatory, objective manner.

This explanation of the search consultant's role in facilitating nego-tiations between boards and CEO candidates is a plausible one, and in several other settings, such as divorces and labor-management negotia-tions, seems to be a principal reason why third parties are brought into tense negotiations. However, we can look at the intermediary in an ex-ternal CEO search in another way by considering the hesitancy that both firms and candidates express about actively participating in this market at all. We have just seen how the involvement of an executive search firm in an external CEO search helps protect participants from risk. Yet the executive search firm's role also helps allay concerns about how the appropriateness of their actions will be perceived both by their peers and by outsiders. For example, both directors and candidates feel constrained by norms concerning the propriety of contacts, in the course of an external CEO search, between board members and CEO candidates who belong to competing firms. In the face of such con-straints, the search firm protects both parties from appearances of im-propriety by eliminating the need for direct contact between the two in the early phases of a search. That directors and candidates, in turn, are generally linked to one another by personal connections creates an-other legitimacy issue that the executive search firm helps to resolve. In this case, the mere presence of a third party mediator lends an appear-ance of distance and objectivity to what otherwise might be suspected by outsiders to be an essentially social exchange.

In view of these realities, a more far-reaching interpretation of the search consultant's role than the "marriage counselor" one would start with the supposition that the gap between buyers and sellers in a mar-ket is, in part, institutional, and is linked to the degree to which par-ticipation in a market is normatively legitimate. In legitimate markets, buyers and sellers can engage openly (and presumably with less height-ened emotions) in exchanges without fear of repercussions. By contrast, in markets of questionable legitimacy, actors may be unwilling or hesitant to engage or participate, even if their interests suggest that an exchange would be mutually beneficial.[33] The role of the executive search firm thus is to help both searching firms and candidates to overcome their ambivalence about participating in a market of this particular kind.

The concern with market legitimacy on the parts of buyers and sellers, in turn, highlights an important fact about interaction, even in markets: it is shaped by a collective, communal structure. Some interactions that could take place in a market do not, in fact, do so because all interaction occurs in a context of institutional constraints, including rules and roles.[34] Rules impose some of these constraints: for example, the rule that organizations cannot exchange cost information with competitors. Role expectations impose constraints as well: directors, for instance, are asked to resign or to recuse themselves from decisions when their memberships on other boards present the potential for a conflict of interest. Under conditions in which a market is perceived as illegitimate, actors may be unwilling to make even initial contact or to engage in ephemeral transactions with others unless there is a means of keeping appropriate distance until a transaction can be consummated. Indeed, in the external CEO market, the role of legitimacy concerns is underscored by the numerous informal restrictions and rules that influence the manner in which interactions must take place. The enforcement of restrictions on, for example, the ways that candidates can be approached is part of this market's distinctive character. In the external CEO market, legitimacy concerns are particularly acute because market decisions occur not only at the level of the individual organization but also at the organizational field level, in which other actors evaluate the outcome.[35]

Under these circumstances, the best searches serve to legitimate both the search process itself and the final choice of the search committee and board so that a new CEO can have a smooth transition into the position. Missteps during the search process can leave organizational observers and constituents alike seething about the search and hostile to its outcome.[36] The search ends up an abysmal failure, not because the wrong candidate was selected, but because someone who may have been right for the organization is handicapped by the mishandling of the process.[37] The outcome of a search that, from a strategically sound perspective, may be seen as appropriate may be rejected by both internal and external constituents because of the manner in which the process was executed.

Much of the board's concern with legitimacy in external CEO search stems, in part, from a weakening of the boundaries and secrecy that once surrounded CEO succession. Naming a new CEO is no longer considered a divine right of the CEO or even of the board. Whereas in the past CEOs or boards of directors could be allowed to choose the successor because of the perceived validity of peer review—the thinking being that people who have been in positions of leadership are best positioned to decide who can run the corporation—the internal succession process now has the aroma of a smoke-filled room. CEO succession is increasingly treated as an event in which external constituencies have both a strong interest in the outcome and a right to influence it.

These external constituencies, namely Wall Street analysts and the business media, now constitute a legitimating authority for most organizations. Ezra Zuckerman, a sociologist of markets, has documented the increased power of Wall Street analysts in the determination of an organization's stock performance. He argues that investors, especially institutional investors, increasingly rely on the judgments of these analysts when making investment decisions.[38] Board members, as a result, must now pay more attention to them, too. "If you go back a few years ago," notes George Kennedy, a director of several public firms, "I don't recall reading the analyst reports on the boards that you served on, everybody else's view as to how things were going. You might read the articles in the *Wall Street Journal* if you are on the board, obviously, but I don't remember reading all those reports." Other directors observe that, through clipping services, they now receive almost every newspaper or magazine article that mentions companies on whose boards they serve. The cumulative result of these changes is to focus directors' attention away from the immediate situation of the firm and toward the externally relevant actors. Directors who control organizations now try to interpret their external environment and then make succession decisions based on their reading of those external actors whose opinions they most value—and with good reason. (Again, the example of AT&T's 1997 CEO search—and the subsequent search the firm had to undertake nine months later—provides a vivid illustration of this point, one that I provide in chapter 4.)

A market characterized by small numbers of buyers and sellers, high risk to both, and such concerns about legitimacy as those outlined above, does indeed bear little resemblance to what is most often meant by a "market," even though previous observers have generally described it as such. The reason for the current lack of understanding of the true nature of the external CEO labor market is that none of the lenses that have been used for observing and analyzing it are adequate for perceiving, much less comprehending, its complexity. Before looking in more detail at how this market actually works, we must explicitly consider the various frameworks that have been used to study it, and outline the perspective that will be used in examining it here.

The External CEO Market as a Socially Constructed Institution

For neoclassical economists, the external CEO labor market is a market like any other.[39] In their view, markets are constituted by large numbers of individuals acting primarily in pursuit of individual self-interest and engaged in relatively anonymous, friction-free exchange. Neoclassical economics also argues that social relationships and institutions do not matter. Society stands apart from the economic transaction. Parties other than the immediate buyers and sellers do not alter the choices and subsequent actions of economic actors, since perfect information and stable preferences are assumed. The story of the Bank One search obviously belies this perspective in many ways.

The other group of social scientists who have studied the external CEO labor market consists of sociologists who use a structural perspective. In contrast to neoclassical economics' individualist framework, the structural perspective—building on the remarkable discoveries of recent sociological, economic, and historical research—views actors in a market as submerged in social relationships.[40] From a structural point of view, certain actors are connected to certain others, trust certain others, receive information from certain others, give information to certain others, are obligated to support certain others, and are dependent on exchange with certain others. This recognition points away from economic calculations and toward patterns of social relationship, reputation, information flow, constraints, opportunities, and the determining roles of community and power. It also points toward the fact that individuals, in pursuing and safeguarding their own interests, often act as much, if not more so, to safeguard their social assets and relationships. To take one example of how much more accurately a structural perspective accounts for the character of the external CEO market than the conventional economics perspective does: although external CEO searches are widely considered to be broad ranging in the way that the neoclassical economic view of the market would suggest, they are in fact (as the Bank One case illustrates) confined within the relatively narrow bounds of inter-firm networks. To take another example: while neoclassical economists' accounts of the external CEO labor market have presumed this market to be "institution free," external institutions such as executive search firms, interlocking directorates, and (as in the Bank One case) investors, analysts, the press, and other groups of actors, play an important role in controlling access to jobs and facilitating mobility into the CEO position.

The structural perspective on the external CEO labor market represents a considerable advance over the traditional economic analysis in that it recognizes the centrality of social networks and relationships to the search and selection process. This perspective, however, has its own limitations. And what neither view—the mainstream economists' nor the structural perspective used by many sociologists—takes into account is the way that the market is perceived by the actors involved, and the culturally conditioned beliefs bound up with their perceptions. Put another way, the structural perspective is contextually sparse because economic action is restricted to the constraints of networks of relations. Considerations such as societal institutions, the preconditions for market exchanges, and how social practices define appropriate and inappropriate forms of market behavior are simply set aside.

To see how social institutions and beliefs exert their influence on the external CEO market, consider several details of the Bank One story once again. In the Bank One search, the business press and financial analysts both influenced and refereed the search process. Negative press, true or not, played a key role in the removal of John McCoy. Similarly, the ability of financial analysts to drive investors to buy or sell Bank One's stock had a decisive influence on the company's directors. It was essentially social beliefs that led the Bank One directors to limit the candidate pool to individuals who were currently CEOs or chairmen at prestigious financial institutions. Moreover, the selection of Dimon was in part determined by the Bank One directors' desire to appease cultural institutions, such as the press, and was seen as a way to signal to competitors that, in the words of one director, "Bank One is back."

To say that actors' perceptions of the market and of the structural position of actors in it are important constitutive dimensions of that market is also to assert, as I do, that the external CEO labor market is a socially constructed institution. Sociologists will understand my use of the term *social construction*, which comes out of the sociology of knowledge, in a way that those outside the discipline may not.[41] To call the external CEO labor market a socially constructed institution is not to say that it is an institution in the everyday sense of that word. Rather, the CEO labor market is an institution in the way that sociologists think of the term: that is, a pattern of practices, relationships, and obligations that are so taken for granted that they assume the status of rules governing both thought and action.

Socially constructed institutions play a pivotal role in the economic functioning of any society. The ideas of the sociologists Mark Granovetter and Viviana Zelizer have been central in developing this concept. In one case study, Granovetter and his colleagues examine the origins of the American electrical utility industry.[42] Through an examination of the state of technology and the economic costs of producing electricity, the researchers suggest that in the 1880s, when the industry was just taking shape, it was by no means clear that it would be organized in its present, taken-for-granted form of investor-owned utility companies generating power in central stations for large areas. Instead, there were two other possibilities: generation of power at a household or neighborhood level, and public ownership of utility firms. What determined the investor-owned model (which until the 2001 California electricity shortage had been taken for granted as the most efficient model for producing electricity) were a variety of non-market forces that are typically ignored in explaining the economic trajectories of particular industries or institutional arrangements, but which converged and interlocked in

powerful ways to forge the industry structure that exists today. Granovetter and his colleagues find that trade associations, director interlocks, decisions by equipment manufacturers about who to sell equipment to, and the ability to mobilize social, political, and financial
resources, all played a pivotal role in creating an industry that is now
dominated by a few large holding companies using standardized methods of generation and organizational structure, and protected by government agencies.

While Granovetter's research has emphasized that networks of relations constrain and facilitate economic action, Viviana Zelizer has emphasized the role of cultural factors in creating and sustaining markets.
In *Morals and Markets*, Zelizer solves one of the great puzzles of nineteenth-century economic history, the sudden popularity of life insurance in the United States after decades of failure to convince the public of its importance.[43] Based on a careful examination of historical
documents related to the industry, Zelizer finds that public resistance to
life insurance was largely the result of a value system that condemned
putting a monetary value on human life. Many early insurance firms discovered that the juxtaposition of concepts such as death and money
conjured up unpleasant images and seemed to many people to violate
the boundary between the sacred and the profane; indeed, the major religious institutions in the United States officially denounced life insurance as sacrilege, arguing that the very idea was incompatible with the
Christian values of charity and compassion. Not until insurers mastered
the delicate problems of fixing a price on an individual life and learning how to market financial provisions for mortality did the public's
viewpoint evolve and life insurance become a legitimate and acceptable
financial planning product.

Turning again to the external CEO market, one sees that many actors both affect and are affected by that market as an institution. Some
of these actors—employees and shareholders, stock market analysts,
the business press—are indirectly involved in influencing the process.
Others—boards of directors, executive search firms, and CEO candidates themselves—play a more direct role. Their perceptions of the
CEO labor market, including their understanding of the rules that determine who can be considered as buyers and sellers, and of the norms

defining appropriate behavior for participants, are essential to understanding how the process of CEO succession takes place.

To call the external CEO market a social construction is not only to call attention to the roles and perceptions of these actors but also to say that, while this market appears to be an external and objective institution—to have, in other words, what some scholars call facticity—this is merely an illusion, since the process of social construction consists precisely in making an institution look like an objective and external aspect of the environment.[44] One of the important lessons of the sociology of knowledge is that very little in society had to be the way it is. As the sociologists Walter Powell and Paul Dimaggio have found, institutions that have been socially constructed in particular ways probably could have been constructed in other ways as well.[45] Part of the process of social construction is to camouflage this fact, since society becomes more stable when people accept its institutions as simply given and share a common explanation for events.[46]

This type of argument is not usually applied to economic institutions, but there is no reason why it should not be. According to conventional economics, economic institutions, including markets, are simply matter-of-fact solutions to problems (for example, the need to minimize costs or to maximize certain kinds of efficiency) that require them to exist or to exist in the particular forms that they have come to assume. Scholars coming from this perspective have treated economic institutions as if they had been constituted by the laws of physics or chemistry.[47] They conspicuously neglect the fact that the entrenching of an institution is, at its roots, a social process, highly dependent on a complex interlocking of factors, including the specific and shared personal understandings of the human agents involved in the process, the social connections among them, organizational conditions, and historical context.[48] The Panglossian treatment of economic institutions as inevitable and maximally efficient has, to date, hampered the progress of social science and the development of its ability to offer convincing explanations for many important economic phenomena.[49]

For example, during the heyday of the multi-business firm, or conglomerate, in the 1960s and 1970s, several economists maintained that this was the ideal form of organization. They argued that the efficiency of a company lay in the way it was managed, not what businesses it was in. The idea that the conglomerate form was the most efficient gained significant following and was used both to explain and to justify the existence of conglomerates. Some economists argued that conglomerates could use their internally generated cash flow to efficiently allocate resources to exit old businesses and enter new ones.[50] Econometric models of the cost of capital were developed to justify the conglomerate strategy and show that conglomerates had a lower cost of capital, and thereby a competitive advantage over small companies seeking funding.[51] Then in the 1980s, as inefficient conglomerates became the target of hostile takeovers, economists attempted to explain the takeover movement by arguing for the inefficiency of conglomerates.[52] New mathematical models were constructed to show that conglomerates inefficiently allocated resources. Core competencies and focus became the mantras of the economic interpretation of business strategy and contemporary economic strategy research. The rise and fall of the conglomerate actually makes it clear that both the multi-business firm and its more focused, streamlined successor were socially constructed. At the same time, economists' contradictory analyses of the conglomerate show how it is possible—not to say necessary—to ascribe efficiency to any particular form of organization once one assumes, a priori, that economic institutions are organized as they are for the purpose of maximizing efficiency.

The social constructionist perspective is particularly useful for studying the CEO labor market because of a similarly evasive maneuver that economists have used to explain the tendency of large, publicly held corporations in recent years to turn from the internal to the external market when replacing CEOs. During the many years in which new CEOs were selected from inside the firm, economists saw the structure and rules of the internal CEO labor market as having a self-evident rationale.[53] The argument went something like this: CEOs were chosen from inside the firm because this was the most efficient way to select them. CEOs require know-how and skills specific to a firm to run it most effectively. Moreover, when new employees join a firm, it is not clear in advance who will acquire the requisite know-how and be the best person to run the firm. Firms therefore use internal labor markets—which utilize training and promotions—both to impart firm-specific know-how and to learn who is likely to be most effective in the CEO's job. Today, confronted by a more ambiguous situation in which almost one-third of all the CEOs selected by large, publicly traded corporations can be classified as outsiders, students of the CEO labor market often dismiss this change as peripheral, a mere epiphenomenon.[54] A social constructionist perspective, by contrast, allows us to see that the external CEO labor market has its own social structure and way of being that cannot be explained with reference to economic criteria such as efficiency.

This is not to suggest that an institution like the external CEO labor market is completely independent of economic forces. Likewise, I am not suggesting that such economic institutions, once formed, are immune to economic factors. What I do argue is that economic institutions can be understood only within the context of broader social structures. Let me give a concrete example to illustrate this theoretical point.

One of the three critical actors in any external CEO search is the executive search firm. Many economists, and even many sociologists, treat the existence of intermediary institutions such as executive search firms as responses to an economic need. The gist of the economic argument is that when corporate directors need to find a new CEO, they are faced with a "make or buy" decision.[55] That is, they can either undertake the search by themselves or farm it out to a third party. Because executive search firms specialize in search, it is argued, they are likely to have cost or scale efficiencies that the directors do not enjoy. Directors therefore compare the transaction cost of conducting the search by themselves versus the cost of hiring an outsider. The mainstream sociological argument, in turn, suggests that because they know of candidates who are unknown to the firm, executive search firms have an information advantage over the directors for which they can and do extract economic "rent."[56]

One problem with both the economic and the existing sociological explanations of the role of executive search firms is that neither explanation meshes with the facts of how external CEO searches actually unfold. For one thing, boards of directors hire search firms even when they have no intention of looking outside for a new CEO. For another, directors seriously consider only candidates who are known to them from the start, before they have even hired a search firm. On further consideration, the conventional perspectives of both economists and sociologists on executive search firms can be seen to sidestep several important questions. Where did executive search firms come from? Why didn't firms go outside for CEOs in the past? And why would a board hire an executive search firm even when it intended to promote an inside candidate, or when it already knew the identities of the outside candidates whom it would consider? Most social scientists who study the CEO labor market have evaded such questions because they require attention to concrete actors, such as directors and CEO candidates, who are embedded in networks of relationships, expectations about behavior, and uncertainty regarding their proper course of action. Such considerations lie very far outside traditional ways of thinking about the CEO labor market.

The CEO Labor Market as a "Closed" Market

The preceding discussion underscores the fact that key differences between the external CEO labor market and more conventional markets are so great that the former cannot be understood using standard economic concepts and market imagery. The analytical lens of social construction was introduced because the social organization and the culture of the main participants in the external CEO market affect both the organization and inner workings of this market and its outcomes so directly and profoundly that only an approach that explicitly considers the relationship between economy and society is capable of yielding insights and generalizations of importance. One idea that captures particularly clearly how both the structure of relationships and the cultural meaning of economic action are linked to the external CEO labor market is the concept of the *closed market*.

The core idea of closed markets can be found in the sociologist Max Weber's discussion of social closure presented in *Economy and Society*.[57] Weber speaks at a general level of closed and open relationships. Here the terms "open" and "closed" will be applied to a market; no change in meaning is implied. In speaking of open and closed markets I refer to the ease or difficulty of access to the basic market relationship, which, in the CEO labor market, means meaningful access to the position of

CEO.[58] Open markets are those that have the properties assumed in neoclassical economic theory, and the mechanisms that allocate people to positions in such markets are those described by the standard economic theory.[59] In open markets, a very large number of transactions occur simultaneously and independently of one another. They establish equilibrium wage rates, and no one is prohibited from working at some specific wage. No single transaction will affect the market as a whole. Employers can rely on active competition among potential workers to minimize labor costs, and workers can rely on open competition among employers to ensure they get the market wage. While they cannot influence that market wage, they can increase their earnings by working more or by supplying a different and higher quality of work.

In contrast to an open market, a closed market exists whenever the distribution of opportunities is restricted to a narrow set of eligible groups or individuals. In Weber's discussions, closure most often took the form of the singling out of certain social or physical attributes as the justificatory basis of exclusion. Weber provided numerous examples of how groups use caste systems, professional societies, and political institutions to improve their fortunes by restricting to a limited circle access to rewards and privileges. To do this, Weber argued, groups single out certain social or physical attributes that they themselves possess and then define these as the criteria of eligibility. In practice, almost any characteristic can be used to this end, provided that it can serve as a reliable mechanism for identifying and excluding outsiders. Exclusionary social closure is thus action by a dominant group designed to secure for itself certain resources and advantages at the expense of other groups. Where the excluded themselves manage to close off to other groups access to what remains of the rewards, the social system becomes more highly differentiated and the number of strata or sub-strata multiplies. An example of this is the Indian caste system, which is based on a highly codified system of social classes that defines in detail what occupations can and cannot be pursued by each of the castes.[60] Apartheid is a more crude example of closure.

As we shall see, one of the defining features of the external CEO labor market is the way that it restricts access to the CEO position to those who fit certain socially defined criteria. While hardly as dramatic or morally repugnant an example of social closure as many others found in human societies in all times and places, the external CEO labor market, properly understood, offers a stark refutation of much of the received wisdom that surrounds it in contemporary America. For besides contradicting orthodox economic and sociological accounts of this market, the closed nature of the external CEO search process flies in the face of today's near-religious faith in markets as a mechanism for achieving such socially desirable goals as equal opportunity based on open competition, or advancement on the basis of merit.

How have we come to this pass? Although, as I argue, the structures and beliefs constraining the major actors in the external CEO market are what constitute the market as an institution, these actors have not created these structures and beliefs themselves. Rather, they have received them as part of a social and cultural system that has developed over time in a series of steps that can be traced. Before turning to the roles of these actors in the external CEO market, we need to consider the origins of one of the key beliefs coloring their perceptions of this market: the very idea of the charismatic CEO.

THE RISE OF THE CHARISMATIC CEO

NOT THE LEAST remarkable feature of the search that culminated in Bank One's hiring of its star CEO, Jamie Dimon, was the way in which, by choosing Dimon, the board passed up an experienced, highly qualified executive who knew the company and its business well. Verne Istock, a University of Michigan graduate and MBA, was a highly regarded banker who had spent thirty-seven years working his way up the ladder at NBD Bancorp, of which he became chairman and CEO in 1994. NBD Bancorp was considered one of the best-managed regional banks in the country, and after one year at the helm, Istock engineered a successful merger between NBD and First Chicago to create one of the largest banks in the country. After the merger, Istock served as CEO and chairman of the new entity. The combination of the two banks was very successful, and a great deal of credit for this success was given to Istock's willingness to share power with, and delegate decision-making to, the executives from First Chicago.

It is not at all unusual today for companies to pass up CEO candidates of the caliber of a Verne Istock. For even strong insider candidates are now routinely dismissed as unequal to the role of corporate savior or (in the preferred lingo of the boardroom) "change agent," a figure now seen as the key to reviving troubled companies. Indeed, the preference for glamorous external candidates over qualified insiders has now become so common that we need to be reminded that things were not always so. The star CEO of today is, on one level, but another incarnation of the kinds of charismatic leaders that have arisen from time to time throughout history and in every corner of the globe. On another level, however, he is the product of a particular, and fairly recent, set of developments in the history of American capitalism.

The Shift from Managerial to Investor Capitalism

The emergence of the external CEO labor market, and of the charismatic CEOs who are the most visible consequence of it, is intimately tied to historical changes in the ownership and control of large corporations in the United States in the twentieth century. The traditional nineteenth-century manufacturing firm had been a personal or familial operation producing piecework, assisted by local merchants who both supplied it with tools and raw materials and distributed and marketed its products—that is, the shop writ large.[1] Ownership and control rested in the same hands. The founder and the chief executive of the firm were one and the same. At the beginning of the twentieth century, as a result of revolutions in communications and transportation and the development of mass markets, firms grew larger and larger. The management intensity of these large organizations, many of which spanned the North American continent, overwhelmed the traditional owner-manager-led organizational structure.[2] To finance the growth of these firms, founders had to sell an increasing portion of the company to investors and shareholders. As a matter of expediency, founders also had to delegate the day-to-day management of the firm to nonfounders. This "managerial innovation" led to a distinct separation of ownership and control, in which control shifted away from owner-founders to professional managers while stock ownership became increasingly diffused among thousands of anonymous stockholders who were not involved in the day-to-day management of the firm.[3]

In his book *The Visible Hand*, a title that was carefully chosen, the historian Alfred Chandler argued that this new professionally managed corporation was economically superior to the stockholder-controlled corporation.[4] Because of the sheer complexity of large corporations, market forces, particularly the stock market, were no longer effective in guiding organizational activity. Instead, managerial capitalism's cadre of professionally trained executives with firm-specific experience and know-how were better stewards for the nation's private assets than were the egocentric founder or short-term-oriented stockholder.[5] Professionals preferred long-term stability and growth to short-term gains. The result, as Chandler described it, was a virtuous cycle: As businesses grew, the very system by which they were structured evolved, allowing them to become even larger and therefore more efficient, profitable, and powerful.

For several decades, the rise of managerial capitalism described in Chandler's thesis seemed like one of those "end of history" moments, such as political theorist Francis Fukuyama saw in the end of the Cold War.[6] The superiority of managerial capitalism over owner-based capitalism as an economic arrangement was almost a given in any treatment of the modern corporation.[7] The steady, visible hand of the professionally trained manager guiding the corporation toward stability and long-term growth was seen as superior to that of the jumpy manager continually reacting to the unpredictable and fickle "invisible" hand of the market. To be sure, there were portents of risk and danger around the edges of Chandler's thesis—for example, the gradual decline of U.S. manufacturing during the late 1960s and 1970s, when higher prices were accompanied by poorer quality—but these were viewed as temporary aberrations rather than as a harbinger of a changing landscape for U.S. corporations. To the extent that any constraint was placed on managerial authority, it came from the federal government's ability to regulate through antitrust enforcement or the regulatory agencies.[8] Corporate directors, although legally responsible to shareholders, in fact felt more beholden to the CEOs who invited them to serve on their companies' boards.

With the exception of a few vocal academics, most of whom were marginalized in their own fields of study and exiled to second-tier institutions, few saw the insulation from market forces as having a negative impact on corporations. Like any human construction when left unchecked, however, this system showed a natural tendency to accumulate inefficiency as a result of bureaucratic inertia and entropy. Whereas the strength of managerial capitalism was the discretion it afforded professional executives to determine the strategies of the firm, its weakness lay in the temptation it afforded these same professionals to take inefficient actions such as negotiating stronger employment contracts, in-

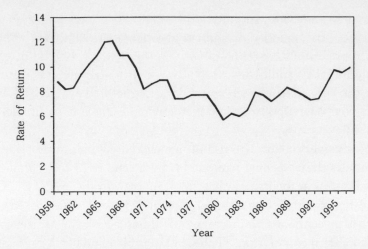

Year

FIGURE 3.1 Corporate Profitability, 1959–1996. Rate of return equals pretax income plus interest divided by tangible assets. *Source:* Poterba (1997) as cited in Baker and Smith (1998)

creasing their own salaries and perquisites, weakening the monitoring power of the board, and ultimately diversifying the firm to reduce their personal risk.[9] In U.S. corporations, this inefficiency manifested itself in the form of a steady decline in U.S. corporate profits beginning in the late 1970s.[10]

Because share ownership of large corporations was dispersed, shareholders were still relatively powerless at this point to exercise any control over management. Thus, if a shareholder was unhappy with the way a particular firm was being run, he or she responded by selling the shares of one company to purchase the shares of another (a maneuver sometimes known as the "Wall Street walk"). This was true even for the largest shareholders, such as pension funds, mutual funds, banks, and insurance companies, which were legally prevented from either owning significant blocks of stock or engaging in collective action to influence management, despite their financial capacity to do so. Exit from holdings in a particular firm, however, increasingly became an ineffective option because of the almost uniform decline in the performance of large corporations. When it came to investing in the stock market, investors had few alternatives. Internationally, for instance, the concerns of shareholders were even more marginal than in the United States.

Investors initially responded to the general decline in corporate performance by siding with incumbent management. Thus, when business executives blamed lower corporate performance on burdensome federal regulations, investors, particularly the increasingly visible institutional investors, joined in the call to roll back government regulation in the areas of the environment, unionization, and occupational safety. Investor loyalty was induced by the belief that deregulation would give existing managers time to restructure and respond to their concerns. Yet despite the significant deregulation of business that began under President Jimmy Carter and accelerated after the arrival of the Reagan administration in 1981, overall U.S. corporate performance continued to underperform. Moreover, the credibility of U.S. executives started to suffer as the business press began to highlight embarrassing examples of senior managers enjoying perks such as fleets of corporate jets, limousine services, executive dining rooms, and so forth, while simultaneously laying off thousands of workers and cutting corporate dividends. The public image of corporate executives began shifting from one of enlightened corporate statesmen who balanced the competing concerns of corporate constituents to that of a self-interested managerial class whose primary interest was taking advantage of weak shareholders.[11] After nearly a half-century of unchallenged supremacy, senior management at many corporations faced a threat to its authority.

Initially, the counterrevolution to the managerial "revolution" was led by outside raiders and private investment groups in the form of leveraged buyout organizations. Taking advantage of financial innovations such as junk bonds and buyout financing, these outsiders began buying poorly performing firms and restructuring them, often by removing incumbent management.[12] Corporate executives, for their part, fought back by adopting a range of defensive measures with exotic names such as poison pills, golden parachutes, fair-price requirements, and supermajority votes. They also turned to the government in an effort to get anti-takeover legislation passed. Although corporate lobbyists such as the Business Roundtable made little headway either with Congress or with the laissez-faire Reagan administration, appeals to state and local governments proved much more successful. In the end, a majority of the more heavily industrialized states adopted anti-takeover legislation that protected incumbent management against unwanted acquisi-

TABLE 3.1
Characteristics and Descriptive Statistics of Mergers by Decade, 1973–98

	1973–79	1980–89	1990–98
Number of Events	789	1427	2040
All Cash	38.3%	45.3%	35.4%
All Stock	37.0%	32.9%	57.8%
Any Stock	45.1%	45.6%	70.9%
Hostile Bid at Any Point	8.4%	14.3%*	4.0%
Hostile Bid Successful	4.1%	7.1%	2.6%

Source: Reported in Andrade, Mitchell, and Stafford (2001).
*Mitchell and Mulherin (1996) report that for the larger, better-known companies listed in the Value Line Investment Survey, 23 percent of these firms received hostile takeover bids during the 1980s.

tions. The strongest of these new provisions allowed directors to consider non-financial factors in accepting or rejecting a takeover. This limited the ability of outsiders to litigate board decisions (such as the adoption of an anti-takeover provision) and—by once again giving managers the upper hand—significantly tempered activity in the takeover markets. Table 3.1 shows that by the late 1980s, hostile takeover activity had declined significantly. However, this did not turn the clock back to the era of managerial capitalism.

Many of the raiders and LBO firms were not self-financed but instead were bankrolled by a set of moneyed actors who enjoyed much greater legitimacy than the greedy takeover artists epitomized by T. Boone Pickens or the "barbarians" of Kohlberg Kravis Roberts.[13] This new set of actors—institutional investors—had almost imperceptibly become the dominant class of shareholders in the United States. Institutional shareholdings, which in 1955 represented 15 percent of the outstanding shares of companies listed on the NYSE, were by the mid-1980s in excess of 50 percent. Today, institutions control some $20 trillion worth of stock.[14]

Whereas exit from unprofitable market positions was the preferred mechanism when institutional investors owned only a small number of shares in the equity market, it was not a real option at this scale of ownership.[15] Institutional shareholders disappointed in a company's perfor-

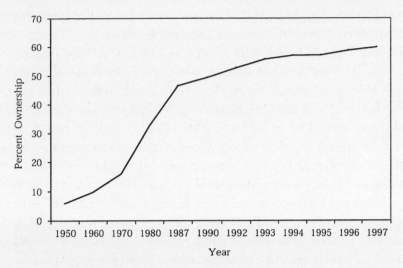

FIGURE 3.2 Institutional Ownership of U.S. Equities from 1950–97. Institutional ownership is defined as private pension funds, open-end mutual funds, state-local government retirement funds, and insurance companies. *Sources*: Data for 1950–80 is from Friedman (1995); data for 1987–97 is from Institutional Investment Report (1998).

mance could not easily sell their block of shares to any investor other than another institution. Moreover, selling even in small increments could significantly damage the price of a holding if it became public that a major shareholder was beginning to exit. While in the past institutional investors had simply sold their shares in one company and invested in another or had loyally supported incumbent managers, they now shifted to a more vocal strategy to force managers to take their concerns more seriously.

The target of most institutional shareholder activities aimed at voicing the views of shareholders became corporate directors. Because directors are at the interface between a particular firm's CEO and its investors, they are the natural targets on which to apply pressure to affect the firm's activities. In 1991, institutional investors such as the College Retirements Equity Fund (CREF), the California Public Employees' Retirement System (CalPERS), and the Teamsters increasingly began to send targeted letters to directors urging them to act to improve performance at a particular firm. Many of these efforts were channeled through intermediary organizations such as the Council of Institutional Investors (CII) and Institutional Shareholder Services, which coordinate and publicize shareholder proxy votes, including those electing directors. If "quiet" pressure did not work, these institutional investors were willing to employ stronger tactics against individual directors. The Teamsters, for example, began to publicly shame directors by publishing an annual list of the worst directors in America. The list, compiled by aggregating data on directors' attendance at board meetings and the number of boards a director sits on, was (and still is) often picked up by the business media and published in outlets such as *Business Week* and *Fortune* magazines.[16] CII puts together a list of "director turkeys" that names board members who serve on the boards of more than one underperforming company. Several pension funds, including CREF, CalPERS, and the Teamsters, now scrutinize the composition of boards to identify directors who are most likely to respond to shareholder concerns.

One of the most awe-inspiring examples of institutional investors' new power over directors was the removal of an entire tier of senior management at General Motors in 1992. The dismissal of Robert Stempel and his top lieutenants that year had no parallel in the history of great corporations. Wholesale removal of executives after takeovers had been known, of course, but boards of directors had usually settled for a single head—and even then with reluctance. As recently as the mid-1980s, not even the constant haranguing of Ross Perot had been able to persuade the GM board to shift gears or change direction. Despite the evidence that GM's market share was rapidly deteriorating and that the company was one of the world's highest-cost car producers in a market with substantial excess capacity, the board had complacently supported CEO Roger Smith and the failed strategy it had approved for over a decade. "I did everything I could to get General Motors to face its problems," Perot later said in the 1992 presidential debates. "They just wouldn't do it."[17] The reason for this was that GM had, in Perot's words, "a Pet Rock board of directors." Rather than heed Perot's calls to cut executive perks and streamline the bureaucracy, the GM board had eventually spent $750 million to buy out his stock and silence him. Even when Smith finally retired in 1990 because of GM's forced retire-

THE RISE OF THE CHARISMATIC CEO

ment policy, the board had agreed to appoint Stempel, his handpicked successor, as CEO, and to keep Smith himself on the board. Thus it is all the more remarkable—and a telling sign of the shift of power from management to investors—that this same supine board, faced with increased pressure from institutional investors, finally dismissed not only Stempel but most of his senior management team.

Encouraged by the corporate upheaval that they helped spur at General Motors, activist investors subsequently zeroed in on other firms.[18] Using new power granted by changes in federal proxy rules in 1992, CII could now solicit proxy votes for shareholder resolutions and against directors. While pension funds exerted pressure through these means, other large shareholders, such as Berkshire Hathaway and KKR, exerted direct pressure through their participation as corporate directors. Although public pension funds were often prohibited by charter and state law from having a board seat on a company they had invested in, Warren Buffett, the chairman of Berkshire Hathaway, and Henry Kravis, the chairman of KKR, did not face any such restrictions. The clearest example of the role of these large shareholders can be found in the recent dismissals of CEOs at two of America's largest consumer product companies, Coca-Cola and Gillette. Insider accounts reveal that the firing of Douglas Ivester at Coke in 2000 was coordinated by two of the company's directors: Warren Buffett and Herbert Allen.[19] At Gillette, where Michael Hawley was ousted as CEO that same year after only eighteen months on the job, accounts from those familiar with the situation highlighted that it was buyout legend Henry Kravis who led the movement for Hawley's dismissal.[20]

These dramatic stories do raise the question of whether such investor-driven dismissals of CEOs were isolated examples, not indicative of any general trend. In response, one could point to tales that have unfolded in the past decade at Apple Computer, Xerox, Lucent, and IBM—all firms in which institutional investors played a role in dismissing what were regarded as underperforming CEOs (that is, CEOs of firms that were underperforming). One could also consider a wider sample of firms. Figure 3.3 examines the rate of CEO dismissals for the 850 largest companies in the United States between 1980 and 1996. Using a statistical technique called hazard-rate analysis, the figure highlights that for the

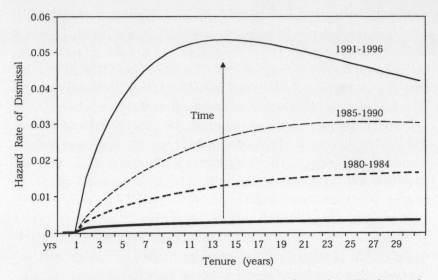

FIGURE 3.3 CEO Dismissal Rates over Time. Hazard rate for CEO dismissals, 1980–96. Note only cohorts for 1975–80 contain complete observation for 1980–96. Subsequent cohorts use both actual data and then predicted values. See the appendix for data sources and model.

same level of corporate performance, a CEO appointed between 1990 and 1996 is three times more likely to be fired than a CEO appointed before 1980.

Even when they have not sought outright dismissal, institutional investors have sought ways to hold CEOs more accountable for poor corporate performance: for example, by actively campaigning against the adoption of anti-takeover defenses or in favor of tighter alignment of CEO incentives with stock performance. All of the forms of pressure applied by investors, via corporate directors, to CEOs—but especially those aimed at achieving CEO dismissals—have revealed a distinctly CEO-centered view of the corporation that, as we shall see, has been another product of the overall shift from managerial to investor capitalism.

In any event, the shift from managerial to investor capitalism has altered the form and boundaries of CEO succession. In particular, CEO tenure has shifted from a time-determined event to a performance-affected event. At the same time, choosing a successor has shifted from a CEO-dominated process to a board-dominated process. As CEOs were held to higher performance standards and the turnover at the top increased to unprecedented levels, boards were now more accountable for the selection decision. Whereas under managerial capitalism, boards typically rubber-stamped the outgoing CEO's choice even when the firm was performing poorly, the search for a CEO successor was now considered the directors' most important job. The job was made all the more challenging by the fact that, in increasing numbers of cases, there was no clear heir apparent. And even when there was, it was now not at all clear to directors whether he or she was the best candidate for the job.

The Liability of "Insiderness"

Particularly in cases in which corporate performance has been mediocre toward the end of a CEO's tenure, or in which the board is forced to remove a CEO, boards now show a strong tendency to assert themselves —and to attempt to reassure investors and other outsiders—by rushing to find a corporate savior from outside the organization.[21] The value of internal candidates is discounted by a belief that such candidates lack the necessary skills to improve organizational performance, if they are not actually seen as part of the problem at hand. Internal candidates, about whom the board knows more than it possibly can about external ones, are considered blemished while external candidates are easily idealized. Directors also tend to believe (mistakenly, as we shall see in chapters 6 and 7) that an insider CEO will be more difficult to control because he or she will be attached to the status quo. By contrast, directors and the external constituencies whom they desire to please view hiring an outsider CEO as a progressive and positive action. The belief in the superiority of outsiders has become so engrained that it was fashionable to portray the legendary Jack Welch—a consummate insider who had spent his entire career at GE before being named the company's CEO—as a de facto outsider. Other such faux outsiders in the ranks of recent CEOs include former Ford chief executive Jacques Nasser and American Express's Harvey Golub.[22]

Things were very different in the era of managerial capitalism, when the board played an essentially passive role in CEO succession, and it was comparatively rare for corporations to hire outsiders. In those days, as now, the choice of a new CEO was influenced by a variety of factors. Many studies of CEO succession have pointed to these influences, which include the strategic direction of the firm, the nature of the regulatory environment, and the performance of the firm.[23] But in the era of managerial capitalism, these factors were all overwhelmed by one critical one: the preferences of the outgoing CEO, as determined by his evaluation of a field of internal candidates.

The importance of the outgoing CEO's preferences in the CEO succession process before the advent of investor capitalism is highlighted in an account by Reginald Jones—Jack Welch's predecessor as CEO of General Electric, who retired in 1981—of how he went about evaluating his potential successors. Jones's account is worth quoting at some length for the insight it provides into not only the process of CEO succession in his day but also the criteria he applied to CEO candidates.

> One technique that I used is what may be called the airplane interview. My predecessor, Fred Borch, used this technique in a somewhat similar situation, but it had impressed me as most helpful, and I had learned much from his effective use of this approach.
>
> I sat down for a couple of hours, unannounced, with each of these seven or eight candidates. They didn't know the purpose of the meeting, and I made sure they didn't tell the others, so that everybody came in surprised. And they wouldn't tell, once they went through the experience, because they wouldn't want the other guy to have the advantage of knowing what this was all about.
>
> You call a fellow in, close the door, get out your pipe, and try to get him relaxed. Then you say to him, "Well, look now, Bill, you and I are flying in one of the company planes and this plane crashes. (Pause) Who should be the next chairman of the General Electric Company?"
>
> Well, some of them try to climb out of the wreckage, but you say, "No, no, you and I are killed. (Pause) Who should be the chairman of General Electric Company?" And boy, this really catches them cold. They fumble around for a while and fumble around, and you have a two hour conversation. And you learn a great deal from that meeting.
>
> When you've done that seven or eight times, once with each of the

leading competitors to replace you, it's amazing what you learn about the chemistry among that group—who will work with whom, who just despises the other guy—and things come out, because this is a totally confidential session you're having with them, totally confidential. Because they've not had any warning that this was going to strike, they blurt things out that you damned well better remember, because sometimes those are more important than the studied comments that you get at a later date.

Now, having done that across the field of candidates, the next thing I did was to call them back three months later, and do it all over again. This time they knew it was coming, and they had been through the experience. Now they came in with sheaves of notes, studied comments; they were statesmen developing, you see, in this process. And we went through the whole thing again—it took a couple of hours.

While I was holding these interviews, I also did the same thing with those senior officers with whom I could talk. These were the ones who were not contenders, the ones who were going to retire before me or with me, whose opinion I valued. They were generally staff people. And you get their reactions as to who should be running the company, what teams will work together, what individuals don't fit, and so on. I shared all this with the five members of the Management Development and Compensation Committee of the board, in depth, and of course with the senior vice president of executive manpower, who was intimately familiar with all these people.

Now, in the next series of interviews—again two in number and again the first one unannounced—you call the fellow in and say, "Remember our airplane conversations . . . ?" "Oh, yeah . . . ," and he starts to sweat a little bit. "Now," you say, "this time, we're out there together, we're flying in a plane and the plane crashes. I'm done, but you live. Now who should be the chairman of General Electric?"

And again, you get a very interesting set of responses. Some don't want any part of it: "Here's the guy you should pick." Others: "I'm your man." And you say, "Okay, if you're the man, what do you see ahead as the major challenges facing GE, what sort of environment do you visualize, what programs would you mount, and who should be the other members of the Corporate Executive office?" Now you're getting very specific about the chemistry, about interpersonal relationships. And then you do that again on an announced basis, just as you did the first time; the second time they come in, they're really ready for you. They've got all their notes and you have a very informed discussion.

Now, that was the way we developed the information, which we shared again with the Management Development and Compensation Committee of the board and, finally, the full board. And the full board, having known these people intimately and been very much involved in the entire succession process, arrived at a set of conclusions as to the three candidates that we should move up to vice chairmen.

We then ran with a Corporate Executive Office of myself and these three new vice chairmen for a period of about fifteen months. . . . Remember, they were attending every board meeting and they were seeing board members in social as well as business situations.[24]

GE's succession process, as portrayed in Jones's account, in many ways bears out the view of CEO succession generally that has become common among economists, inspired largely by Sherwin Rosen and Edward Lazear's theories of "executive tournaments." An executive tournament is an overt contest among internal candidates based on the idea that, given the company's meritocracy, ability largely determines who will be the next CEO of the corporation.[25] Yet GE's process, as Jones describes it, also demonstrates that the abilities required to become the CEO of such an organization go well beyond administrative ones. A successful candidate at GE would also need to have tremendous political skills to navigate a competitive corporate hierarchy in which numerous executives were in competition for the top position.[26]

Within the closed circle of corporate management in the era of managerial capitalism, CEO succession could remain limited largely to internal candidates, almost all of whom had spent their entire careers inside a single firm. Yet a confluence of business trends, coinciding with the rise of investor capitalism in the late 1980s and early 1990s, eventually made it more difficult to simply promote a CEO from within without at least benchmarking an internal CEO candidate against outsiders.

As investors became increasingly restive, the traditional advantages of promoting from within—industry-specific experience and knowledge about a particular firm's culture and political terrain, for instance— were no longer always perceived as advantages. Insider CEO candidates were viewed as suspect and as impediments to organizational change. Analysts and the business media often questioned whether insiders would be willing to make difficult decisions such as downsizing or reversing past strategic decisions that they may have had a hand in making. (GM's Robert Stempel, who had always seconded the plans of his predecessor, Roger Smith, is an example of an inside successor who was now considered compromised by his past as a loyal corporate soldier.) Directors also adopted this more skeptical stance toward insiders. Henry Wendt, a director and former CEO of SmithKline Beecham, describes the change by saying, "The emphasis on reinventing the corporation, on reengineering and restructuring accelerates the pace of change. So the balance has shifted to recruiting from the outside for a change agent." A knowledgeable insider involved with the 1993 selection of Lou Gerstner, IBM's recently retired outsider CEO, states the rationale for bringing in an outsider when the company needs to change in unusually blunt terms.

> The person coming from the outside has a clear mandate, particularly if he is coming into a troubled situation. He is not beholden to anyone. There are so many constraints on the internally-promoted individual. There is so much baggage! Organizational boxes, the people in the boxes, probably half the businesses that were bought now should be chucked, commitments to people on what their future will be. [As an insider], you are part of the process. Now that you are on top, you cannot be a Magnum Prick. You turn to an outsider and then you can watch the blood spray. You don't see many examples of internal candidates getting to the top of the system and then laying waste to the existing culture.

As the shift to investor capitalism gathered steam, a rapidly changing technological environment, continuing deregulation, and industry consolidation also fueled the perception that insiders might not have the right skills to manage in the new milieu. Moreover, choosing an outsider became a way of demonstrating to Wall Street the board's commitment to change. For example, when computer maker Compaq announced in July 2000 that an insider, Michael Capellas, would become CEO, its stock price immediately dropped 4 percent. By contrast, computer maker Hewlett-Packard's shares jumped 2 percent when it was announced in July 1999 that an outsider, Carly Fiorina, would become the next CEO.[27] According to a search consultant with knowledge of the H-P search, business analysts believed that the H-P culture had grown too soft, with too much emphasis on consensus decision-making, and H-P's board had increasingly adopted this view. The directors wanted someone to shake up the traditional culture, which worked to the detriment of inside candidate Ann Livermore (the CEO of H-P's $14 billion Enterprise Computing division), who was said to be the outgoing CEO's choice.[28]

At the level of the board, changes in board practices have also contributed to the increasing willingness of directors to break from past succession policies and bring in outsiders. Two shifts have been particularly important here. The first of these has involved changes in the ways in which board members are compensated. In recent years, almost all the *Fortune 500* firms have adopted some form of stock options for directors. The idea is that if directors are paid in stock, they will act in the best interests of shareholders and thus will be more willing to break with past organizational practices such as hiring insider candidates. The second shift leading to a more independent board has been a change in the way that directors are elected. Traditionally, the CEO of a firm selected a firm's directors. This was usually accomplished by the CEO's serving on the board's nominating committee. In recent years, however, the practice of a CEO serving on a nominating committee has been frowned upon. In a study of corporate boards, Anil Shivdasani and David Yermack have found that when the CEO serves on the nominating committee or no nominating committee exists, firms appoint fewer independent outside directors and more gray outsiders (such as personal attorneys or corporate consultants) with conflicts of interest. Their study has also found a trend of companies removing CEOs from involvement in director selection, leading to the creation of more independent boards.[29]

Impatient investors, an increasingly turbulent business environment, changes in the way that corporate directors are selected and compensated—all of these factors have influenced the turn from inside to outside candidates in the CEO succession process. An equally important consequence of these developments, however, has been a dramatic change both in the way that the CEO position itself is conceived and in the qualities directors seek in a CEO candidate. In the era of investor capitalism, it is no longer enough—or even of the first importance—that a CEO candidate have particular skills as a manager. What matters much more is that a candidate have a particular kind of person.

Charismatic Orientation

Along with the many other changes that the decline of managerial capitalism and the rise, in its place, of the more Darwinian system of investor capitalism have brought for corporations and those who are affected by their actions, these events have led to a greater focus on the individual CEO. As we have seen, the pressures brought to bear by investors, via boards of directors, on CEOs—including demands for their dismissals—have been premised on the belief that the CEO can and should be held responsible for corporate performance, irrespective of his or her *job* performance, or indeed of the many other factors that more decisively influence firm performance.[30]

Corporate directors' adoption of this belief can be seen in, for example, the trend toward making stock options an increasingly important part of CEO compensation packages. Indeed, by supposedly tying CEO pay more closely to corporate performance as measured by the stock market,[31] these new compensation packages have indirectly reinforced the idea that an unsatisfactory stock price is a legitimate basis for dismissing the CEO—even if dismissal becomes, as it does in many cases, an occasion to provide the outgoing CEO with generous financial rewards for failure. The belief that the CEO is individually responsible for the firm's financial performance is also reflected in the increasingly frank way that boards of directors have become willing to discuss CEO dismissals. Of the twenty-two *Fortune* 500 CEOs who suddenly resigned in 1992 and 1993, only two—or so the press releases from those years would have us believe—were actually forced out. The rest, we are meant to conclude, either retired voluntarily or went on to pursue other opportunities.[32] Less than a decade later, the press releases announcing the forced departures of Al Dunlap from Sunbeam, Michael Hawley from Gillette, and Richard McGinn from Lucent struck an entirely different note. In its account of McGinn's firing, Lucent's press release flatly announced, "In a meeting this weekend, the board reviewed

Lucent's recent performance and outlook for the current quarter and determined that an immediate change in leadership was necessary."[33]

In embracing the belief that a company's fortunes depend on who occupies the CEO suite, corporate directors have not, of course, been operating in a cultural vacuum. In what is ultimately the most significant development for CEO succession resulting from the advent of investor capitalism, a distinctly American cult of the CEO has replaced attention and deference to the complex organizations that the CEOs of large companies head. Like corporate boards' assumption of the task of choosing a new CEO, or the growing tendency for companies to turn to outside successors, this development—and the type of corporate leader it has exalted—represents a sharp break with the circumstances that preceded it. For when the era of managerial capitalism ended in the 1980s, the Organization Man, and the business culture that had once sustained him, died with it.

During the era of managerial capitalism, American business was very much conducted within a set of generally accepted rules that maintained an ordered, stable business environment.[34] The government regulated many industries, including trucking, communications, and airlines. A few giant companies dominated many markets, such as for automobiles, steel, and consumer electronics, while foreign trade was relatively slight and foreign competitors were not considered a threat. In this period, corporations were run by a professional class of conforming managers, who were willing to sublimate their individuality in exchange for the security of corporate hierarchy and steady promotions. Their uniformity was perceptively captured in classic texts such as William H. Whyte's *The Organization Man*, C. Wright Mills's *The Power Elite*, and David Riesman's *The Lonely Crowd*.[35] These men shared a common bureaucratic culture and viewed business as having reached a détente or rapprochement with government and labor.

This world changed during the 1970s and early 1980s, as a radically different business environment came into being. The country was on the brink of what some have called the third industrial revolution. Smokestack industries were being replaced by services. Technology began to move from the back office to the boardroom. Chips were products made from sand instead of from potatoes. Foreign competition, first from Japan and then from Europe, landed on the shores of North America with a ferocity and strength so completely unexpected as to raise fundamental questions regarding the organization of the American economy.[36] Moreover, the deregulation that corporate chieftains had literally begged Congress for had once again opened the American market to the war of all against all that characterizes unbridled capitalism, but meanwhile failed to boost corporate profits. The gentleman's capitalism that had characterized the era of managerial capitalism was gone, and a new type of leadership seemed called for.

The new corporate leadership that began emerging in the 1980s was in many ways a throwback to the swashbuckling Robber Barons of the late nineteenth century. This group, however, tended to be more public-relations savvy and psychologically attuned to the zeitgeist, thus avoiding being vilified as the Robber Barons had been. The new CEOs were portrayed as entrepreneurial. Like Steve Jobs and Bill Gates, they founded new companies. Or, like Jack Welch and Lou Gerstner, they rejuvenated old-line firms. These new members of the business elite were no longer defined as professional managers but instead as *leaders*, whose ability to lead consisted in their personal characteristics or, more simply, their charisma.[37]

The turn toward charismatic authority in business, while in part a reaction to a rapidly changing economic and business environment, was also reinforced by a changing cultural context. The term *charisma* was introduced into the common lexicon by the sociologist Max Weber, who transferred it from its original religious context to the examination of political regimes. Political scientists have found that a turn toward charismatic leadership is most likely at times of dramatic changes in the social or economic order. Such major disruptions are said to create a cultic milieu favoring the appearance of leaders who can give a society a new vision while providing an outlet for the expression of the anger and frustration generated by the collapse of an old order.[38] Sociologists, meanwhile, have pointed to the role of more subtle cultural factors that increase the predisposition toward charismatic authority.[39] In the case of the business world in the era of investor capitalism, the turn toward charismatic CEOs has been partly rooted in a changing conception of business and its role in society.

Over the last twenty years, business has been elevated in American society into an activity transcending the profane task of making money.

Business is now portrayed as having a moral dimension. The change can be seen in the publicity materials of companies such as the cigarette manufacturer Philip Morris, which claims to be motivated by higher purposes than a mere desire to sell cigarettes. Instead, Philip Morris is supposedly guided by the values of "Integrity, trust, passion, creativity, quality and sharing," as well as by a "belief in adult choice."[40] DuPont doesn't just produce chemicals anymore, but has instead dedicated itself to "the work of improving life on our planet."[41] While one might argue that the social criticism directed for many years against industries such as tobacco and chemicals is the cause of this emphasis on mission, companies in other, seemingly much less socially and ethically questionable industries also now tout themselves in such high-flown terms. *Fast Company,* the business magazine created for the "New Economy," describes itself as not just a magazine but "a movement . . . [striving] to help people in the new economy discover the tools, techniques, and tactics they need to succeed at work and life."[42] ServiceMaster, which is in the business of industrial cleaning and facilities management, described its mission thus in its 1995 annual report:

> At ServiceMaster, the task before us is to train and motivate people to serve so that they will do a more effective job, be more productive in their work, and, yes, even be better people. . . . It is more than a job, a means to earn a living. It is, in fact, our mission. . . . [I]f we focused exclusively on profit, we would be a firm that had failed to nurture its soul.[43]

Couched in psychological and humanistic terms, this new orientation has adopted the mantra that employees are the most important resource of the company—an idea that companies can now embrace for solidly self-interested reasons. One distinguishing feature of today's business landscape is that the best way to achieve high returns for shareholders is to maximize the efforts and commitment of employees.[44] In the new ideology created to serve the corporation's ends in this changed environment, employees are no longer subordinates or workers, but rather "partners," "owners," and "associates." Whatever the euphemism, the purpose of this terminology is to create the impression that employees are participants in a grand social experiment in which each and every individual makes a difference. In the 1960s, the sociologists David Riesman and Nathan Glazer foresaw this transformation in which a job is no longer about economic sustenance but is said also to be a source of meaning. More recently, the social commentator David Brooks has provided important insight into the new counter-cultural capitalist ethos in which work has been transformed into an intellectual and spiritual calling.[45] In business schools, meanwhile, the advice given to students is that they need to be "passionate" and "ecstatic" about their jobs. The corporation, commitment to the job, and teamwork have become substitutes for the increasingly fractured and transient communities in which many people now live. Their significance has become quasi-religious, as suggested by the importation of terms such as *mission* and *values* into the contemporary corporate lexicon.

This changing definition of business has also changed the definition of an effective CEO from that of competent manager to charismatic leader. Given the new conception of the corporation and its role in society, a CEO must now inspire. To motivate employees to devote long hours to the company, the CEO must convince them that the firm is not simply a profit-making enterprise but that it fulfills a larger, more exalted mission. The new CEO's role has been portrayed in a variety of ways: visionary, evangelist, role model, coach. Whatever the precise job description, the charismatic CEO stands in stark contrast to the professional Organization Man who toiled in anonymity during the era of managerial capitalism. The pages of *Business Week, Fortune*, and *Harvard Business Review* are now filled with stories about heroic leadership, the habits of successful people, and the personal characteristics displayed by leaders.[46] Becoming a CEO is now about communicating an essential optimism, confidence, and can-do attitude. In the process, individuality has become a desired attribute, not a liability. (One need only look at the books of management gurus such as Tom Peters or Stephen Covey to see this transformation.)

Future scholars of organizations may well date the advent of this new breed of corporate leader to September 1979, when Lee Iacocca was elected chairman and CEO of Chrysler Corporation. Not since the heyday of the Robber Barons, when Rockefellers, Fords, and Carnegies ruled the business world, had a CEO so captivated the nation. Before Iacocca ascended to the leadership of Chrysler, the company had appeared doomed. Yet within a few short years, under Iacocca's leadership and with the help of $1.2 billion of government-guaranteed loans, the company appeared vigorous again.[47] Its K-car was a bestseller and the Chrysler minivan would forever change the landscape of suburban driveways. Chrysler's profits were so large, the company hardly knew what to do with the money. In 1984, Iacocca's autobiography became the best selling business biography of all time. Two years later, standing at the base of the newly refurbished Statue of Liberty on a warm Fourth of July evening, Iacocca received more cheers than the man he was standing next to, President Ronald Reagan. Indeed, at that moment, many influential political people had initiated a movement to recruit Iacocca to run for president in 1988. Certainly his rhetorical powers were magnificent, and any other corporate chief appeared positively bland standing next to this son of Italian immigrants and personification of the American dream.

Today, with corporations' need for "vision" and "leadership" having become axiomatic, more and more CEOs pattern themselves on charismatic leaders such as Iacocca. Some play the role naturally; others are still rehearsing. Yet comparing today's new CEOs with the directors who appoint them—many of the latter retired CEOs who rose through the corporate ranks during the heyday of managerial capitalism—one discerns clear differences. Whereas most of the older, former executives are quiet, politically skilled, and studied in their comments, the new CEOs are more verbal, controlling, and abrasive. The new CEOs also display a brash self-confidence and even flamboyance that can be very seductive and inspiring.[48]

It is also clear that at least some of today's celebrity CEOs would not have succeeded in the world of managerial capitalism. The tantrums and tirades John Byrne described in *Chainsaw*, his book on the supposed turnaround master Al Dunlap, for example, would surely not have been tolerated in that earlier era:

> In Dunlap's presence, knees trembled and stomachs churned. Underlings feared the torrential harangue that Dunlap could unleash at any moment. At his worst, he became viciously profane, even violent. Executives said he would throw papers or furniture, bang his hands on his desk, and shout so ferociously that a manager's hair would be blown back by the stream of air that rushed from Dunlap's mouth. "Hair spray day" became a code phrase among execs, signifying a potential tantrum.[49]

In more skeptical and socialized conditions, such people were often described as eccentric, unstable, and unpredictable, rather than as the "out of the box" or "emotional" thinkers who are so venerated today.[50]

Although this startling transformation in the type of person now entrusted with the job of running America's major corporations is primarily cultural in origin, the cultural influences at work have been powerfully reinforced by institutional changes in American society and American business coinciding with the rise of investor capitalism. In particular, institutions such as the business press and financial analysts have become powerful mediating influences that command great attention and increasingly arbitrate, shape, diffuse, filter, and focus attention to business organizations. They have acquired this power owing to the same changes in the ownership of American corporations that created investor capitalism in the first place. An account of these structural changes forms the last part of the story of the rise of the charismatic CEO.

The Changing Institutional Context

CEOs could afford to be bland and colorless when they were less visible in society, and they became more visible as investors both became more demanding and came to represent a broader swath of the American public. As the economist Robert Shiller has argued, changes over the past two decades in the nature of employee pension plans have encouraged people to learn about and accept stocks as investments. The most revolutionary change, according to Shiller, has been the expansion of defined contribution plans; the most common of these, 401(k) plans, are weighted heavily in favor of stocks. The second vehicle through which the broader American populace has invested in the stock market is mutual funds, which began to enjoy wide popularity in the early 1980s. In 1982, Shiller has found, there were only 340 equity mutual funds in the United States; by the end of 1998 there were 3,513—more mutual funds than stocks listed on the New York Stock Exchange. And whereas there were only 6.2 million equity-mutual-fund shareholder accounts in the United States in 1982 (one for every ten U.S. families), by 1998 there were 119.8 (nearly two accounts per family).[51] (Between 1990 and 1996 alone, assets in equity-based mutual funds grew from $249 billion to $1.7 trillion.) In less than two decades, investing had become America's most popular participatory sport.

As ordinary Americans have become investors, there has been a corresponding explosion in the numbers of stock market analysts and business media, which now serve as the primary source of news about corporations for most investors. These developments (which have made following business and the stock market into another form of media-based entertainment), coupled with the individualistic bias of American culture, have given a strong impetus to the cult of the CEO in American business and society.

Consider, for example, how the American business press now filters and transmits information on organizational performance and strategy. With an eye to a national audience, the business media focus not on the complexities of organizations or on rapid changes in the business environment, but rather on the actors involved. This approach personifies the corporation, making much of winners and losers, of who is up and who is down, of who is a good CEO and who is not. The press has thereby turned CEOs—once as unknown to the American public as their secretaries, chauffeurs, and shoe-shiners—into a new category of American celebrity. Many business articles now emphasize the personal habits and attributes of individual CEOs, often going into more depth about these matters than about details of a firm's strategy or finances. Whether portraying CEOs as "magnetic" personalities or "bland" bureaucrats, they powerfully reinforce not only the myth that the CEO is the hinge on which the entire organization turns but also the concept of corporate leadership as a function of personality. And whether their judgments about particular individuals are taken at face value or not, these portrayals—once they have been complacently reproduced by business news channels such as CNBC and MSNBC—serve by their very ubiquity to increase the attention paid to individual CEOs and their personal traits. (Figure 3.4 presents a simple count of the number of CEOs who have appeared on the cover of Business Week over the past twenty years.)

To take an example of this new tendency (and how it mirrors attitudes in the corporate world itself), Fortune magazine in its May 2000 issue asked rhetorically if John Chambers, CEO of the then high-flying

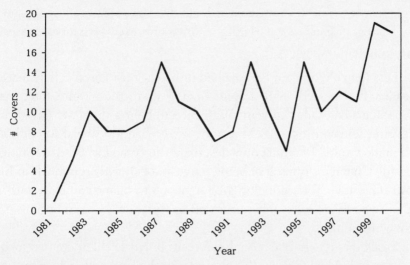

FIGURE 3.4 Number of *Business Week* Covers Featuring CEOs from the *Fortune* 1000 from 1980–2000. Excludes covers in which multiple CEOs appeared.

Cisco Systems, was the greatest CEO ever, and whether it was too late to purchase Cisco stock. The author described Chambers in almost reverential terms: "Chambers has an open face and looks you in the eye when he speaks. His accent isn't the pinched Appalachian you might expect but more a gentle Piedmont." The article then went on to describe a speech that Chambers had recently given:

> On this early April evening, big wheels from a group called the Financial Services Roundtable, including Dick Kovacevich of Wells Fargo, Allen Wheat of CSFB, and Robert Herres of USAA, seem to be actually intrigued by the program's pre-dinner speaker. The execs have donned their blue blazers (and brought their spouses too!) and are rapidly filling the Casa Grande Ballroom. The speaker is John Chambers, and when he gets going the group hangs on his every word, because they believe Chambers can explain how to harness the power of the Internet.
>
> It's powerful stuff. The Internet will become completely pervasive, says Chambers, working the room like a preacher. "Your franchises are under attack. Prices will fall. Margins will decline. You must get on the Net and find new ways to add value." You can almost see the mental note taking in the audience: "Monday: Ramp up Internet effort. Ask IT guys

about Cisco." It's a wake-up call, but the crowd seems to love the messenger. Chambers gets a big hand. Afterwards, execs press forward to soak in some Net karma.[52]

Less than a year later, *Fortune* had turned against Cisco's charismatic leader. It appeared that, despite having up-to-the-minute forecasts, Chambers had failed to warn Wall Street about a dramatic fall-off in revenue and earnings. (By May 2001, Cisco had lost over $400 billion in market value.) *Fortune* now described the company as arrogant, accusing Chambers himself of being naive and believing too much in his own fairy tale. "Those looking for someone to blame can start with a CEO who didn't seem able to turn off the spigot of his own optimism," the writer opined.[53]

Stock market analysts, too, have contributed to the increased focus on the individual CEO and—by virtue of the very real influence that they wield—have made a certain kind of personality part of the new CEO job description. Once largely ignored by CEOs and corporate boards, analysts have become an important part of the way financial markets work, and their numbers have increased markedly (see figure 3.5).

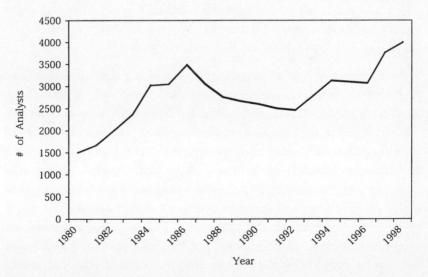

FIGURE 3.5 Total Number of Equity Analysts Employed in the United States from 1980–98. *Source:* Groysenberg (2001)

Although analysts have traditionally been portrayed as orienting their research and opinions toward institutional investors, Robert Shiller has argued that their recommendations are now consumed by the entire investment community.[54] Analysts have therefore emerged as important intermediaries between investors and the firm. A particular analyst's recommendations can dramatically affect short-term trading volume and the price of a stock.[55] This is especially true when his or her voice can be amplified by the business press, which has stoked competition among analysts to make headlines with their upgrades and downgrades.

Analysts, that is to say, now compete actively to be interviewed on CNBC and quoted in the *Wall Street Journal*. One consequence has been that analysts, bowing to the media's biases as to what makes for interesting reading or viewing, have increasingly replaced technical analysis of a company with focus on the person running it. In the business press, statements about a particular firm's prospects that are grounded in narratives of success and failure and managerial legend and myth are more compelling than technical analysis. By focusing on the individual running the corporation, analysts and media rely on a type of shorthand that simplifies communications about complicated subjects such as financial statements, business strategies, or industry conditions. Given this orientation, what a CEO says in a CNBC briefing or a meeting with analysts becomes part of a story that is quickly diffused and can affect evaluations of a company's future prospects.

To see how this substitution of personalization for analysis is effected in practice, consider the reaction of stock market analysts in 1993 to Eastman Kodak's appointment of the first outsider CEO in its history, George Fisher. Fisher had been president of Motorola, for whose strong performance at the time he was widely credited even though—in light of Motorola's problems today—it is apparent that much of the company's earlier success was actually due to telecommunications deregulation's having increased competition in local cellular markets and lowered prices for consumers, leading to a more rapid adoption of the technology. Fisher had reportedly been courted by IBM for its top job, but had declined. When the announcement of his appointment by Kodak was made, a CS First Boston analyst told Dow Jones Newswires: "We're psyched. The stock is going higher and we think it is an excellent choice."[56] Investors then responded to Fisher's selection by immediately bidding up Kodak's stock 15 percent.[57] A similar response from analysts (and subsequently from investors) occurred when AT&T brought in C. Michael Armstrong from Hughes Electronics in 1997 and a Dillon Read analyst enthused: "AT&T appears to have gotten the superstar CEO it needs to firmly guide the company through the transition from the current long-distance oligopoly environment to a fully competitive U.S. and global telecommunications world."[58]

The rise of the business media and analysts, with their fixation on the CEO, has, in turn, introduced a new set of informal ground rules to CEO succession: a critical consideration in evaluating a potential CEO today is his or her ability to command attention from the media and stock market analysts in a way that will establish credibility for the firm and inspire confidence in both investors and others. How analysts are likely to react to a new CEO has become a principal concern of directors conducting a search. In a reflection of this trend, the closed-circulation magazine *Corporate Board Member* devoted the cover story of its Spring 2001 issue to the subject of attracting favorable attention from analysts and the business media. The story argued that directors now have to think of the CEO as the most visible symbol of the firm and its "star storyteller":

> There is no better messenger than your CEO, though the CFO can be a close second. Institutional investors expect quality time with the top brass. . . . In one form or the other, they should be spending 40 percent of their time on investor relations. That means a major commitment to investor conference calls, presentations at banking and industry conferences, in-person visits to major shareholders, and last but hardly least, media appearances.[59]

In such an environment, directors need to consider how effective CEOs will be in conveying confidence to analysts and attracting attention from business media outlets such as MSNBC. In a sidebar in the *Corporate Board Member* article, Tyler Mathisen, host of CNBC's *Marketwatch*, described the characteristics he looks for in a guest, and offered advice to executives on how to handle themselves in an appearance on television:

Remember that television tends to "bland out" even the most energetic speaker. So be animated; wave your hands if that is your wont. Never forget that your voice is a musical instrument. It is meant to be played, loud as well as slow. Your tone matters. It is no coincidence that many of the CEOs who come across best on TV are the ones whose companies are in the communications business. Think Michael Eisner of Disney, Barry Diller of USA Networks, Sumner Redstone of Viacom, Ted Turner of AOL Time Warner. These men not only know their businesses cold, they also know the value of a compelling performance. And they don't shrink from an opportunity to be provocative, even combative, if the occasion warrants.[60]

As the emphasis on image-projection and image-reception has become so prevalent, directors have come to place correspondingly less emphasis on individuals' particular experiences or training when evaluating candidates for the CEO job. Personality and image are now widely believed to be more important not just than particular business abilities but also than firm- and industry-specific knowledge and experience. The result has been to reinforce directors' tendencies to actively pursue outsider CEOs who possess the elusive characteristics of charisma that have become so highly valued, rather than the concrete experience that inside candidates would be more likely to possess. In this sense, the emergence of the ideal of the charismatic CEO, like the circumstances that began to make CEO tenure more unstable in the 1990s, has been a precipitating factor in the very development of an external CEO labor market.

Viewed in this cultural and historical context, the external CEO market turns out to be truly inseparable from a variety of influences not normally associated with markets. Structural influences such as the major shift in the ownership of major American corporations over the last generation have combined with culturally conditioned beliefs about the nature of leadership in organizations to create a market for CEO candidates with particular personal traits, drawn from a pool of external candidates—a market that simply did not exist before. Besides creating the elementary conditions of this new market considered in chapter 2 (small numbers of buyers and sellers, high risk to participants, and concerns about legitimacy), these structures and beliefs influence the behavior of the major actors in the market—directors, executive search consultants, and candidates—at every step of the process of external CEO search. It is to the roles of each of these actors that we must now turn our attention.

CHAPTER 4

BOARD GAMES:
THE ROLE OF DIRECTORS
IN CEO SEARCH

THERE ARE two ways of understanding the role of corporate directors in external CEO search. One is based on the prevalent belief that actors in the external CEO market are what neoclassical economists say that actors in markets generally are: autonomous individuals rationally pursuing their self-interest in a context with a high degree of transparency. This approach focuses on the motives and behavior of the individual director. Today, this is perhaps the most commonly used method of accounting for directors' roles in corporate governance. It is linked to the view that directors are fully motivated to act in the interests of the firm and its shareholders only when they have a financial interest in so doing. Advocates of this perspective have argued that without financial inducements such as stock options or share grants, directors "have little incentive to extend themselves beyond relatively superficial oversight of their firms' affairs. They mechanically fulfill their specified duties (certain approvals and audits) and watch for egregious derailments, but not much more."[1]

An emphasis on director shareholding has become all the rage in recent prescriptions for improving corporate governance. Today, almost all publicly traded corporations have adopted some type of director stock plan. Despite the proliferation of such plans, however, little evidence supports the belief that they have any effect on director behavior or firm performance. In one of the largest sample studies on the subject, John Core and his colleagues found that "percentage ownership per outside director . . . has little effect on the monitoring role of the board of directors." The researchers concluded that there is no empirical support for "recent conjectures suggesting that outside directors should be forced to hold a greater amount of the firm's shares in order to ensure that they have a financial stake in the outcome of their monitoring."[2]

The focus on financial incentives for individual directors misses the truly critical point about director behavior: a board is not simply an aggregation of individuals, but in fact constitutes a complex group. The actions of a board, therefore, cannot be viewed as an aggregate of individual directors' behaviors. A second and, I argue, more powerful way of understanding the role of directors in external CEO searches sees their actions as growing out of the connections and relationships in which individual directors are embedded, and that reach beyond the confines of any particular boardroom.

The Social Character of the Board

Once one moves beyond the standard individualistic models for explaining the behavior of corporate directors, it becomes apparent that group- and community-oriented behavior takes the place of calculations of self-interest when directors undertake an action such as searching for a new CEO. The nature of board membership, combined with the small size of the overall director community and the embeddedness of directors within a larger social system of third parties (such as analysts and the business media), results in an ingrained mutual dependence among people who share many relationships: those with whom board members are economically involved are the same as those with whom they are socially linked through shared status, organizational affiliations, and social standing. Several scholars have noted that directors are often connected to other leaders in the business community by virtue of their common residence in elite neighborhoods and membership in social clubs, professional associations, and public-policy committees.[3] Directors' actions in external CEO search are fundamentally regulated by these massive social facts of structural relationships and shared values.

Directors, to begin with, are highly cognizant of their membership in the communities to which they belong by virtue of their service on a corporate board. Like members of other close-knit communities, they have a clear sense of their own social domain—how far it extends, who belongs in it, and who does not.[4] There is a social map, a list of members, and a system of gradations, hallowed by time and sanctioned by tradition. Whereas most of us are often only vaguely aware of our membership in social communities and of our place in a particular social system, directors explicitly know which groups they belong to, what communities they serve, where they are in the status hierarchy, and what their roles are. Two groups to which directors belong are particularly relevant to explaining directors' role in CEO search and therefore are worth describing in some detail.

The first membership group with which a director identifies him or herself is a particular corporate board. Individual boards of directors are characterized by a high degree of internal cohesion, facilitated by several structural factors, the first of which is group distinctiveness. By distinctiveness I mean how easily a group can be defined and how easily members of the group can identify one another.[5] Tom Piper, a board member at companies including Marriott Corporation, describes the "groupiness" of board meetings: "It is hard to explain to a person who is not a director. It is in many ways a club. You have a group of highly respected individuals who you work with. Each board I belong to has its own norms and ways of doing things, we value this. . . . We are conscious that being a director constitutes a unique set of roles and responsibilities." The centrality of this distinctiveness is so strong, according to Piper, that there are "many people whose identities get caught up in being a board member of one or another particular firm." The distinctiveness of a particular board is not only expressed in the group consciousness or "we-feeling" of directors but is also apparent to outsiders (such as researchers or investors), who can easily identify a firm's directors through a search on a corporate website or in the pages of an annual report.

The second structural quality that lends a board its cohesiveness is the small number of people who constitute the group. Today, the average board consists of thirteen people, only one less than the average board in 1980. This smallness of scale gives rise to particular interpersonal and group processes. As social psychological research on organizational groups has shown, the smallness of a group heightens the members' awareness of one another not only as professionals but also as private individuals.[6] One director describes what he sees as the advantages of a small board by saying, "There is less formality in the smaller board. We can engage in more constructive and frank discussions with the CEO. Also, it is easier to develop a working relationship and team feeling with the other board members when the number of participants is smaller."

The third structural factor leading to high cohesion among members of a board is homogeneity. Homogeneity in a group, the sociologist C. Wright Mills noted, eases role-taking and identification both with other individuals and with the collectivity.[7] Although not one director I met (including the one woman and one African-American I interviewed) made reference to this obvious fact, board members are similar along a variety of observable demographic dimensions such as gender (they are almost all males), race (they are almost always white), age (they are in their fifties and sixties), occupation (most occupy or have occupied the highest administrative positions in organizations), class (most are quite wealthy), and status position (they are affiliated with high-prestige institutions and clubs, and almost all have a biographical sketch in Marquis's *Who's Who in America*).[8]

The sense of internal cohesion on a corporate board created by these three structural factors is reinforced, in turn, by the existence of group norms of a kind that can be found within any face-to-face group. These norms guide both directors' behavior and their evaluations of others' behavior. Many board norms are oriented specifically toward promoting board cohesion. There is a strong emphasis on politeness and courtesy, and an avoidance of direct conflict and confrontation. Aside from legally required committees, boards avoid specialization of any kind. In their face-to-face interactions, board members also show a tendency to shun distinct honorary titles of any kind, including Dr., Professor, or even Mr. or Ms. Seniority on the board is rarely discussed among directors. As such conventions suggest, boardroom decorum seeks to avoid the emergence of prestige groups of any kind within the group. Moreover, board members tend to hold in low regard members who are boastful about individual accomplishments. Making a big fuss over some individual accomplishment is considered brash and rude. In its own particular way, each board is a gentleman's club, in both the best and worst senses of the term.

Structural factors and group norms thus combine to give members of a corporate board a strong sense of group identity. Yet because many directors serve on multiple boards, they are inevitably members of a second group: the broader director community. By "community" I mean a group that exists in such a way that its members share not this or that particular interest but rather the basic conditions of a societal position and a common perspective.[9] In a landmark 1984 study, Michael Useem presented overwhelming evidence for the existence of this broader director community. Combining in-depth interviews and multiple data sources, Useem found that board members shared remarkably similar attitudes and beliefs regarding their roles as directors, and that they were highly conscious of themselves as a community and of their roles in this community. The foundation upon which this community rested, according to Useem, was the overlapping ties of directors created through interlocking board memberships. (An "interlock" exists when a person affiliated with one organization sits on the board of directors of another.) Directors who sat on multiple boards, especially those of prestigious companies, enjoyed particularly high status and influence. It is through these interlocks that director values and beliefs are both shaped and diffused. It is also through these interlocks that information about board practices is diffused.[10]

At the time when Useem conducted his study, a director's loyalty to his particular board and his loyalty to the larger corporate community rarely came into conflict. Useem found that those directors who would have faced the greatest potential for conflicting loyalties—those with multiple board memberships—easily navigated between their roles as board members of particular firms and as members of the inner-circle group of directors who represented broader, inter-corporate interests.[11] This situation was soon to change as the era of managerial capitalism gave way to the new era of investor capitalism.

Although not recognized at the time, the absence of role conflict that Useem observed was dependent on the institutional autonomy enjoyed by many corporations during the 1970s and early 1980s, the period of his study. As documented by Alfred Chandler, the managerial corporation was organized for autonomy, relying on its own retained earnings to fund operations and giving managers full discretion in deciding how much to return to shareholders and how much to invest in new ventures.[12] Corporations were institutionally complete. Directors and managers were institutionally autonomous because they contained within themselves the necessary resources and organization for dealing with all aspects of corporate existence, obviating the need for the organization to be too dependent on other actors. Nowhere was this corporate autonomy more evident than in the marginal role boards played in CEO selection.[13] Except in cases of overt crisis, boards played almost no role in shaping the CEO succession process or influencing its outcome in any meaningful way. Philip Caldwell, CEO of Ford Motor Company in the early 1980s, aptly summarized the CEO succession process for the boards on which he had served during the heyday of managerial capitalism: "[T]he incumbent CEO is the designer of a selection process that ultimately produces his successor."

The shift from managerial to investor capitalism (described in chapter 3) that began in the 1980s created an environment in which corporations lost the autonomy they had previously enjoyed. The threat of corporate takeovers, the emergence of a shareholder rights movement spearheaded by institutional investors, and the increased influence of Wall Street analysts and the business media are just some of the many factors that ended the insulation of corporate management and directors from the turbulence of market forces. Change in CEO succession and search set in abruptly. CEOs, who previously had insulated themselves from the authority of directors in choosing their successors, were increasingly challenged by board members, who themselves were being pressured by institutional investors to take greater control over the CEO succession process, particularly when firm performance was unsatisfactory.

In this environment, the demands of external actors began to penetrate the boundaries of the director community. The previously insular culture of the board increasingly became an aspect or dimension of the societal context of which it was part. Directors' actions were still influenced by the social dynamics of the individual board, but were now increasingly oriented toward reacting to the concerns of actors outside the immediate corporate environment. One consequence of this new orientation was the adoption of a widespread ethos among the director community exalting the creation of shareholder value to the virtual exclusion of other, potentially competing, corporate objectives.

This new orientation toward shareholder interests sometimes directly opposed the loyalty that board members felt toward the particular boards on which they served. For example, taking control of the CEO succession process—which boards were now under increasing pressure from outside forces to do—was an action that directly challenged past corporate practices and the authority of the incumbent CEO.[14] Outside forces gained leverage, however, from the presence on boards of outside directors, who felt their responsibilities to the larger community of directors (e.g., the responsibility to show that the corporate world as a whole was mindful of shareholder interests) more keenly than did others on the boards on which they served, and who were less invested in the maintenance of past practices. Table 4.1 summarizes the changes in board composition between 1980 and 1990, and shows that, by 1990, on average one less insider served on a corporate board than a decade before. (As noted earlier in this chapter, average board size also decreased by one member over the same period. Both changes were the result of pressure from institutional investors.) Table 4.2, which summarizes the variables that predict the likelihood of CEO dismissals, shows that in addition to poor performance, the percentage of outside

TABLE 4.1
Changes in Board Characteristics over Time

	Year					
	1980		1985		1990	
	(M)	(SD)	(M)	(SD)	(M)	(SD)
Inside Directors	4.20	2.20	3.73	2.18	3.24	1.86
Outside Directors	10.16	4.60	10.40	4.91	10.16	4.56
Entire Board	14.36	4.37	14.14	5.18	13.40	4.79
Board Interlocks	12.02	11.52	10.92	11.24	11.12	9.89
Fraction: Inside Directors	.307	.152	.281	.162	.262	.161

TABLE 4.2
Maximum-Likelihood Estimation of Effects on Transition Rate toward Forced CEO Turnover, 1980–96, using a log-logistic model. For specification of model, see appendix.

Coefficient	Exponential	Model 1**	Model 2**	Model 3**	Model 4**	Model 5**	Model 6**
a-vector							
Constant	−5.57***	−5.39***	−4.80***	−4.66***	−4.71***	−4.91***	−4.61***
	(.114)	(.153)	(.116)	(.112)	(.114)	(.136)	(.120)
Performance	−.831***	−.830***	−.615***	−.552***	−.564***	−.587***	−.319***
	(.162)	(.163)	(.127)	(.123)	(.123)	(.124)	(.137)
Employees (ln)	.018	.016	.024	.025	.028	.037	.003
	(.039)	(.038)	(.030)	(.029)	(.029)	(.029)	(.032)
Founder				−.995***	−.967***	−.991***	−.929***
				(.217)	(.216)	(.216)	(.215)
Separate Chairman					.327***	.300***	.278***
					(.092)	(.092)	(.091)

	(1)	(2)	(3)	(4)	(5)	(6)	(7)
Pct Outside Directors						.578***	
						(.193)	
Interlocks							.098**
							(.044)
Interlocks × Performance							.454***
							(.077)
b-vector							
Constant		.045	.193***	.234***	.235***	.222***	.229***
		(.037)	(.045)	(.045)	(.045)	(.045)	(.045)
Cohort before 1980			-.243***	-.248***	-.244***	-.243***	-.245***
			(.043)	(.043)	(.043)	(.043)	(.043)
Cohort after 1985			.338***	.321***	.326***	.346***	.330***
			(.044)	(.044)	(.044)	(.045)	(.044)
Log-likelihood	2953.14	-2949.58	-2829.17	-2811.61	-2805.74	-2801.51	-2786.75

*$p < .10$; **$p < .05$; ***$p < .01$.

directors and the number of other boards on which a firm's directors serve are key predictors of CEO dismissal: the greater the number of outside directors and director interlocks on a particular board, the greater the likelihood that the CEO will be fired if performance falters.

Even as individual boards, in their local operation, still retained much of their old identity, integration, and attachment to board cohesion and loyalty to the CEO, the broader director community had lost the autonomy and self-sufficiency of Useem's inner circle, and the war over corporate control now knocked on the boardroom door. As we saw in chapter 3, institutional investors—once passive custodians of their clients' accounts who tended to automatically vote their shares as management recommended—were no longer passive. And while hostile takeovers subsequently waned in the 1990s, many institutional investors did not return to their old ways. In many cases they became the ones targeting underperforming companies through coordinated action, such as that directed at General Motors in 1992 and at Digital Equipment that same year. As a *Fortune* magazine headline put it, the "big owners" had begun to "roar,"[15] and their roar was directed at outside directors who had the formal authority to exercise control over CEO turnover and succession. In the relatively short span of a decade—and despite having exercised almost no influence on the choice of a new CEO for the better part of a century—boards came to regard CEO succession as part of their job. Today, directors are almost unanimous in their view that choosing a new CEO is among the most important decisions made by a board.[16]

Emboldened to exert real control over the CEO succession process, directors now try to interpret their organization's external environment, then make succession decisions based on their reading of those outside actors whose evaluations they most prize. This reliance on external judgments stems partly from the fact that in actually choosing a CEO (rather than simply rubber-stamping the outgoing CEO's choice), directors have no habits or settled procedures to fall back on.[17] External succession is different from internal, so boards have no existing version of the CEO succession process that readily solves the problems posed by external search. As the social psychologist Leon Festinger and others have discovered, when objective or institutionalized processes for evaluating a course of action are not available, individual actions and opinions as to the rightness of those actions are strongly influenced by the opinions and evaluations of relevant others.[18] In the case of CEO succession, Wall Street analysts and the business media have become the relevant others.

This way of reading and responding to the external environment has had significant consequences for CEO succession, as is illustrated by the search that resulted in Jamie Dimon's hiring by Bank One. For another example, consider the process that led first to the appointment in October 1996 of John Walter as AT&T's president, COO, and CEO-designate, then to his firing by the AT&T board less than nine months later. On the day that Walter's selection was announced, telecommunications analysts described it as "a mistake,"[19] the CNN anchor commenting on the selection called Walter "a puzzling choice," and AT&T's market value fell by $4 billion.[20] As the immediate plunge in the company's stock price suggests, this initial judgment by Wall Street analysts and the press became a self-fulfilling prophecy. Walter was described in the press as lacking credibility among the executives who worked for him, and quickly lost the confidence of the board. After less than nine months as company president, John Walter was dismissed by AT&T's board in July 1997. He was replaced three months later by a name-brand CEO whom many influential analysts felt should have originally been selected, C. Michael Armstrong.[21] Walter's fate convincingly demonstrates how the perceptions and judgments of opinion leaders in the external environment can and do weigh more heavily in the external succession process than do the individual judgments of the directors themselves.

The influence that external actors such as analysts and the business media exert on an external CEO search offers a particularly clear example of how directors act not as autonomous individuals but rather as members of groups that are, in turn, firmly embedded in larger social networks and relations. Yet in many other ways that may not be so readily apparent, directors are strongly influenced at every step of the external CEO search process by the social dimensions of corporate boards.

Launching the CEO Search

The importance of the social factors discussed above—the cultural forces of board cohesion, the structural roles of interlocking directorships in channeling both values and information throughout the broader director community, and the institutional context within which directors operate—can be seen not just in the increased involvement of corporate boards in the CEO succession process, or in the dramatic, highly publicized firings and hirings to which that process has increasingly given rise. These factors can also be observed at work throughout the external CEO search process, including those phases of it that are generally hidden from outsiders. Indeed, right from the start of the external CEO search as typically conducted today, we can see directors organizing and carrying out their deliberations in ways that defy what we would expect if the external CEO labor market were a "market" of the kind that most other observers have described, with individuals acting rationally to advance their own interests.

ORGANIZING THE SEARCH: THE SEARCH COMMITTEE

The process of board-led CEO succession, whether internal or external, starts with the board's appointing a search committee, which manages the administrative tasks of succession. The chair of the search committee is usually the director responsible for the executive development and compensation committee. Among its other tasks, the search committee hires the executive search firm that now almost always assists with the search.

Whether a search committee exercises significant control over the succession process is most dependent on the recent performance of the firm—as is the decision about whether to conduct a serious external search. If the firm has performed satisfactorily, the outgoing CEO is asked to participate but not allowed to take control of the process. In such cases, the appointment usually passes to the internal heir apparent, whose identity has been known well in advance. To the extent that the board conducts a search in this situation, it is fairly superficial and merely symbolic. This was recently the situation at a Northeast bank, where the outgoing CEO, who by all accounts had performed well, had made his preference for his successor clear to the board and to financial analysts. The board went through the motions of forming a search committee and conducting a "search." One search consultant hired to bless the heir apparent admitted that there was no serious data gathering or comparison of this candidate against others, either inside or outside. The consultant summarized the process in this way:

> We had a short list, some internal and external candidates, but I can't say it was meaningful. Everyone knew that [D] was [M]'s favored chosen successor. The search committee went through the motions and I was asked to evaluate the internal candidates..... I went around to talk to the other executives about [D]. I asked them to provide examples of when he had been visionary, his leadership style. As you can imagine, everything was described very positively. When I asked for negative examples and feedback, people were silent. They knew the end game. . . . The board acted upon the outgoing CEO's recommendation and appointed his successor with little reaction from either the press or Wall Street.

In some internal successions, there is a horse race between known competing candidates. This has been General Electric's historical succession practice (as described in longtime CEO Reginald Jones's own words in chapter 3). In the most recent instance, GE's current CEO, Jeffrey Immelt, was explicitly pitted against two other internal candidates. While GE's board and its search committee made an admirable show to investors and the business media of having been actively involved in the search, the decision to elect Immelt was mostly made by the retiring CEO, Jack Welch. Not surprisingly, GE's press release on Immelt's appointment described the decision as having been supported unanimously by the board.[22]

GE, of course, has been a high-performing firm for many years. When firm performance has been poor, or no obvious successor or potential successors to an outgoing CEO have emerged, the search process takes on a quite different character.

When a CEO is thought to be performing poorly (generally because firm performance itself has slipped), or when the CEO position has become unexpectedly vacant, boards come under tremendous pressure to appoint a new CEO. A firm pays a price financially and in terms of organizational image when it remains leaderless for too long. Directors know that a firm's executives, managers, and line employees all experience a great deal of uncertainty when the CEO position is empty. Moreover, Wall Street and the business media both exert unrelenting pressure on boards to announce a new chief executive as quickly as possible. One consequence of this pressure to expeditiously announce a new CEO is that the board's search process is oriented toward completing the search as quickly as possible.

In such circumstances, boards tend to try to adapt to an external search many of the forms and practices developed for internal succession. Because most boards have not had extensive experience with outside succession, they fall back on more familiar processes. Internal succession thus becomes the template from which the external succession process is developed. In many cases, it offers a quick and apparently viable solution with little expense, since boards are in a rush to complete the search. This is not to say that directors are not consciously aware of this copying process. As one director says, "Once you've done a search, you have a sense of what one should look like. This then becomes the basis upon which you do other searches." One consequence of this approach is that, because many large companies share directors with one another, there are few major differences among companies in terms of how the search committee is organized for an external search.

One of the first questions the search committee chair faces is what the committee's size should be. This question is often vigorously debated by the board. Some board members argue that a large committee will better represent the interests of the board as a whole. Others argue that a small committee will be more focused and efficient. Interestingly, these debates do not drastically affect the outcome. In 75 percent of the field cases I examined, the search committee had between four and seven members. The smallest committee I found consisted of three members, and the largest of eleven.

Consistent with the taboo on creating distinctions among board members, as well as with the usual practice in internal searches, the composition of the search committee is not as vigorously debated as is its size. The most common method for determining the composition of the search committee is asking for volunteers. The individuals who volunteer for the assignment are disproportionately directors who are retired executives or directors from non-business backgrounds such as nonprofits and education—essentially, directors who have more time than do their peers to devote to the search. In the field cases I examined, on average only one non-retired director served on the search committee.

One unintended result of the uniform application of the practices used for internal searches to external search—particularly the voluntary method for composing a committee—is that boards do not always pay as careful attention to the composition of the search committee as the ramifications of the search process would suggest that they should. The composition of the search committee is critical to succession outcomes. In some cases that I studied, however, search committees were composed of members who had little familiarity with the company and its history. In these cases, most of the information committee members had about the company, its products, and its other executives, was limited to the information received in quarterly meetings. Meanwhile, the predominance of retired directors on search committees impedes the effectiveness of the external search process in a particularly significant way. Because the future CEO will want some familiarity with the board members with whom he or she will work, the search committee needs individuals who are likely to stay on the board for some time. This is unlikely to be the case when most of the search committee is made up of executives who have already retired.

Search committees also need directors with diverse functional backgrounds. In several instances, the narrow range of committee members' backgrounds bias CEO succession decisions. Consider the case of one technology company with a strong engineering culture. Although the company's products were considered the most technologically advanced in its market, poor marketing had slashed its market share. Yet the search committee, made up largely of directors with backgrounds in operations or research and development, recommended a CEO with a strong technical background but little marketing experience. Of course, it is human nature to gravitate toward persons like oneself. Yet it is also unsurprising that the company's market share continued to erode after the appointment of the search committee's choice of a new CEO.

DEFINING THE POSITION: THE SPECIFICATION SHEET

Even though the composition of the typical search committee seems to belie directors' stated belief in the importance of the job of choosing a new CEO, board members are not utterly oblivious of the needs of the firm as a factor in a CEO search. Directors, in fact, portray the CEO succession process as a unique chance for them to assess the firm's situation. The opportunity to search for a new CEO, in the words of one director, is "a clean slate to find the person to help meet the company's objectives." CEO succession, according to another director, offers one of the few real opportunities for board members to assess the current state of the organization and the future that they desire for it.

Such statements notwithstanding, there is little evidence that board members engage in any extensive discussion of a firm's objectives during the actual search process. Even in cases in which the firm has been performing poorly, or the organization needs a new strategic direction because of a changed environment, most CEO searches do not begin with an analysis of the problems facing the organization. Instead, many search committees jump immediately into the task of writing a specification sheet.

The specification sheet is a formal document that describes the requirements for the new CEO. It is usually developed with the assistance of an executive search firm (which conducts one-on-one meetings with each of the board members to get their ideas), and is considered a critical element of the search process. Al Zeien, the former CEO of Gillette and a member of several corporate boards, emphasizes the importance of the specification sheet for the search process. "From my own experience on an outside board," Zeien observes, "the search firm [and the search] is only as good as the spec that the board agrees upon at the outset, and the spec has got to be pretty specific because that is really the basis by which the process is going to take place."

Search consultants also stress the importance of the specification sheet; according to one, the spec sheet "lays out the required qualifications . . . the desired qualifications . . . and forces the client to prioritize and focus." Because of the commonly held view that the specification sheet provides the guidelines against which candidates can be both identified and evaluated, executive search firms emphasize its development as a strategic component of the search process, and their particular approach to assembling a specification sheet as an important way for them to differentiate themselves from their competitors. Preparation of the specification sheet is, as one consultant put it, "the consultative component of the process, and perhaps our most value added."

In view of these descriptions, it comes as a surprise that search committee members rarely refer back to the specification sheet once it has been drawn up and initially circulated. Instead of functioning as a set of guidelines for the search, the specification sheet assumes importance only during the process of compiling it, when it acts as a Rorschach print on which directors project their hopes, desires, fears, interpretations, and solutions. In discussions ostensibly devoted to identifying the qualities that the search committee should seek in the next CEO, some directors privately air their grievances against the outgoing CEO and blame him for the firm's problems. Others use the process of compiling the specification sheet to engage in self-congratulatory behavior—for example, by describing their roles in ousting the previous CEO. Almost every director also uses it as a chance to discuss his or her "theories of leadership" and ideas about the qualities of a good leader. The resulting list is usually so long that, if taken seriously, it would deter many candidates by its sheer length. In compiling this list of desired qualities, moreover, directors give little attention to their relative importance.

Figure 4.1a presents a specification sheet for a CEO search at an insurance company, and figure 4.1b presents a specification sheet for a search at a major software company. Both of these lists are entirely typical of those used in external CEO searches. Three aspects of these specification sheets immediately stand out as noteworthy.

The first striking feature of these specification sheets is their emphasis on individual characteristics. The content of both lists consists largely of a collection of personal traits rather than a set of concrete skills or a discussion of the situational context of the search. The CEO should be "aggressive." The CEO should be able to "balance reward with risk." The CEO should be able to "provide direction." The CEO should be able to "work closely with the team to develop a direction." Judging from these lists of qualities, a CEO's ability to perform effectively in the position is determined entirely by individual attributes, with no reference to the particular challenges facing the firm.

The second noteworthy feature of the two sample specification sheets is the similarity between them. A blind read would make it difficult to know that one sheet comes from a software firm and the other from an insurance company. Part of this similarity stems from the fact that each of the characteristics listed is so vague—traits such as "proven leader" and "motivator" apparently do not need to be defined. Yet such

9273-002

PSP-80%/MEL-20%|MEL|PSP-45%/JEB-20%/REH-5%/MEL-20%/TNJ-10%|CLH

Function code:111,113
Industry code:631,632,FSP

Client: ████████████████████████INSURANCE CO OF AMERICA
(GENERAL MANAGEMENT)

Position: PRESIDENT & CEO

Compensation: $500,000 to $1,000,000 + $150,000 Bonus

Duties: REPORTING TO THE BOARD OF DIRECTORS, THE SUCCESSFUL
CANDIDATE WILL BE RESPONSIBLE FOR ALL OPERATIONS OF
████████████████████ INSURANCE COMPANY. THIS INCLUDES
ALL DIVISIONS, SUBSIDIARIES, AND/OR OTHER VENTURES. DUTIES
WOULD INCLUDE DEVELOPING A STRATEGIC PLAN TO ADDRESS A
CHANGING INDUSTRY AND MARKETING ENVIRONMENT; MANAGING THE
EXECUTIVE AND MANAGEMENT STAFF; ANNUAL TACTICS AND BUDGET;
LONG-TERM TACTICS AND BUDGETS; GAINING CONSENSUS WITH THE
BOARD AND ████████████████ FOR PRESENT AND FUTURE DIRECTION
OF THE COMPANY. THIS INDIVIDUAL SHOULD ESTABLISH
CHALLENGING GOALS FOR THE CORPORATION IN SAFELY OBTAINING
ROE OF BETWEEN 13 AND 15 PERCENT. ALSO, THIS INDIVIDUAL
SHOULD CONCENTRATE ON INCREASING MARKET PRICE AND DIVIDENDS
WHICH MAKE UP STOCKHOLDER VALUE. ONE OF THE CRITERIA FOR
CEO SUCCESS SHOULD BE DEVELOPING MARKET PRICE ABOVE BOOK
VALUE. THESE MARKET IMPROVEMENTS HAVE TO BE BALANCED
APPROPRIATELY WITH RISKS. THEREFORE, THE SUCCESSFUL
CANDIDATE MUST HAVE MARKET AND GROWTH SKILLS WHILE AT THE
SAME TIME BE ON THE FOREFRONT OF INSURANCE ISSUES AS THEY
ARE IMPACTED BY EXTERNAL ISSUES (I.E. A CHANGING
ENVIRONMENT IN GROUP HEALTH, INCREASING COMPETITION FOR THE
QUALITY CUSTOMER, AND BUSINESS OPPORTUNITIES IN PERIPHERAL
PRODUCTS). ACCOMMODATIONS CAN BE MADE IN INDUSTRY KNOWLEDGE
FOR THOSE CANDIDATES OUTSIDE THE INDUSTRY. BUT GENERAL
FINANCIAL INSTITUTION ACUMEN IS REQUIRED. PARTICULAR
ATTENTION SHOULD BE PAID TOWARDS BRINGING THE FOUR CORE
BUSINESSES UNDER ONE CORPORATE MENTALITY.

Organization:

	Location	Sales Volume	# Employees
Client:	████████████	$2 billion	

Product/Service: LIFE AND HEALTH INSURANCE

The person:
Min. experience: 25 YEARS

Education: UNDERGRADUATE DEGREE, A GRADUATE DEGREE OR OTHER ADVANCED
EDUCATIONAL DESIGNATION SUCH AS CLU OR FSA WOULD BE
CONSIDERED A PLUS.

Other
characteristics: A MATURE, HIGH ENERGY, PROGRESSIVE, STRATEGICALLY ORIENTED
EXECUTIVE. THE PERSON MUST BE INTELLIGENT, ARTICULATE, AND
HAVE SIGNIFICANT STATURE. A MANAGER WITH A TAKE-CHARGE BUT
PARTICIPATIVE MANAGEMENT STYLE, THIS INDIVIDUAL SHOULD BE
SOMEONE WHO CAN MOTIVATE, DELEGATE, AND RECEIVED IN-DEPTH
INVOLVEMENT FROM SUBORDINATES. THIS INDIVIDUAL MUST HAVE
THE HIGHEST PROFESSIONAL AND PERSONAL STANDARDS. THIS

FIGURE 4.1a Specification Sheet for Insurance Company CEO Search.

9273-002
Continued:
Other
Characteristics:

PERSON MUST BE STRATEGIC AND BE ABLE TO ARTICULATE A
CORPORATE VISION TO ALL CONSTITUENTS. IT IS MOST IMPORTANT
THAT THIS PERSON BE PERCEIVED AS FITTING THE CULTURE, BOTH
IN THE CORPORATION AND COMMUNITY. IMPORTANT CONSIDERATIONS:
A COMMITMENT TO CUSTOMER SERVICE, EMPLOYEE RELATIONS,
CONSENSUS BUILDING, AND SUCCESSION PLANNING. THE INDIVIDUAL
MUST BE WELL BALANCED, CONFIDENT BUT WITH A SENSE OF
HUMILITY. THE SUCCESSFUL CANDIDATE WILL HAVE A TRACK RECORD
IN PORTFOLIO DECISIONS, SUCCESSION PLANNING, AND BUILDING
ROI.

Experience: A PROVEN EXECUTIVE FROM A SUBSTANTIAL, RESPECTED,
HIGH-PERFORMING ORGANIZATION. AN INDIVIDUAL WITH STRONG
LEADERSHIP AND MANAGEMENT ABILITIES, THE CANDIDATE SHOULD
HAVE KNOWLEDGE OF THE INSURANCE INDUSTRY, BUT COULD QUITE
POSSIBLY COME FROM AN AREA OUTSIDE THE INDUSTRY IN SOME
OTHER FINANCIAL INSTITUTION ENVIRONMENT. THE INDIVIDUAL
WILL PRESENTLY BE FOUND IN A NUMBER ONE OR NUMBER TWO
POSITION, COMFORTABLE IN DEALING AT THE HIGHEST LEVELS,
DEALING WITH A BOARD, DEALING WITH THE "PUBLICS." THE
PERSON SHOULD HAVE A PROVEN TRACK RECORD IN SUCCESSFUL
STRATEGIC PLANNING, MARKETING, AND RISK/ASSET MANAGEMENT.

Targets:

PSP
04/29/93

FIGURE 4.1a Continued.

descriptions are, indeed, in many ways irreducible to more particular requirements because their rightness appears to be grounded in nature and reason. After all, who is against leadership and motivation? The individual characteristics that search committees seek in a CEO represent society's idealized definitions of leadership writ small. They are congruent with prevailing notions—those found in the business press, for example—of what a CEO should be like. Thus, this laundry list of characteristics sheds light on how societal beliefs permeate the CEO search process.

The third remarkable feature of these specification sheets is the ambiguous and contradictory nature of many of their requirements when considered in relation to one another. For example, the board of the insurance company (fig. 4.1a) was looking for a CEO who would both "establish challenging goals" and "safely" deliver a return on equity of "between 13 and 15 percent." This individual was expected to "concentrate on increasing . . . stockholder value," but to make only such changes as would be "appropriate with risk." The incoming candidate was to be at the "forefront of insurance issues," but "accommodations

8650-001 MENLO PARK
JTT-67%/DBK-33% | DBK | JTT-50%/DBK-50% | PNL

Function code:113,112
Industry code:7371

Client:

Position: PRESIDENT CEO AND CHAIRMAN

Compensation: $350,000 + $150,000 Bonus

Perqs: STOCK OPTIONS ON 1,000,000 SHARES

Duties: REPORTING TO THE BOARD OF DIRECTORS, THIS INDIVIDUAL WILL
HAVE FULL RESPONSIBILITY FOR THE COMPANY'S STRATEGY AND
OPERATIONS. INCLUDED IN THE LATTER ARE THE VARIOUS BUSINESS
UNITS, OPERATIONAL UNITS IN NORTH AMERICA, ASIA/PACIFIC,
AND EUROPE, FINANCE, CORPORATE MARKETING, RESEARCH AND
DEVELOPMENT, INFORMATION SYSTEMS, OPERATIONS, LEGAL AND
HUMAN RESOURCES DEPARTMENTS. THE CEO'S RESPONSIBILITIES
WILL INCLUDE STRATEGIC PLANNING, BUDGETING, PRODUCT
PRIORITIZING, AND THE DEVELOPMENT OF METHODS, MEASUREMENT
SYSTEMS, AND POLICIES FOR CONTINUING THE COMPANY'S RAPID
GROWTH. AN IMPORTANT PART OF THE JOB IS BEING THE COMPANY'S
VISIBLE REPRESENTATIVE TO EMPLOYEES, THE FINANCIAL
COMMUNITY, COMPANY MANAGEMENT, VENDORS, CUSTOMERS,
STRATEGIC PARTNERS, AND THE DISTRIBUTION CHANNELS.
ADDITIONALLY, THE CEO IS RESPONSIBLE FOR THE FOSTERING OF
LEADERSHIP, MANAGEMENT DEVELOPMENT PROGRAMS, AND TEAM
BUILDING. THE CEO WILL BE CHARGED WITH ESTABLISHING A
LONG-TERM COMPETITIVE STRATEGY, AND WILL BE THE KEY COMPANY
SPOKESPERSON WITHIN THE INDUSTRY.

Organization:

Client:

Product/Service:

The person:
Min. experience:

Education:

Other
characteristics: ASTUTE INTELLECT, DECISIVE, ACTION ORIENTED AND PERSONABLE,
WITH THE HIGHEST INTEGRITY AND AUTHENTICITY; ABLE TO
OPERATE PROFESSIONALLY IN A FAST PACED, FLEXIBLE
ENVIRONMENT. COMMITTED TO EXCELLENCE AND TOTAL QUALITY IN
PRODUCTS, SERVICES AND SUPPORT. A PROVEN LEADER AND
MOTIVATOR; HIGHLY PROFESSIONAL, AND CONFIDENT WITH AN OPEN
STYLE. MUST INTERACT PRODUCTIVELY WITH DIVERSE MANAGEMENT
TEAM AS WELL AS BROAD BASED EMPLOYEE GROUPS, CUSTOMER
GROUPS AND FINANCIAL COMMUNITY. SUCCESSFUL CANDIDATE WILL

FIGURE 4.1b Specification Sheet for Software Company CEO Search.

8650-001
Continued:
Other
Characteristics:

HAVE A STRONG EQUITY MOTIVATION AND UNRELENTING COMMITMENT
TO MAKE THE COMPANY WORK. MUST BE ABLE TO SELL IDEAS/PLANS
INTERNALLY; COMFORT WITH DEVELOPMENT ENVIRONMENT IS
CRITICAL. WILL PURSUE AGGRESSIVE RESEARCH AND RIGOROUS
DEVELOPMENT PROCESS. CAN QUICKLY AND ACCURATELY ASSESS NEAR
AND LONG-TERM OPPORTUNITIES AND THREATS. MUST BE ABLE TO
ANALYZE AND INTERPRET INDUSTRY TRENDS. CAN ARTICULATE
━━━━━━━━ VISION/MISSION WHICH CAN BE EXECUTED BY STAFF
AND MANAGEMENT. SHOULD BE A SUCCESSFUL SENIOR EXECUTIVE, A
QUICK STUDY, WITH BUSINESS JUDGEMENT. HAS A GLOBAL
VIEWPOINT; INTERNATIONAL PERSPECTIVE AND UNDERSTANDING.
MUST BE AN INNOVATIVE LEADER, AND DEMONSTRATE A PASSIONATE
ATTENTIVENESS TO CURRENT AND FUTURE MARKET REQUIREMENTS.
SHOULD BE STRONGLY ENTREPRENEURIAL--PURSUES CALCULATED
RISKS FOR SIGNIFICANT GAIN. SHOULD HAVE A DEMONSTRATED
ABILITY TO BUILD COHESIVE TEAMS. MUST HAVE THE BEHAVIORS,
PHILOSOPHIES, AND VALUES THAT WOULD BE A CULTURAL FIT AT
THE COMPANY. APPROACH SHOULD BE CREATIVE WITH A DESIRE TO
SET HIGH STANDARDS. READILY ADJUSTS TO RAPID CHANGES IN
TECHNOLOGY, PRODUCTS, AND MARKETPLACE. SHOULD HAVE
INTERPERSONAL SKILLS THAT WILL ALLOW THE PERSON TO BUILD
EARLY CREDIBILITY. MUST BE WILLING TO STAND UP FOR BELIEFS.
IDEALLY, THIS INDIVIDUAL WILL HAVE MANAGED THROUGH
DIFFICULT PERIODS SUCCESSFULLY. COMPANY CULTURE REQUIRES A
HIGH SENSE OF URGENCY AND A VERY HIGH COMMITMENT LEVEL.
WILL ASSURE HIGH LEVEL OF VISIBILITY AND ACCESSIBILITY
INTERNALLY AND EXTERNALLY. DEDICATED TO STRONG MANAGEMENT
DEVELOPMENT AND PROFESSIONAL GROWTH PROGRAMS.

Experience: REQUIREMENT THAT CANDIDATE HAS HAD SIGNIFICANT P&L
EXPERIENCE WITHIN THE COMPUTER (OR OTHER
COMPLEX-TECHNOLOGY) INDUSTRY; PREFERENCE TOWARD INDIVIDUALS
WHO HAVE OPERATED SUCCESSFULLY IN A LARGE COMPANY, AND THEN
MADE THE TRANSITION TO A SMALLER ORGANIZATION; PREFERENCE
FOR SUCCESSFUL TRACK RECORD IN A HIGH-GROWTH COMPANY WELL
RESPECTED FOR ITS PRODUCT INNOVATION AND LEADERSHIP. SHOULD
BE FAMILIAR WITH DIVERSE AREAS OF THE COMPUTER INDUSTRY,
SUCH AS INTERNATIONAL DISTRIBUTION, SYSTEMS INTEGRATORS,
END USERS, SOFTWARE HOUSES, AND HARDWARE VENDORS.
EXPERIENCE IN A SOFTWARE COMPANY NOT A REQUIREMENT PROVIDED
INDIVIDUAL UNDERSTANDS THE INDUSTRY. CANDIDATE'S PRIOR
CAREER EMPHASIS COULD BE IN OPERATIONS, TECHNICAL
DEVELOPMENT, OR MARKETING AND SALES. STRONG PREFERENCE FOR
EXPERIENCE AND COMFORT WITH HANDS-ON TECHNICAL DEVELOPMENT
AT SOME POINT IN CAREER.

Targets:

JTT
11/13/91

FIGURE 4.1b Continued.

[could] be made in industry knowledge for those candidates outside the industry." Looking at either of the sample specification sheets, one can only conclude that no one person could fulfill all of the requirements on either one of them. How is it possible, for example, to be team oriented and a consensus builder while being directive? To be a risk taker without taking too many risks? To be flexible and yet stand up for one's beliefs? This would be a no-win situation for candidates and board mem-

bers alike—if anyone ended up taking the specification sheet the least bit seriously.

How to account for these anomalies and deficiencies in the specification sheet? A knee-jerk explanation might be that the people conducting the search have not worked hard enough, or been given the appropriate incentives, to pinpoint the precise traits or skills necessary to the organization's near-term success. Yet such an interpretation ignores the context formed by the contemporary view of the CEO. Because it is assumed that the quality of the CEO determines firm performance, while—in the absence of any demonstrable link between the two—it is difficult, if not impossible, to know ex ante what characteristics in a CEO are needed to improve performance, directors are left to guess about which criteria are likely to be associated with success. Consequently, they resort to using the difficult-to-define buzzwords that we see on specification sheets—terms such as "leadership," "team builder," and "integrity."

Moreover, even if directors could more precisely define the qualities they were seeking in a new CEO, the search process would continue to exist in tension with the information problems associated with external CEO search. Selecting a CEO is an information-intensive decision. The information required for this task is also highly particular and fine grained. That is, it usually can be derived only through direct experience in working with and observing the candidate. Some examples of particular information include candidates' dispositions, working styles, and mannerisms; how they work with others; and, most importantly, whether they are really capable of doing what they say they can do. For internal candidates, this information is more easily gathered than for external ones, since the board and the sitting CEO have better knowledge and experience of the individuals under consideration. Moreover, a detailed record of an insider candidate's promotion history, performance reviews, and accomplishments can be found in the firm's own personnel records.

For outside candidates, however, this kind of particular information is not so easily gathered. Because of the requirements of confidentiality inherent in CEO search, it is not possible for directors to interview peers or subordinates for particular information about the candidates. Instead, particular information needs to be ascertained and assembled through more informal means. Before directors undertake the difficult search for such information, however, they narrow the pool of candidates on the basis of the much less fine-grained information available from the start. With careful consideration to how both internal and external—but especially external—constituents will perceive the search, directors use structurally and culturally derived attributes to create a pool of candidates that these constituents will see as legitimate and defensible.

Creating the Candidate Pool: The Social Matching Process

For boards to consider the interests of outside parties when selecting a new CEO is, of course, potentially desirable. After all, both a company's shareholders and the larger community for which the press is writing will be affected in some way by the decision. Yet the focus on external constituents does have some important unintended consequences. Most significantly, it has led to an emphasis on the "acceptability" of a candidate at the expense of considering whether an individual possesses the skills necessary for the position. As a result of this emphasis, search committees focus on a fairly narrow pool of candidates and evaluate them by means of a very conservative decision process. These features of the search process, in turn, are evident in the final choices that directors make when selecting a new CEO.

While the CEO succession process appears, at first glance, to offer limitless opportunities for invigorating an organization or introducing fundamental change, many search committees express frustration with the limited pool of candidates from which they end up choosing, often lamenting that candidates are seemingly indistinguishable from one another and even from the predecessor CEO. The reason for this outcome can be found in the process that search committees use to identify and qualify the candidate pool.

IDENTIFYING THE CANDIDATES

Following the compilation of a specification sheet, directors, often with the assistance of an executive search firm, begin putting together an initial list of candidates. Board members themselves, based on their knowledge of the industry and of the profiles of CEO talent at other firms, suggest the majority of these candidates. As Michael Useem and others have found, just as the leading internal candidates for a vacant CEO position are already board members at other companies, those considered plausible external candidates are also already board members.[23] While executive search firms will sometimes add one or two names, their contributions to this phase of the process are negligible.

One director of several public firms, William Pounds (the former dean of MIT's Sloan School of Management), provides a general description of the process for compiling the initial list of candidates:

> The first hurdle for myself is the laugh test: if we actually named this guy and told the employees and shareholders that he was the new boss, what would they think? Then there is the tendency to find people who look like the job. You start by whacking down the job to a set of alternatives. So you consider things like performance . . . the company they are coming from, who they have worked with. From there you start to find people who look like the position.

Consider the entirely typical case of a search at a publishing firm. Here, the search committee came up with a list of forty names, thirty of which came from the directors themselves, who were asked by the search firm to list potential candidates. The search firm added ten names to the list, including those of four women or members of minority groups. Within a few days, with the help of the search firm, the search committee narrowed the initial list down to twenty candidates, almost all of them actively employed. The search firm then gave the search committee a booklet containing a photograph and a short profile of each of these candidates. The profiles included only general information on the candidates' work histories and educational credentials, as well as estimates of their most recent compensation. One director described the booklet as a "Who's Who of global publishing that included high-profile CEOs of other prominent publishing firms and promising top executives from related industries such as entertainment."

The search firm then began to contact candidates listed in the book. Without revealing the identity of their client, the search consultants sought to identify candidates who would seriously consider moving from their existing positions. When the consultants came back with a short list of ten candidates, the board narrowed the list even further. Throughout this process, the board was guided by three criteria for winnowing the candidate pool: the current position of the candidate, the performance of the candidate's current firm, and the stature of that firm.

These criteria form the critical matter of the CEO labor market. At one level, as we shall see, they represent apparently reasonable responses to the elementary conditions of the market outlined in chapter 2. The relevance of these criteria—prior position, firm performance, and firm status—seems so self-evident, so reasonable, that directors rarely question them or feel the need to justify using them.

At the same time, however, these criteria form the basis of a durable sorting process that results in a narrow definition of the candidate pool, and a distinct privileging of one set of candidates over another. Examined with a critical eye, the standards by which candidates are sorted turn out not to be aligned with the technical or efficiency goals of the CEO search. Rather, they are essentially extraneous considerations that cause search committees to shine a spotlight on certain candidates, thereby leaving others in the shadows. The mechanism governing this sorting process is one that can best be described, using James C. March and James G. March's term, as "social matching."[24] Social matching is a filtering process that takes place when individual and organizational actors are confronted with choices that are difficult to select among because of limited information, and because the choices themselves cannot be reliably distinguished from one another. At a minimum, social matching is a convention. Its impact, however, is not benign. Social matching is one of the basic mechanisms that contribute to a closed CEO labor market, because directors seize upon one or more easily identifiable external characteristics of potential candidates to construct a narrowly defined candidate pool. By relying on social matching to identify the plausible candidate pool, directors are caught in an unforeseen trap of focusing on a small set of candidates and unwittingly undermining the original intent of a broad search.

Directors' tendencies to fasten on particular characteristics are also conditioned by what the anthropologist Mary Douglas calls "habits of thought."[25] Habits of thought are organizing and classificatory principles that appear to be endowed with the character of common sense, theories that seem self-evident. In the case of external CEO search, the external environment furnishes many, if not all, of the habits of thought on which directors rely in what is, at its core, a thoroughly social process. Directors' socially derived ideas about the criteria necessary to be included in the candidate pool then actively influence both directors' perceptions of candidates and the composition of the pool. For example, as a result of limiting the pool to candidates from organizations that have been performing well, many firms pass over talented executives from underperforming firms—all because their directors accept the widespread idea that organizational performance is a direct result of the ability and efforts of the CEO. Other circumstances (such as market conditions or the skills and experience of a company's senior management team) that are known to have a profound impact on corporate performance are not considered in sorting through the candidates. Thus, reliance on the performance of the firm from which the candidate is coming for evaluating a candidate's record—although at one level a perfectly defensible response—is actually problematic.

Let us examine each of the three criteria that directors employ to sort external CEO candidates at greater length.

POSITION MATCHING: ALREADY A CEO OR PRESIDENT

Many search committees feel that a potential CEO candidate needs to have previous experience leading a large corporation. Fully 75 percent of outsider CEO appointees during the period between 1985 and 2000 were either CEOs or presidents in their previous jobs. According to one director, a candidate's having already been in the CEO position or its equivalent "gives you a sense of how they are likely to act. It reduces uncertainty." Directors point out that the fact that an individual is already a CEO indicates that another board has already rendered a favorable judgment about that person. From the directors' point of view, coding a candidate on the basis of his previous position saves effort and energy. As Gigi Michelson, a longtime director at GE and other large firms, puts it, a board would not appoint someone to a CEO position if it "did not already have a judgment about the person, their personal stability, some knowledge of [their] family life and outside background, outside activity, outside of the corporation and so on." In using position matching to sort external CEO candidates, directors effectively trick themselves into thinking that already occupying the CEO (or president) position is a reliable signal of leadership abilities.

Directors' reliance on position matching in identifying candidates also makes it easier for the board to eventually defend its chosen candidate to the outside world. By choosing a candidate who has already had experience as a CEO or president, the board conforms to expectations concerning the traits or characteristics a legitimate candidate will need. Board members thus externalize what should be their own responsibility for choosing among available candidates.

Of course all of the expectations to which directors want candidates to conform create advantages for certain classes of candidates and disadvantages for others, which makes focusing on candidates with prior CEO experience—particularly at large companies—a potential liability. This is a problem that directors seem to be aware of at some level. While no two CEOs are the same, and each will have a different personality and style of leadership, such differences are often minor. And although directors do not make a link between their selection process and the uniformity of candidates that they observe, they do often comment on this uniformity and describe it as a problem. Several directors I interviewed complained about the shortage of "real leadership" and the "cookie-cutter" character of several of the CEO candidates whom they had considered. "A lot of the candidates are corporate survivors, not leaders" corporate director George Kennedy said of a search he had led at the industrial conglomerate Brunswick. Similarly, Henry Wendt, former CEO of SmithKline Beecham and a director on other companies' boards, commented:

> We're in the most severe shortage of CEO talent in corporate history. Most of the people I see are not leaders, they are managers who know how to work the system and have worked it well. Times are different. We need leaders, not politicians. We need to find people who can define what the organization is about. Charismatic people who help people understand what they need to do. Executors who know how to get things done. People who integrate leadership into their everyday activities. It is really difficult to find a real leader based on my experience in searching for CEOs.

Such observations are not surprising, given the candidate pool that directors themselves typically create. As C. Wright Mills noted years ago, in an observation that still applies today, "The top executives of the big companies are not, and never have been, a miscellaneous collection of Americans; they are a quite uniform social type which has had exceptional advantages of origin and training, and they do not fit many of the stereotypes that prevail about them."[26] Whatever their origins, CEOs of large corporations settle into the executive suite after a selection process lasting years. Socialization in the executive suite and self-selection en route to it significantly reduce the variability of the types of candidates who are seriously considered for vacancies in the CEO job. Those at the top of an organization are all corporate survivors. Of course, the skills possessed by all such survivors—specifically, their ability to comprehend and navigate a complex corporate bureaucracy—were once considered desirable in a CEO, inasmuch as the CEO's job, before the rise of investor capitalism, was thought to require understanding how complex organizations function and being able to work with the people in them. Yet directors shun such qualifications now that they are in search of the elusive personal characteristic called "leadership."

Directors' categorizing of candidates according to whether they have already been CEOs also highlights the fact that the social matching process that directors use is not so much one of consciously excluding candidates as it is one of creating expectations that can be fulfilled by only a small number of them. This has the consequence not only of narrowing the candidate pool but also of narrowing the directors' own thought processes. In their social matching process, directors pick and choose among the criteria that they believe will give due weight to the concerns of external parties. Yet by selecting candidates on the basis of socially legitimated classifications, such as already having occupied a position of corporate leadership, they are at the same time establishing a pattern of thought and action that is adhered to in the rest of the selection process. That is, these classifications, though grounded in pragmatic reasoning, also straitjacket the minds of directors—the more so, precisely because they do not *appear* to be unreasonably narrow. The convention of choosing an individual who has already occupied the position of CEO overcomes any tendency that individual board members might have to select candidates who deviate from the externally derived orthodoxy. Board members thus substitute a social convention for deliberative thinking and decision-making.

PERFORMANCE SORTING: COMING FROM A HIGH-PERFORMING COMPANY

In almost every external CEO search I studied, candidates were categorized according to the performance of their current firms. In the minds of directors, sorting candidates along the criterion of firm performance is a reasonable means of gauging the quality of a potential CEO. In the case of Hewlett-Packard's most recent CEO search, for example, several H-P directors described choosing outsider Carly Fiorina over several internal candidates because they associated Fiorina with the strong performance of Lucent Technologies, her previous firm. Lucent's stock had indeed performed extraordinarily well since the company had been spun off from AT&T. Yet while the H-P directors had attributed Lucent's success to its executives, much of this "success," it was later revealed, was due to creative accounting and liberal financing of sales to customers. Another relevant factor that these H-P directors seemed to ignore was that investors had bid up almost every technology-related stock in 1999.[27]

Yet despite such considerations, directors everywhere admire CEO candidates whose firms have performed at a level above the average for their industry. In choosing among external CEO candidates, directors attach great value to observable performance metrics in making their selection decisions. Consequently, firms choosing a CEO from outside usually select candidates from firms that are performing well relative to their industry. An examination of all outsider CEO appointments in the S&P 500 companies during the period I have studied finds that at the time of their appointments, 70 percent of outsider CEOs are moving from companies that are in the top quartile of performance in their industries.

What is striking about this performance sorting is the casual assumption that CEOs directly affect organizational performance—an assumption that, as we saw in chapter 2, has found little empirical support in scholarly studies on the topic. Directors, however, rarely cast a critical eye on the supposed connection between firm performance and executive quality, and dismiss as inherently flawed any research that questions it. One director describes any such research as "inherently unscientific, since you can never run the controlled experiment of what the firm would have been like without the CEO," and dismisses statistical techniques—as well as studies that match comparable firms to one another to gauge the impact of an individual CEO on performance—as "academic mumbo-jumbo, with no regard for reality." It is as if when directors don't like the empirical facts, they simply create their own narratives (admittedly a common enough human trait). In such a milieu, any theory or causal relationship that one cares to posit is justifiable. Meanwhile, there is little evidence of directors' trying to deconstruct the performance of a candidate's organization into its constituent parts, to determine what role the candidate may have played and what might be attributable to factors such as the environment, the quality of the company's employees, the competitive structure of its industry, or even luck.

Even granting, for the sake of argument, the possible validity of the contention that the research showing little or no connection between firm performance and executive quality is inherently flawed, a question arises as to why directors so resist any suggestion that the widely credited relationship between the two might be spurious. It is difficult to convey to the reader how deeply rooted this belief in the dependent relationship between CEO quality and firm performance is among members of corporate boards, who hold it with virtually religious conviction. To openly question it is taboo.[28] One reason it may be difficult for directors to talk objectively about the relationship between CEOs and firm performance is that it touches on fundamental, deeply held beliefs about, for example, corporate meritocracy and the reasons for their own ascensions to the top rungs of the corporate hierarchy. Directors have internalized the link between CEOs and performance to the point of sacralizing it. Every director defends the logic. Thus, directors' existing theories about the relationship between CEO quality and firm performance pre-condition their responses to a challenge and even determine what can be counted as a reasonable question. Their ideas place firm limits on their ability to make objective judgments about the posited relationship.

Another reason it is difficult to question the belief in the relationship between CEOs and corporate performance is because it enjoys such broad external support and legitimacy—especially among constituencies such as the business media and analysts, who, as we saw in chapter 3, often reduce firm performance to the qualities of a single individual. The sociologist Robert Merton has written about the power that a social fact can have over human behavior.[29] Once a complete and self-reinforcing system of opinions has been formed in a society, it offers strong resistance to anything that contradicts it.[30] Thus the external institutions of the business media and analysts systematically reinforce the individual perceptions of directors. They fix and routinize dynamic thought processes, making them part of an invisible social structure. They hide their influence and rouse emotions to a heightened pitch when these perceptions are questioned.

As in the case of position matching, the belief in the link between CEO quality and firm performance is not without its substantive consequences. Without directors' explicitly realizing it, this emphasis on the performance of the firms with which CEO candidates are linked sometimes leads to the inclusion of otherwise mediocre candidates, and to the exclusion of candidates who may actually have performed admirably under challenging circumstances. By connecting firm performance to CEO quality as a sorting mechanism for eliminating potential candidates, directors create a system for segmenting people on the basis of a measure that from an empirical standpoint is inherently flawed.

STATUS MATCHING: COMING FROM A FIRM OF SIMILAR OR HIGHER REPUTE

Prestige is particularly important in CEO searches, and search committees see the status of the firm from which a CEO candidate comes as amplifying or reducing the status of their own organizations. They also see the status of a firm as a property of individual executives who have worked for it. One director summarizes the effects of this outlook on external CEO searches:

> While the search process is becoming professionalized, the way things work at this level is a lot on the basis of appearances. The process is basically driven by the board, and most boards are looking for either one or

two things in a CEO—peers, which suggests executives who are similar to them, or more higher [sic] profile people who bring prestige and stature to the company simply because of who they are and their obvious accomplishments. So by and large, this is a biased set of selection criteria.

Faced with the need to defend their firms' current positions in the corporate status hierarchy, or desiring to move up the ladder, boards recruit CEOs from organizations with status comparable to, or higher than, that of their own companies. In the external CEO searches I studied, 80 percent of firms recruited their new CEOs from such companies.[31]

Directors' concern with the status of the firm has parallels with concerns about status in most areas of society. Status, as the economist Thorstein Veblen noted, can be used to signal quality, wealth, and, by inference, power.[32] In sociology, Joel Podolny's research has strongly underscored the importance of status in markets.[33] Podolny argues that under conditions of uncertainty, organizations use their affiliations with other economic actors as signals of their own quality and worth. This reflected legitimacy or status may, in turn, have a number of positive economic benefits for the actor, ranging from survival to organizational growth to profitability. In the case of an organization whose future is uncertain, appointing a CEO who is from a high-status firm can produce advantages for the organization such as increased confidence in its prospects.[34]

One of the basic insights of research on status, however, is that a tight coupling between the status of individuals or organizations and their underlying quality may not always exist, a point illustrated by the case of auto parts manufacturer Federal Mogul. The firm's appointment of Richard Snell, formerly CEO of Tenneco Automotive, as its own CEO in November 1996 prompted a Merrill Lynch analyst to write: "Frankly, we are surprised and somewhat relieved that the company was able to secure someone of Mr. Snell's stature." Federal Mogul's stock price jumped to $25 per share from $22 as a consequence of Snell's appointment. As he had done in his previous position at Tenneco, the new CEO then went on an acquisition spree. In the process, he turned Federal Mogul from a $2 billion company into a $6 billion company, while its stock price plummeted from $70 per share in mid-1998 to just $1 in February 2001.[35]

Yet despite such cautionary tales, board members have their own version of Q ratings, and hiring a high-status CEO is viewed as an indication that a company belongs to a particular class of firms. One notable expression of the American corporate ethos is the tendency to form ranks and lists. *Business Week* and *Fortune* magazines, for example, continually generate lists of the "100 Best Companies to Work For" or "America's Most Admired Companies." *Fortune's* survey of "Most Admired Companies" is typical of how such tabulations are assembled. The magazine creates its ranking through a survey of executives, directors, and financial analysts in which respondents are asked to rate companies along the criteria of: (1) quality of management; (2) quality of products and services; (3) financial soundness; (4) long-term investment value; (5) use of corporate assets; (6) innovativeness; (7) responsibility to the community and environment; and (8) ability to attract and retain talented people. Such lists, in turn—although generated, in part, by directors themselves—then form part of directors' view of which corporations and executives are inherently the best. Meanwhile, the notion that CEOs have a status that can be transferred from one company to another has become deeply ingrained in directors' new view of the role of the CEO. And while CEO candidates might appear to most outsiders to be similar with respect to their prior titles, education, and background—just as they appear similar to board members, as we have seen, in terms of their "leadership" abilities—from directors' perspective, no list of candidates can be described as flat or undifferentiated along the lines of status.

Directors' placing of a primary value on status is a gesture that is aimed, in turn, at outside audiences, who are presumed to be capable of discerning the same status differences that the directors themselves do. In a reaction against what external observers see as the uniformity of the candidates in the firm's internal labor market, directors seize on status considerations partly as a way of giving these outsiders a choice from what to the directors (although not necessarily to anybody else) seems a varied menu. Ironically, this decision has the effect mainly of limiting the external candidate pool. Yet relying on status considerations constrains directors significantly in other ways as well. The sheen of a candidate's status often dazzles directors and reduces the level of questioning they will direct at him or her. In the pursuit of status, directors stop trusting their own responses to particular individuals, even feigning indifference to candidates whom they secretly admire and in whom they have reliably based confidence. In the quest for a high-status CEO, directors forego the opportunity to choose a candidate who might truly represent "new blood" and be "reinvigorating" in favor of one who, but for his celebrity, might not even be considered qualified for the job.

Directors' Connections as a Source of Information

Social matching is a relatively crude way of sorting candidates for a position such as CEO. One reason that directors resort to it—in addition to the pressure they feel from internal and external constituents to produce a defensible choice for CEO—is the relative difficulty of obtaining more useful kinds of information about CEO candidates. The means that directors do use for acquiring such information, meanwhile, also restrict their focus to a relative handful of candidates.

Fine-grained information is critical to the outsider CEO selection process. As one director of a $2.6 billion manufacturing concern states:

> As a person responsible for the fiduciary interests of the company, I can tell you that going outside the firm for a CEO is a very difficult decision. . . . While people think there is always a potential person out there who can do the job, this is hard to prove. For example, going outside for the bottom line is fine, but once you start considering issues such as corporate culture and norms, etc., you recognize that you don't want a bull in a china shop, like that guy at Sunbeam [Al Dunlap]. Instead, making that outsider decision requires knowing as much as possible about the person from the outside as you can.

To get such fine-grained information on external candidates, directors rely largely on their connections to other directors. Since a large number of CEO candidates are themselves on boards, they are often connected to other board members. These connections, in turn, make the interlocking directorate particularly well suited for transferring spe-

Table 4.3
Logit Model for Predicting Outsider CEO Succession, 1980–96

	Model 1	Model 2	Model 3
	Conditional on CEO Turnover (n = 1520)	Conditional on Forced Turnover (n = 496)	Conditional on Natural Turnover (n = 1024)
Performance (Lag 1 Year)	−5.02***	−3.82**	−5.57***
	(1.23)	(1.99)	(1.59)
Ln (Employees)	−1.48**	0.91	−.163*
	(.067)	(.117)	(.084)
Pct Insiders Directors	−1.42***	−.824	−2.16***
	(.590)	(.828)	(.857)
Board Centrality	1.47***	1.71***	1.21***
(using Bonacich Centrality)	(.333)	(.552)	(.417)
Constant	−.936***	−1.10***	.775**
	(.246)	(.383)	(.329)

For specification of model, see appendix.
**p < .05; ***p < .01.

cific information about potential candidates. One director describes this process of information transfer in a search in which he participated:

> After we had narrowed down our list of candidates to the finalists, I began to make phone calls. While we liked [David] in particular, we were worried that he would try to change the company culture rather than adapt it. We were looking for a person who would change what was not working well in our culture and keep what was [working]. I made a phone call to a director of another board I sat on who had been his former boss and began to verify my assumptions about this individual and what he thought of this individual's abilities. I did not reveal the name of the company, but described what we were looking for. He allayed our fears and we eventually selected this person because we were able to find out in fairly accurate ways what he was like and would be like once he got here.

The reliance on director ties for particular information about candidates is an important element facilitating the creation of a CEO labor market. The importance of having access to particular information about candidates is highlighted in table 4.3. This table shows that those boards that have a high level of connectivity to other boards through prominent directors are more likely to appoint outsiders than those boards that do not have such connections. This is true independently of whether the outgoing CEO was fired.

The irony inherent in directors' reliance on social ties and in their use of the social matching process in external CEO searches is that even when directors have gone outside the firm to get away from the restrictiveness of the internal market, they often end up duplicating a similar structure in the external CEO selection process. Social matching, in particular, creates a contradiction between the ideal of opening the CEO labor market beyond the relatively narrow confines of the firm and the reality of external searches' focus on a narrow set of candidates. One might say that the external succession process runs in the rut of social matching. The criteria used in the directors' social matching process are harmful not least because they are substituted for others that might measure such truly individual characteristics as ability or industriousness.

The criteria employed in the social matching process that characterizes external CEO succession not only shed light on the closed nature of the CEO labor market but also account, in particular, for the durable homogeneity we observe in the nation's CEO suites despite dramatic changes in the composition of the work force.[36] When directors use these criteria to identify a legitimate set of candidates, they are at the same time maintaining and reproducing a social structure. Through their concern with maintaining group cohesion, their connections with other directors that channel information and values throughout the broader director community, and their attention to the external institutional context in which they operate, directors develop beliefs and social codes that focus their attention on a homogenous set of candidates whom they believe share these beliefs and codes. One of the most perceptive directors I spoke with understood this process. "Do you miss something by not having different criteria or a broader cross-section?" he asks. "Yes, you probably do. You should understand that I am not making any value judgments as to whether the system necessarily is right or wrong or the way it should be. This is the way that it is."

The outcome to which social matching in CEO searches leads is not intentional, but it is locked into external CEO search by the social matching process itself. And because this process is now so routinized in external search—that is, it is taken for granted, rarely questioned, and close to universal—it reproduces a strikingly similar set of candidates in one search after another. Although directors play the most active role in this self-limiting, self-replicating selection process, they are not the only actors in external CEO search to play this particular part. To see how boards of directors receive critical reinforcement in keeping external CEO search focused mostly on a small group of the usual suspects, we need to examine the little understood role of the executive search firm.

CHAPTER 5

THE GO-BETWEENS: THE ROLE OF
THE EXECUTIVE SEARCH FIRM

In CHAPTER 4, we saw corporate directors engaged in the external CEO search process in ways that belie both conventional accounts of how that process works and existing theories purporting to explain it. Directors, we observed, give surprisingly little thought at the beginning of the search process (or at any point thereafter) to the strategic situation and needs of the firm, focusing their time and energy instead on creating a list of ill-defined, often contradictory qualities to be sought in a candidate and then ignoring these supposed requirements throughout the rest of the search. In defining and narrowing the pool of candidates, directors evaluate prospective CEOs based not on their individual abilities and achievements but according to a set of essentially extraneous criteria employed in a process of "social matching."

Yet if these behaviors appear anomalous, it is only, as we also saw, because of our failure to understand the nature of corporate boards and the constraints under which they operate in external CEO searches. In the first place, far from being the autonomous, self-interested individuals of conventional economic theory, directors are members of social groups possessed of their own distinct structures and norms, groups which in turn are embedded in social networks extending beyond the community of directors. Second, the typical corporate board engaged in an external CEO search is essentially flying blind, confronting what is usually, for any given board, an unprecedented situation, and attempting to adapt to the attendant uncertainty with the only ready means it finds at its disposal.

Among many other apparent anomalies that emerge from a close look at the external CEO search process is the role played by a third party to that process, the executive search firm. A simple anecdote conveys the essential strangeness of this role. During a dinner at a meeting of the Business Council (an exclusive group of CEOs), a director from a telecommunications firm that was about to launch a CEO search sat next to a CEO from another firm. Six weeks later, the CEO found himself interviewing for the vacancy at the director's firm. Although, at the time of the Business Council meeting, the search was only a few days from being officially initiated, at no time during the dinner was the candidate given any reason to suspect this. The candidate informed me that he became aware of the search only when an executive search consultant subsequently contacted him. Similarly, the director relayed to me that at no time during the dinner did the CEO candidate "give the slightest indication" that he would ever consider leaving his current firm. Why did the company looking for a new CEO hire a search firm to contact a candidate one of its directors knew, with whom the director could have directly discussed the opening?

As with directors, the role and behavior of executive search consultants in a CEO search turn out to be quite different both from what is widely perceived and from what is predicated in existing economic and sociological theory. As noted in chapter 2, both economists and sociologists generally explain the role of third parties in market exchanges as a response to an economic need. For economists, the function of a third party such as an executive search firm (ESF) in a CEO search is to match the supply of executive talent with the demand for it. The search firm would be said to possess critical information about candidates, such as which are willing to leave their current positions. An economist's view of ESFs would also point to the advantages of scale that they derive from maintaining up-to-date databases about candidates. Sociologists who study markets would follow a similar line of reasoning in describing the role of third parties such as ESFs, but would also stress that buyers and sellers in the market for CEOs are disconnected from each other and that the search firm acts as a broker, using its extensive network of contacts to bring the supply side and the demand side together.

It is true that for a market to function well, buyers and sellers need to know one another's identities and to have good information about one another. Yet as we saw in chapter 4, these requirements explain nothing about the actual division of labor between directors and ESFs in most CEO search engagements. For one thing, directors are in most cases connected from the outset to the potential candidates, if not directly then through a fellow board member who knows a candidate quite well. For another, the detailed information about candidates in a CEO search is gathered not by the search firm but by the directors themselves. If the proponents of either the economic or sociological perspectives on the role of third parties in markets were asked why a company involved in a search cannot obtain information about candidates and connect with them on its own, the answer would be that while the company could in fact do this, it would be more expensive than hiring a third party. Both the economic and sociological lines of argument, in other words, suggest that companies that hire an executive search firm are making an essentially economic decision as to whether to "make or buy" the search.

A closer look at the CEO search process than most social scientists have undertaken, however, reveals many anomalies in the function of ESFs that such a purely economic perspective cannot explain. Like the role and behavior of directors, the involvement of ESFs in the external CEO search process needs to be understood in its social dimensions, structural and cultural, as well as in relation to the unique characteristics of the external CEO market. To understand the social relations and belief systems in which ESFs and those with whom they interact in the CEO search process are embedded, it is useful to look at where the executive search industry came from and how it came to be a player in the external CEO market.

A Brief History of the Executive Search Industry

Executive search firms are professional service firms whose primary mission is to assist organizations in the search for, and recruitment of, executive management. Globally, executive search is an $11.5 billion industry; more than half that revenue is generated in the United States, where search firms are used about four times more often than in Europe, where inter-firm mobility has remained relatively low.[1] The largest ESFs, a subset of the broader recruiter category and the object of my focus here, are most significantly differentiated from others in the industry by their geographic reach, private-sector focus, multiple-industry experience, retainer-based fees, and specialization in the recruitment of senior management and boards of directors. These firms are distinct from the contingency-fee recruiters who usually fill mid- and lower-level managerial jobs as well as technical and office-support jobs.

The earliest executive search firms did not emerge overnight. Rather, their roots lay in an industry that boomed in the post–World War II period—management consulting. In the industry's early days, Booz Allen Hamilton and McKinsey & Co. dominated management consulting, and by the 1940s were advising top executives on corporate strategies. As management consulting continued to gain legitimacy within corporate America, the question often arose as to who would actually implement the necessary strategies that these consulting firms recommended. The implementation issue gave rise to the externally facilitated executive search in its initial form, as consulting firms including Booz Allen and McKinsey developed in-house executive-search capabilities. Independent search firms soon followed.

While these new search firms were successful in building legitimacy among corporate chieftains for externally facilitated executive searches (except in the case of the CEO position, as we shall see momentarily), most remained relatively small, confining their searches to particular localities and charging on a contingency-fee basis. Throughout the 1950s, the executive search industry as a whole was fragmented and business was generated largely as a consequence of the founder's connections. Most firms did not survive beyond the retirement of their founders, but others sprang up to replace those that folded.[2] (With low barriers to entry into the business, there are even today literally thousands of search firms in the United States.)

Not until the 1960s did some rationalization of the industry begin to take place. This second phase was marked by the formation of the four large, retainer-based executive search firms that still dominate the industry: Heidrick & Struggles International, Spencer Stuart & Associates, Russell Reynolds Associates, and Korn/Ferry International. Three of these firms can trace their origins to the search departments of major professional services firms: Heidrick & Struggles and Spencer

TABLE 5.1
Worldwide and U.S. Revenue of the Four Largest U.S. Executive Search Firms, 1993–2000

Firm	Worldwide Revenues ($ Millions)						
	2000	1999	1998	1997	1996	1995	1994
Korn/Ferry International	$576.4	$418.4	$339.1	$301.1	$256.8	$215.7	$168
Heidrick & Struggles Int'l	$574.2	$429.2	$324.8	$258.0	$199.8	$161.0	$131
Spencer Stuart	$345.0	$259.5	$238.8	$244.7	$178.0	$158.5	$127
Russell Reynolds Associates	$305.3	$240.0	$189.8	$184.3	$147.3	$132.1	$104

Source: Kennedy Information Inc.'s Executive Recruiter News.

Stuart emerged from the management consulting firm Booz Allen Hamilton, and Korn/Ferry from the accounting and consulting firm Peat Marwick. The fourth major ESF, Russell Reynolds, emerged from the financial services industry.

Today, these large executive search firms are sophisticated service organizations whose resources extend well beyond those of the sole proprietorships they originally were. Those earlier, entrepreneurial firms needed only a convincing salesman with a telephone and a carefully collected Rolodex. Today's large search firms, by contrast, are extensively computerized and professionally managed. Their research staffs use sophisticated computer directories to map the latest changes in large company organization charts. Consultants handle up to five or six searches simultaneously, for a variety of firms.

Although rooted in the management consulting business, the modern executive search industry grew into its own as a result of several developments connected with the post–World War II economic boom. With the European economy in ruins at the close of the war, American industry found itself confronted with an unprecedented demand for its goods and services, which in turn fueled a demand for a large number of new executives to accommodate large corporations' requirements for general managers to run the booming factories of the United States. Increased demand for executives also came from the emerging service sectors of transportation, communications, and retail, and from the powerful global financial industry, which had completely shifted its center

U.S. Revenues
($ Millions)

2000	1999	1998	1997	1996	1995	1994	1993
$339.6	$218.5	$177.0	$157.2	$126.2	$103.8	$90.1	$55.6
$341.6	$256.4	$178.0	$154.0	$123.1	$99.3	$85.1	$69.4
$192.4	$140.3	$126.0	$131.1	$97.7	$78.3	$68.6	$48.7
$160.2	$123.1	$93.4	$94.1	$78.5	$69.7	$60.6	$40.4

of activities from London to New York. While many of the companies in such industries had traditionally prided themselves on training and nurturing their own people to fill positions within the firm, the growth pressures on U.S. industry forced firms to turn to other organizations to recruit for their top slots (although it would be many years before looking outside for a new CEO would become acceptable).

That executive search firms sprang up to satisfy a demand from companies for executives, rather than a demand from would-be executives for jobs, accounts for what remains a critical difference between ESFs and traditional employment services. While the latter serve people looking for jobs, ESFs handle jobs looking for people—usually people who are already employed and not actively seeking a job.

As the executive search industry as a whole continued to grow in the postwar years, three institutional changes in the business environment had a particularly dramatic impact on the growth of the Big Four firms. First, out of concerns about conflict of interest and the maintenance of professional objectivity, management consulting firms exited the search business. Since the demand for executives, however, did not decline, corporate America's need for executive-search services was now filled by firms focused only on executive search. The firms that proved to have a distinct advantage in serving large, lucrative, steady, and geographically dispersed clients were those that (a) emerged out of consulting firms with established relationships with clients, (b) were organized as partnerships rather than sole proprietorships, thus enabling them to create a career path for search consultants, and (c) had developed branch offices around the country enabling them to serve the largest corporations and tap a broad labor pool.

The second institutional factor that fueled the growth of the Big Four executive search firms was the exclusion of the formal personnel function in large corporations from the task of senior executive search, even as personnel departments were rapidly proliferating. Researchers have noted the dramatic increase in personnel departments across the corporate landscape in the postwar period because of changes in U.S. employment law and the professionalization of the personnel function.[3] What these researchers fail to make explicit, however, is that even as the personnel function was becoming more complex, most personnel officers were viewed by their firms as ancillary and marginal to the strategic mission of the company. While personnel departments could effectively recruit junior employees and managers, design salary grades, and write job descriptions, they were not instrumental in promotion or selection decisions related to senior executives. The mere fact that the human resources department of today is considered one of the lowest-prestige divisions in most major companies makes the priorities plain. The personnel function was (and continues to be) peripheral to the senior executive team, and did not often have representation on a firm's management committee or board. Even when personnel departments were asked to search for and select executives for positions with considerably more formal and informal authority than anyone within human resources possessed, most lacked the ability to make effective decisions because of their status as a staff function and cost center, as opposed to an operating function and profit center, for the corporation. Moreover, new, complex government regulations concerning employment made personnel work more complex and managerial recruitment more difficult. For example, out of a concern for both maintaining privacy and preventing discrimination, many personal questions could no longer be posed to a prospective employee—a problem that could now be partially overcome by employing a search consultant as an intermediary. In his book *The Headhunters*, John Byrne quotes a search consultant describing this aspect of what an ESF could now offer its clients:

What can a headhunter ask a candidate that a client legally cannot? "Almost everything," replies Brenda Ruello, of Heidrick & Struggles. "My attitude is that I can ask a candidate any question I want to ask. I work for my client and the more I know about a candidate is better for my client. And I don't like surprises. I don't think a client can ask all those questions like 'Who's going to take care of your children. Tell me about your divorce' or any of those things. I can set up an interview in an environment that encourages you to talk. By the fun of it, the warmth of it and the non-threatening way of asking a question."[4]

The third institutional factor in the growth of the Big Four was the dramatic rise of the MBA as a professional credential. The notion that MBA training created a "general manager" altered the prevalent assumption that all executives had to be home-grown talent, as MBA education at the elite business schools shifted from an orientation of training managers for specific functions, such as finance and marketing, to producing leaders whose skills could be generalized across functions and industries. As a result, the corporate landscape was characterized by a new class of mobile managers willing and able to move from one firm to another for the sake of promotions and raises. This group was distinctly different from the loyal corporate executive described in William Whyte's classic 1956 text The Organization Man.[5]

These developments, while allowing the Big Four executive search firms to grow in size and influence, also helped pave the way for the eventual emergence of an external CEO market. Yet it is important to observe that with only a few notable exceptions, the CEO position remained sacrosanct and outside the purview of ESFs until the early 1990s. Up to that point, the idea of an outsider coming into the organization as CEO without at least a few years in the firm's own senior executive ranks was close to heresy. The appointment of an outsider was seen as suspect and a failure on behalf of a company's board and top management to develop competent executives.[6] For example, Wall Street analysts jeered at the 1978 appointment of an outsider CEO, Edwin Gee, at International Paper. Commenting on the fall of the company's stock price after the announcement, analysts criticized the company for its failure to generate top management from within the firm.

"They've had to go outside the company for nearly every recent top management change," one analyst stated.[7] He asserted that the most recent appointment "is the wrong decision for a company which has visibly underperformed in the paper market. They need [someone] who had [sic] experience in the forest products industry as well." As one of his first moves to placate such critics, Gee vowed to analysts that he would start developing a pool of internal candidates and that the next chief executive would come from inside the company.[8]

This preference for insiders was soon to change, however, as CEOs of *Fortune* 100 companies began to be forced out of their jobs in 1992 and 1993, marking a seismic shift in corporate governance and creating what would become a universally recognized role for ESFs in the CEO search process. A CEO search by a major east coast retail bank in the early 1990s presaged this new function for the ESF. The bank's CEO, though a poor performer by almost all measures, continued to enjoy enough support from a board with which he enjoyed a cozy relationship to avoid dismissal. Moreover, through a series of political actions, the CEO had had a hand in removing all but one of his potential replacements from within the company, leaving this sole survivor as the favored choice of the board. The board, however, came under "a lot of pressure from institutional investors who thought that the current situation was one of sub-optimization of assets and gross underperformance," according to one director. When the incumbent CEO finally announced his retirement date, the board quickly appointed a search committee while also agreeing to benchmark the inside candidate against outsiders—it being generally understood among the board members, although never explicitly stated, that this would be an exercise with a predetermined outcome. Surprisingly, however, one of the first actions of the outside director who had been appointed to head the search committee was to announce that the company would employ an ESF. The local newspapers applauded the apparent decision to consider outsiders, viewing this as a sign that the board was exerting more authority and control over the bank. Three of the largest and best-known search firms—Russell Reynolds, Heidrick & Struggles, and Spencer Stuart—were invited to compete for the business. (Russell Reynolds was eventually awarded the job.) After a seemingly extensive external search lasting six months, the board named the inside candidate to the CEO position. Yet even this ultimately perfunctory exercise proved to be an important step in establishing a role for ESFs in the CEO search process.

The situation at a large Massachusetts computer company at about this same time was similar in some ways, yet led to a quite different result that saw an ESF brought into the middle of the CEO search process. The company's CEOs had always come from within the organization, and had tended to bring with them circles of associates who were often longtime friends as well as colleagues. The rationale behind the practice was that successful teams should be kept intact. In the early 1990s, however, as the company began to face dramatically changing markets, the collegiality prevailing in the CEO's inner circle prevented significant change and the replacement of weak performers. After a series of missed performance targets and a great deal of internal debate, the existing CEO recognized that the mood in the boardroom had changed seemingly overnight. Many board members were savvy enough to recognize that the environment had changed. As one director puts it, "The widows and orphans were no longer the shareholders." Meanwhile, the dismissal of Robert Stempel (who had been the handpicked choice of his predecessor, rubber-stamped by the board) at General Motors, as well as the debacle at American Express in which James Robinson had been rewarded with the title of chairman after years of disastrous performance as CEO, had seized the board members' attention. So did a scathing series of stories in the media, and accusations from investors that the board was asleep at the wheel. When the directors publicly announced that they would immediately begin the search for a new CEO, the first order of business was to find an ESF to lead it. Again, the largest search firms were invited to compete for what the media described as "the search assignment of the decade." During the entire process, the firm and the ESF were able to maintain the confidentiality of the search, despite intense media speculation. After four months, the firm chose an outsider for the CEO position.

Given the critical importance that, as we have seen, issues such as confidentiality have for firms conducting external CEO searches, the ESF that led the computer company's search would appear to have acquitted itself well in at least one major part of its job. And ever since the two CEO searches described above marked the entry of ESFs into this strategically key area, hiring an ESF has come to be regarded as an entirely normal and even necessary part of conducting an external CEO search. It is therefore surprising, and significant, that ESFs are viewed skeptically and even suspiciously by those who hire and work with them. The precarious position of ESFs in the system of social structures and beliefs governing the external CEO search process offers an important clue, in turn, to their role not just as facilitators of an economic exchange but also as functionaries in an elaborately staged and choreographed ritual leading to social closure.

The Marginal Status of Executive Search Consultants

Although executive search consultants are commonly credited with playing an important role in helping firms identify executive talent, they are viewed warily by the directors who have hired them. One director I interviewed commented on the "sleaziness of the whole search business" (by which he meant the executive search industry). While some board members' assessments are considerably less harsh, almost all of the directors I interviewed were nevertheless critical of the industry and the increased level of search firm activity over the last two decades.

Many directors see search firms as contributing to disruptive job-hopping and the spiraling salaries of CEOs. "Of course, how much you pay depends on the worry that you might lose the individual. To the extent that ESFs are constantly tempting an executive with illusions about greener pastures, we have to respond," explains one director. It would appear to be true that ESFs today are extremely active and even aggressive in their efforts to learn which executives might be interested in leaving their current firms: a recent, much-discussed *New York Times* article cited a survey indicating that nearly half of all American managers over the age of thirty-five speak with executive search consultants at least quarterly—and it is not the executives who are placing the calls.[9] It is also true that, hardened by the downsizings, "rightsizings," outsourcings, and restructurings of the late 1980s and the 1990s—developments standing in stark contrast to the long-term commitments on the part of employers to employees that were the rule during the era of managerial capitalism—executives, while still proclaiming the importance of institutional loyalty, often demonstrate little such loyalty themselves. Yet it would seem, at the least, difficult to determine how much ESFs are actively contributing to diminished loyalty on the part of executives as opposed to merely exploiting it for their own purposes.

Whether such attitudes are justified or not, executive search consultants recognize the wariness with which their clientele regards them. Indeed, they may be highly attuned to it, for search consultants are likely to harbor considerable professional insecurity to begin with. This insecurity arises from both the dubious status that ESFs have historically possessed and the backgrounds of the individuals who have traditionally entered the profession.

John Beck, a director at Russell Reynolds Associates, recalls an incident during the early 1980s in which the founder of the firm, Russ Reynolds, approached the Harvard Business School about undertaking some joint activities. "He was told that the business school didn't consider executive search a business but sort of a group of parasites who were kept at bay or entertained or whatever by the corporations that used them," Beck relates.[10] This ungentlemanly reception must have come as a rude surprise to Reynolds, who, in his firm's self-published history, described his original vision of creating a firm that would be the equivalent of Morgan Stanley in the executive search business:

> We wanted to be the *best*, and that means you have the best people, the best office, the best staff, the best equipment. Quality attracts quality. I think the choice of an office—the appearance of the office, the ambiance of the office—is a very important ingredient in the life of the company.[11]

Faced with the suspicion and even disparagement that continue to this day to dog the executive search industry, Reynolds set out to elevate and cleanse the early image of search consultants as panderers and parasites. Beth Green Olesky, a Russell Reynolds consultant, describes the imprint that the founder attempted to give to his firm:

> Russ would pick people in his image, for the most part, which wasn't a bad image. I think we became known as a kind of white-shoe . . . firm. This was a great help in the early days when the recruiting industry did not quite pass the "smell test." Everyone was very credentialed. Russ always tried to pick people with high personal standards and was always very careful about who he brought into the firm: he viewed it as a privi-

lege to work here. Our offices looked like Morgan Bank's offices. Russ was always repeating Morgan's motto, which is something like, "First-class people doing first-class business, in a first-class way." He believed it and promulgated it.[12]

Notwithstanding Reynolds's high aspirations for his firm, and for the entire search industry, executive search consultants have sometimes been thought—by themselves as well as others—to fall short of the highest standards of personal integrity. Indeed in the 1980s the industry faced a minor crisis when its self-appointed watchdog newsletter, *Executive Recruiter News*, reported on several cases in which high-profile search consultants had inflated their educational credentials. After the publication of these reports, the Association of Executive Search Consultants began requiring member firms to check the credentials of their consultants. Search consultants themselves, meanwhile, frequently tell stories about members of the profession who have misrepresented their backgrounds, and cite this as the reason for the poor image many outsiders have of their profession.[13]

Yet even when they are truthful about their backgrounds—as the overwhelming majority of them surely are—search consultants have reason for insecurity about their credentials compared with those of their corporate clients' other highly paid advisers. This is because the candidate pool for consultant positions in executive search firms is composed primarily of former management consultants and investment bankers—including many who have failed to make partner in these occupations—as well as executives who have topped out at their current firms. The global executive search firm Egon Zehnder, for example, highlights the fact that 40 of its 270 professional staff in 1999 were alumni of the illustrious consulting firm McKinsey & Co.[14] And if search consultants can be accused of contributing to the prevalence of job-hopping among executives, it is in part, perhaps, because they lay themselves open to this charge by being frequent job-hoppers themselves. A search firm looking to enter new markets or quickly develop a client base will often try to hire top consultants from a competitor.[15] Moreover, most new search firms are founded by experienced search consultants.

Not surprisingly, given their marginal status in the world in which they operate—and perhaps in their own eyes as well—search consultants exhibit a heightened self-consciousness and are experts at managing image and presentation of self. For example, they dress in expensively tailored clothing like that of the clients and candidates with whom they interact. One might argue, of course, that because search consultants' lives are suffused with corporate values and they constantly interact with the corporate elite, such traits represent not conscious attempts to create an image but rather mimetic processes, such as those by which real-life investment bankers can't help looking and acting like Gordon Gekko in the movie *Wall Street*. In my interviews with search consultants and discussions with them of ESF hiring practices, however, it became clear that there are specific policies and profiles directed toward hiring people in the image of the corporate chieftains whom search firms seek to serve. John Byrne paints a portrait of one of the large executive search firms that describes the results of such policies:

> The typical headhunter here is white, male, and prep-school-Protestant. [The] firm is populated by a sea of Ivy Leaguers in neatly pressed pinstripes and monogrammed shirts. Of the 114 consultants portrayed in [the] brochure, 74 boast graduate degrees from some of the world's most distinguished universities. There are 45 M.B.A.s alone, a third of whom hold the golden passport stamped at Harvard. Among those 114, only one is black; 20 are women, and seven are bald.[16]

The heightened self-consciousness found among search consultants is evident not only in their physical appearance and concern with credentials but also in their behavior. Few things betray social insecurity as pointedly as name-dropping, a practice in which search consultants engage quite overtly. They also highlight their associations with important organizations and individuals, not only joining the same exclusive clubs as do top executives, but advertising these affiliations in both their conversation and their biographies on their firms' Web sites. For example, one search consultant whom I met sought, within a few minutes of our introduction to each other, to assure me of his insider status among the corporate elite, making overt references to his "recent golf game" with IBM's Lou Gerstner, his "recent lunch" with a president of one of GE's divisions, a "drink at the Yale Club" with another "well-known executive," and "the board infighting" at a prominent computer firm then undertaking a search. Such behavior—which one encounters as a matter of course among search consultants—suggests high-status associations in which the consultant anxiously suspects that his or her place in the winners' circle is close to the periphery.[17]

Search consultants' concern with appearances as a means of gaining acceptance as legitimate players in the high-stakes game of executive placement also extends to the location and physical decor of executive search firm offices. Three of the four largest ESFs are headquartered in midtown Manhattan, while their satellite offices are located in the centers of the major cities of the world, on the highest floors of the highest-rent buildings. The office decor combines features of a *Fortune* 500 headquarters and an Ivy League club: dark wood, antique oriental rugs, and decorous paintings of quaint New England towns. On the burnished coffee table are copies of the firm's brochure and of the day's *Wall Street Journal* and *New York Times*. In an effort to recruit the "very credentialed" people (particularly from management consulting firms and investment banks) who once tended to shy away from executive search, the elite firms have created environs designed to reassure such individuals and, more generally, to professionalize an occupation that has historically lacked such legitimating features as certification, links to an academic discipline, or a strong professional association. Like search consultants' aping of the physical appearance and lifestyles of the corporate elite, the imitation of corporate decor forms part of a painstaking, decades-long attempt to construct an image of trusted corporate adviser and consiglière to the board—not fast-talking headhunter with a Rolodex and a phone working out of a one-room office.

Although it is easy to mock search consultants for the kinds of traits and behaviors described above (to join in the disdain, in other words, that many corporate directors show toward them), they appear in a more sympathetic light when one recalls that third parties or middlemen have been considered suspect in many cultures and historical periods.[18] The third-party role has often been occupied by people who are marginalized in their societies to begin with. For example, sociologists have found that a number of marginalized ethnic groups in the world have occupied a middleman position in the economic structure. Some of these groups include the Jews in Europe, the Parsis in India, Indians in South Africa, and the Chinese in Southeast Asia, all of whom have tended to concentrate in occupations such as agent, rent collector, moneylender, and broker.[19] When borrowing or lending money, European monarchies often used Jewish middlemen to distance themselves from, or cleanse themselves of, aspects of the transaction that they could not own up to or openly participate in. Parsis in India often performed similar functions in trade.[20] These middleman occupations, in turn, tend to fall between the cracks of the economic structure, are considered marginal activities, and occupy the lowest rungs in terms of occupational status. At the same time, it is critical to recognize that those who serve in these intermediary roles perform an important function. For example, as sociologists have tended to emphasize, marginalized groups in middleman positions buffer elites from the hostility of those they dominate by doing what is seen as their dirty work for them.[21] In other words, middlemen bear the status consequences of engaging in actions that are seen as unbecoming or unworthy of high-status actors.

The marginal intermediary also serves another, less recognized function: because they are not subject to the same constraints as are other members of society, intermediaries are often the source of new and innovative practices. The low-status intermediary has a freedom of action that is denied to the norm-bound members of a particular social structure: because their status is already marginal, intermediaries can engage in practices that are not yet legitimate in society, thereby initiating certain kinds of changes in the social structure. Some scholars have noted, for example, that the great financial innovations of the 1980s, such as high-yield debt and leveraged buyouts, were inventions of second- and third-tier investment firms such as Drexel Burnham Lambert, while first-tier firms such as Goldman Sachs initially dismissed the use of such instruments as something that "their class of firms" would not engage in.[22] This traditional function for middlemen, in turn, points to the fact that in legitimating themselves both in their own eyes and in the eyes of those with whom they conduct business, these intermediaries are also legitimating certain processes for the other actors involved.

Search consultants must concern themselves with appearances because both their clients and the candidates whom these clients are attempting to woo are themselves particularly sensitive to appearances of both competence and legitimacy on the part of the ESF, and to appearances of propriety in the search process generally. To point to this concern with appearances on the part of all three major parties to the external CEO search is also to confront, once again, the disparity between the ostensible and the actual roles of the ESF in the search process. This disparity is evident throughout a CEO search, starting at the point at which a company seeking a new CEO decides to hire an executive search firm.

Choosing a Search Consultant: The Shootout

By the time a company calls in an ESF, the current CEO may have unexpectedly announced that he or she is leaving, or the board may have decided that the CEO needs to be replaced. Whatever the reason for the CEO's impending departure, the board may decide to bring in an ESF either because an internal successor is not available, because the directors wish to benchmark their insider candidate or candidates against outsiders, or because they are inclined from the beginning to seek an outside successor. Because of the importance of the CEO position, as we have seen, the board feels that it is urgent to fill the vacancy as quickly as possible. As one search consultant remarks, "Wall Street, the directors, and the remaining company executives are nervous until they know who is going to be steering the ship."

After the decision to enlist the aid of a search firm, the usual next step is to hold a ritual competition among ESFs, an event known in the search industry as a "shootout." The shootout is essentially a process in which search consultants argue for why their firm should be chosen for a particular assignment. Typically, only the largest and most prestigious firms compete to handle CEO searches. Increasingly, even companies at which a particular search firm has successfully placed senior executives, or even directors, in the past will ask that firm to compete against others in a shootout. The ritual aspect of the shootout is clearly brought out by the fact that even when a company seeking a new CEO has already decided to use a particular search firm, it will still go through the exercise of a shootout.

Three firms are typically invited to compete in a shootout.[23] To prepare for this event, the search consultants attempt to develop an understanding of the hiring firm's current situation and recent history, including its political dynamics. A consultant at Heidrick & Struggles describes his preparation for the shootout as "homework": "Homework, for recruiters, means undertaking a rapid fact-finding mission and presenting an initial plan of a CEO profile." Another consultant describes this preparation by saying, "We try to develop an understanding of the business." Like much else about the ESF's contribution to the CEO search process, however, this diligently pursued activity seems to take place largely for the sake of appearances. For as we saw in chapter 4, neither a search firm's "understanding of the business" nor any "CEO profile" that it develops will play any significant role in the actual CEO search.

During the shootout, search firms attempt to differentiate themselves from the other ESFs competing to handle the search. Retainer-based search firms do not compete on price, so price comparisons do not figure in the competition. (The Association of Executive Search Consultants requires that its members charge fees on a retainer basis regardless of whether the search consultant successfully places a candidate. In addition to its retainer, an ESF handling a CEO search also receives one-third of the successful candidate's negotiated cash compensation plus expenses.) Instead, the consultants representing the various ESFs stress their own firm's unique approach to executive search—although each competing firm turns out to have the same reasons as the others for claiming uniqueness. That is, all the major search firms stress their global reach, consultative approach to search, and team-based operations, as well as the business experience of their consultants. Here is how Russell Reynolds and Spencer Stuart, respectively, describe their basic approaches to executive search assignments on their firms' Web sites:

> Every client has different needs, and each assignment conducted by Russell Reynolds Associates is unique. What remains constant are the high standards we apply throughout the course of all assignments. We employ a systematic approach that is both comprehensive in scope—involving an in-depth investigation of a targeted group of well-qualified individuals—and swift. We recognize the urgency of our clients' needs and we aim to meet those needs quickly and effectively.[24]

> Corporate leadership and governance is as important an element of corporate strategy as deciding how to introduce new products or raise capital

for expansion. Our role is to be a consultant and strategic adviser in this vital area by providing judgment, market intelligence and insight, not just a list of names. Before a prospect becomes a candidate, we perform an in-depth analysis of the executive to document accomplishments, management style, leadership philosophy and personal and professional ambitions. We maintain a close relationship with the client throughout the search process, from our initial meeting to closing the offer.[25]

Here is how the two firms describe the caliber of their consultants:

The quality of our recruiting consultants is the key to the service excellence we provide. Our consultants are highly informed and most have firsthand experience in the industries and markets they serve. The consultants in all of our 33 wholly owned offices work in global teams so our clients benefit from the collective knowledge of our entire firm.[26]

The quality, integrity and expertise of our consultants ensure that we provide the best leadership solutions for every assignment. Many Spencer Stuart consultants have previous experience at some of the world's top corporations and management consulting firms; others have owned or operated their own businesses. None has ever sat on the sidelines.[27]

Despite their efforts to distinguish themselves from one another, however, search firms cannot be easily differentiated on process, for there are very few real differences among the practices of these firms. While all the major ESFs emphasize that their consultants have special expertise in evaluating leadership talent, most search firms hire their consultants from the same candidate pool of ex-management consultants, investment bankers, and executives. The similarity in the practices of these firms is further reinforced by the fact that a firm's senior search consultants often have worked at other search firms. Given all these homogenizing influences, it is hardly surprising that all of the major ESFs follow a similar process in the early phases of a search, beginning with the drafting of a specification sheet and ending with a short-list of candidates. Owing to these similarities across ESFs, meanwhile, most of their clients would agree with the statement of one director that the top-tier search firms are "essentially indistinguishable."

If executive search firms are really indistinguishable from one another, then on what basis do companies decide which ESF to engage? As it happens, which search firm a company selects often depends on the search committee members' knowledge of, and experience with, the competing ESFs. According to Steve Scroggins of Russell Reynolds, "the [prior] relationship tends to be a critical tipping factor" in deciding which search firm a company will go with. For example, a member of the search committee in the 1997 CEO search at Stanley Works explained the selection of Heidrick & Struggles as the executive recruiter by saying, "I had done a lot of work with Heidrick in the past and felt comfortable in [*sic*] their assistance for the search." If no prior relationship exists, search firms may well be selected on the basis of past search assignments at well-known, prestigious firms. Thus, for instance, Heidrick & Struggles will point to its placements at Home Depot, IBM, and Eastman Kodak. Of course, most ESFs have placed so many executives that all the elite firms can point to resounding successes. (As almost goes without saying, each of these firms has also placed its share of spectacular failures, although these are not discussed in brochures or on Web sites.)

If companies choose which search firm to work with on such bases, why go through the ritual of the shootout at all? In essence, the shootout is the first act of an elaborate drama designed to disguise the social nature of the external CEO search process and dress it up as objective and market based. This same kind of game is played again when the search firm and its client create the impression that the role of the ESF hired after the shootout is to help the searching company identify and evaluate candidates, whereas the real—and absolutely critical—function that the ESF performs is of another kind altogether.

The Executive Search Firm as Intermediary

As noted in chapter 4, the first step in the CEO search process, once a search committee has been formed and an ESF has been engaged, is the compilation of a specification sheet, which turns out to be a laundry list of desired qualifications and traits that is never actually used in most CEO searches. The second step (which is especially important if the board is seriously considering an outsider candidate) is the ESF's solicitation from the directors of the names of potential candidates. This point is critical: as search consultants themselves emphasize in describing the process, very few CEO searches start from scratch, and the suggestions of names by directors constitute the crucial input. This is illustrated by an unsuccessful search at a large regional financial services firm in which many of the directors were local businessmen and acquaintances of the incumbent CEO. "We had a hell of a time even generating a preliminary candidate list here," the search consultant responsible for the search remarked. "The board was of little help, since many of them were 'local boys' and had little knowledge about who were the other leading figures in the [financial services] industry."

Insofar as ESFs actively participate in the process of identifying and then evaluating candidates, moreover, they operate only at a general level. As shown in figure 5.1, the CEO search process involves both extensive and intensive phases.

In the extensive phase of the search, candidate specifications and candidate pools are defined, and general information about potential candidates is gathered. Examples of general information include the educational backgrounds and work histories of persons in the initial candidate pool. These tasks typically are divided between directors and the ESFs. Most of the search consultants I interviewed agreed with the view of this phase of the search provided by one of their colleagues:

> Our primary responsibility in the research phase is to get the factual, exact information on the preliminary list. Our responsibility is to make sure [that] what is presented to the client with respect to the background and experience of the candidate is factual and verified. . . . [This information is gathered] from our library or research group, who collect general information on every major company and their executives.

Executive search firms can assemble this information quickly because they are continually generating and replenishing their candidate lists. The ESFs in my sample interviewed, on average, two thousand executives a year. Consequently, ESFs have an up-to-date record of most candidates' work histories, personal information, and salary. Having this information enables an ESF to quickly trim a preliminary candidate list by removing candidates who would be "too expensive," "are nearing retirement," or "are untouchable because we placed them in their current position within the last three years."

EXTENSIVE SEARCH

- Define Specifications   +

- Define Candidate Pool   +   +

- Gather General Information   +

INTENSIVE SEARCH

- Gather Particular Information   +
  About Candidates

- Check References   +

FIGURE 5.1 Executive Search Firms' and Directors' Roles in CEO Search.

In the intensive phase of the search, specific information about candidates is gathered and references are checked. Most of this process is conducted by the directors, who, as we saw in chapter 4, rely on their personal contacts with other directors who have direct knowledge of a candidate under consideration to collect detailed, concrete information about the candidate's capabilities.

Corporate directors, for their part, clearly understand that the role of the ESF in a CEO search is not really to identify and evaluate candidates. What then is that role? Gigi Michelson, a director of several *Fortune* 500 firms who has been involved in several CEO searches, explains one of the important functions that the ESF does perform quite plainly:

> To expect the executive search firm to do the board's job is a miscalculation. The most effective use of a search firm that I have found on numerous occasions is that there are . . . search firms who can open the door to candidates that otherwise are likely to turn you down. There are individuals in search firms who could open the doors, where other individuals, including our own directors and other search firms, simply cannot do it. I could name names. People who can get you to the right guy who, in the meantime, has been approached 35 times in the last year-

and-a-half and has turned them all down and has a standard speech for the purpose, but the right firm can get to him.

Now consider a description of the ESF's role in the CEO search process offered by a recent CEO candidate:

> There is a big difference in taking a call from an executive search firm than [sic] taking a call from another firm, especially a competitor, talking to you about a job. I can toy with the search firm, get some information about the opportunity, find out how much I'm worth in the market. . . . Talking to a director is a whole new ball game . . . and a serious one. . . . You don't play around once these kinds of conversations start taking place.

In contrast to economic and sociological accounts of third parties in markets, which discuss the third-party role in terms of providing information and matching supply with demand, these descriptions of the function of ESFs by actual participants in the CEO search process point to a different kind of activity altogether. As one search consultant puts it, "If you look at this as some simple type of information gap that we fill, you are missing the big picture." The accounts given by those who know the process first-hand suggest that ESFs are first and foremost actors dealing in one particular commodity: intermediation. The intermediary role, which in fact sharply distinguishes ESFs from mere information brokers, arises in turn from the three distinctive characteristics of the external CEO market as described in chapter 2: small numbers, high risk, and concerns about legitimacy.

The intermediation that ESFs perform—as search consultants themselves describe it—can be broken down into three primary elements: (1) coordinating the activities of a searching firm's board to create cohesion and help rapidly develop candidate specifications and identify a candidate pool; (2) mediating the exchange between the searching firm and the candidates to manage a gradual commitment process in which neither the candidates nor the searching firm are unduly exposed to risk should a deal fail to materialize; and (3) legitimating the search process by signaling to constituents that it was conducted professionally and with the participants' best interests in mind. Let us consider each of these elements in turn.

COORDINATING

Outsourcing is a common means of getting business done. In the CEO search process, firms outsource the coordination of the search to ESFs. Coordination in the search process entails managing both the inter-dependent activities of the search and the heightened emotions that external CEO search tends to arouse in directors and candidates.

One aspect of the ESF's coordination role in a CEO search arises from its specialization in executive search. Directors are often involved in a CEO search only as part-time governors. Boards usually meet only quarterly and do not have large administrative staffs reporting to them. Consequently, search firms have advantages in terms of both experience and scale over any searching firm in managing the administrative tasks associated with a CEO search. If carrying out this aspect of the coordination role were all that ESFs did, the hiring of a search firm could accurately be described as a make-buy decision.

The ESF's coordinating role in a CEO search, however, involves much more than the management and performance of administrative tasks. Given the nature of the CEO position and its importance—both strategic and symbolic—for organizations, a CEO search is a disruptive process that, as directors and search consultants both stress, is closely connected to the internal workings of the searching firm. The anxiety and enthusiasms that a search can engender among directors, and the controversies generated by conflicts between various constituencies and purposes, are part and parcel of any CEO search and must be skillfully managed. Thus, in addition to managing the administrative activities of a CEO search, ESFs focus a significant amount of attention on help-ing a firm's directors "keep their act together."

Consider two examples of how ESFs carry out this second, often del-icate aspect of their coordinating function. Because the number of po-tentially qualified candidates for the CEO position in a large corpora-tion is considered small, executive search consultants want to ensure that the actions of the board do not inadvertently result in the loss of a candidate. According to consultants, the most common way that boards unintentionally sabotage their own searches is when an overly exuber-ant director contacts a candidate directly to discuss an opportunity. (This is a blunder because it can cause the candidate to fear that rumors about his candidacy will leak out prematurely and jeopardize his current position, in which case the candidate will publicly announce that he is not interested in any other position and reaffirm his commitment to his existing firm.) Thus, part of the ESF's role is to make sure that board members understand the rules of the high-stakes game that they are playing and the importance of observing them. Moreover, as we saw in the story of the Bank One search in chapter 1, boards can be riven by factions (despite the high value placed on board cohesion in directors' culture). This makes blending the various factions of the board into a single voice another key part of the ESF's coordinating function.

Corporate boards' reliance on an intermediary for coordination in external CEO search highlights the fact that when organizations confront ambiguous and complex market exchanges, social arrangements can become critical for directing activities toward the realization of economic objectives. They are equally important with respect to the second intermediary role played by the ESF in an external CEO search, the role of mediating itself.

MEDIATING

As suggested by the candidate quoted above who spoke about the difference between taking a call from a search firm and talking directly with a searching company itself, ESFs play a critical role as both a channel of communication and a buffer between high-status actors who, without a third party's intervention, would not engage in the risky business of external CEO search at all. This is the aspect of the intermediary's role that involves mediating per se.

Most of the current literature on social actors who bridge otherwise unconnected parties focuses on information flow.[28] This emphasis on information, although important, has drawn attention from the interactions between actors involved in a strategic situation. Consequently, much of this literature misses the rich, complex, micro-level interactions among the three parties to an external CEO search as they seek to "make a deal."[29] Much of what is taken for granted or ignored in standard sociological and economic treatments of third parties is, in fact, a delicate and emergent social process that relies heavily on the third party to help create a working relationship between the two principal participants in the exchange. As the CEO of an ESF emphatically reminded me (after I had informally lectured him on the academic literature on brokers and structural holes), "We are not talking about the relationships between positions, but relationships between people. We are talking about real people here. People with egos, often fragile egos. People with career concerns. People whose greatest asset is their reputation."

As we saw in chapter 2, an external CEO search is risky for both the searching firm and the candidates. Both parties have a strong interest in ensuring confidentiality: firms because they wish to avoid commitment to a specific individual too early in the process, and because they do not want to risk the embarrassment and difficulty of not obtaining their first-choice candidate; candidates because their careers may be at risk if their interest in another firm is disclosed prematurely, or because they fear embarrassment for having pursued a job without receiving an offer. ESFs go to great lengths to ensure that such desires are respected. When visiting a search firm, one will not usually see more than one person waiting in the reception area. ESF offices have private rooms where candidates can meet with consultants, and schedules are carefully coordinated to avoid the embarrassment of candidates running into people they know. In the case of a CEO search, search consultants are particularly careful to arrange private meetings. (Recall how the Russell Reynolds consultants involved in the CEO search at Bank One used such means to shield the candidates from unwanted exposure.) One search consultant comments on this need for confidentiality by emphasizing the importance to both parties of maintaining what are generally very high reputations and status:

> There are a lot of repercussions if the process comes out in the open. Those candidates who didn't get the job are seen as somehow defective to the outside world and disloyal in their own companies. Those directors who didn't get their first-choice candidate are also seen as ineffective. The whole process is risky for all involved. You have to remember, these are not your everyday people here. They are highly regarded people who are influential in their companies, government, and their communities. The risk to all parties is very high.

Because of the risk and the potential threat to careers, reputations, and status for both parties to an external CEO search, ESFs must ensure that all parties to the exchange are serious in their intentions. Therefore ESFs, once retained, are careful to probe directors about whether they are in earnest about hiring an external candidate. If a board is not serious about external candidates and if it is likely that a particular insider will be hired, the ESF usually conducts only a superficial search. In such situations, one consultant remarks, "We bring in a couple of young people that we might have our eye on just to see how they come across to a board. These are the people who are probably not ready for a CEO job just yet, but this is more of an exercise for the candidate . . . to see how they perform." When an external search is serious, the ESF is very diligent about ensuring that a candidate who shows interest is not simply trying to use a potential job offer as a negotiation tactic with his or her current employer. Many search consultants agree with the view expressed by one of their fraternity that "getting at the intentions of the candidates is key." Another consultant describes how he is able to learn the intentions of a candidate who may be very desirable but is also known as a savvy negotiator:

> We ask questions about when they would be willing to start, what their expected compensation is, how they would feel about resigning from their current firm . . . and would they be willing to meet [in person] for an interview. The purpose is to make the job real to them. . . . The candidates, too, are not stupid. They know if they screw around with this, we won't be calling them back. Reneging on an offer is a pretty bad move in a world where your word is taken as an oath.

Once one realizes how much is at stake for both searching firms and candidates in this process, it becomes apparent how essential the finely honed interpersonal and diplomatic skills of the search consultants are to its successful conclusion. The potential threat to both status and careers faced by a searching board and by external candidates as a consequence of participating in an external CEO search is reminiscent of Clifford Geertz's notion of "deep play." For Geertz, a "deep play" is a situation "in which the stakes are so high that it is, from [a] utilitarian standpoint, [almost] irrational for men to engage in it at all." As Geertz also observes, however, individuals engage constantly in deep plays of "status gambling."[30] Yet the kind of status gamble that Geertz describes can take place only through a mediator.

In the external CEO search, it is the ESFs that play this crucial mediating role. Specifically, the ESF mediates the status gamble through a gradual and synchronized commitment process during which the candidates and the searching firm each gain the other party's trust through increasing exposure to similar levels of risk. During the search process, ESFs go to extraordinary lengths to ensure that neither side will be more vulnerable than the other should a deal fail to be consummated. This requires the search consultants to maintain a careful balance in their dealings with both sides. As Tom Friel, a senior search consultant at Heidrick & Struggles, states, "The unique aspect of [search firms] is that, unlike other business transactions . . . the executive placement consultant is required to play both an advocacy role for the client and an advocacy role for a candidate. Essentially, you have to be a mediator. This is a tricky position." Almost every consultant emphasizes the overriding importance of "fairness" and "saving face" for all parties involved in the transaction.

One of the main ways in which ESFs manage the status gamble for all parties is by limiting direct contact between candidates and the searching firm. This strategy is first apparent in the fact that the ESF and not the searching firm approaches the prospective candidates to gauge their interest in the job. Asked about the reasoning behind this procedure, one search consultant explains, "It's obvious. It is the first step we take to protect our client's interests." Another consultant expresses a similar sentiment while also pointing to the interests of the candidate: "If the candidate is clearly not interested, he doesn't need to know the name of the firm . . . they remain anonymous. Similarly, the candidate is also protected because they [sic] didn't pursue the matter. Nobody is exposed." Indeed, every consultant I interviewed described the initial probing of the candidates' interest by the ESF as a means of ensuring anonymity and protecting the interests of both the parties to the exchange.

An ESF mediates between candidates and clients throughout the search process, continually moving back and forth between the parties, "identifying concerns, overcoming roadblocks, making sure each side is comfortable," as one search consultant puts it. At every point in a search, the ESF must display sensitivity to the risk faced by each of the parties as their commitment gradually escalates. As the process unfolds, says one search consultant, typically the original list of "15 to 20 candidates will become whittled down as several candidates realize that they really aren't ready to leave their current job if an offer was made or [if the firm ascertains] that the candidate is not the right type of person for the job." Consultants state that a final candidate list of three or four candidates emerges through this process of "shuttling back and forth between candidates and client." Then and only then will the ESF arrange a time and place for an interview between the candidates and the searching firm.

The idea that a searching firm's directors would interview candidates only once before making a decision seems quite surprising in light of the broad responsibilities of the CEO position. Executive search consultants make it clear, however, that this practice rests on an important reason. The face-to-face interview is a particularly intense exchange in which both the searching firm and the candidates are in a risky and vulnerable state. During their interviews with the candidates, directors usually are quite frank about their dissatisfaction with the previous CEO. Similarly, candidates are aware not only that they are displaying disloyalty to their current employers by accepting an invitation to interview but also that they face the possibility of rejection. (This play is "deep" in the Geertzian sense because all players are showing their hands.) In the words of one search consultant, although the candidates at this stage of the game could "technically refuse an offer, they are not likely to do so. Otherwise I would not have brought them in for the interview."

Georg Simmel observed the intensity and commitment of the kind of face-to-face interaction of which an interview consists:

> Of the special sense-organs, the eye has a uniquely sociological function. The union and interaction of individuals is based upon mutual glances. This is perhaps the most direct and purest reciprocity which exists anywhere. . . . [T]he totality of social relations of human beings, their self-assertion and self-abnegation, their intimacies and estrangements, would be changed in unpredictable ways if there occurred no glance of eye to eye. This mutual glance between persons, in distinction from the simple

sight or observation of the other, signifies a wholly new and unique union between them.[31]

The sociologist Erving Goffman, in his analysis of "face engagements," discusses the escalation of commitment that arises as a consequence of face-to-face interaction. He writes:

> Once a set of participants have avowedly opened themselves up to one another for an engagement, an eye-to-eye ecological huddle tends to be carefully maintained, maximizing the opportunity for participants to monitor one another's mutual perceivings. The participants turn their minds to the same subject matter (in the case of talk), their eyes to the same subject. . . . A shared definition of the situation comes to prevail. This includes agreement concerning perceptual relevancies and irrelevancies, and a "working consensus," involving a degree of mutual considerateness, a sympathy and a muting of opinion differences.[32]

Goffman also notes the peril of face-to-face engagements with respect to their effect on escalating commitment. In a face-to-face meeting, he states, "a kind of implicit contract or gentleman's agreement" arises.[33] In an external CEO search, both parties seek to defer such an agreement until both sides are ready to "commit to a marriage." The mediating role of the ESF involves reliably ascertaining when this mutual readiness exists.

Like its coordinating role in the external CEO search, the mediating function of the ESF is an example of the importance of social structures in helping actors confront complex and ambiguous market exchanges. In the third intermediary role played by ESFs in the external CEO search, it becomes clear that not only social structures but also the actors' socially conditioned perceptions and beliefs are critical to understanding the external CEO market.

LEGITIMATING

As we also saw in chapters 2 and 4, concerns about the legitimacy of the external CEO search process on the part of directors, candidates, and the external actors whose beliefs influence them are a defining feature of the external CEO market. Because of their business and social ties to the larger director community, board members are greatly concerned about maintaining appearances of propriety in contacts between themselves and potential candidates. Because of the influence wielded by external actors such as analysts and the business press, directors also wish to ensure that these observers will view the external search process as having been objective and proper. In these circumstances, the ESF's participation is a key means by which a searching firm can legitimately find a suitable person to fill its CEO position. Barbara Seidel of Russell Reynolds summarizes board members' concerns about legitimacy and the role of the ESF in helping to allay them: "The board sometimes already knows what it wants to do, but will hire a search firm anyway. They feel a sense of fiduciary responsibility. They do it as a stamp. Russell Reynolds is a name brand that offers both comfort and legitimacy to the whole process."

The signaling of legitimacy that the engagement of an ESF accomplishes in an external CEO search takes place, first of all, between firms and candidates. Both of these parties implicitly accept that a firm that uses an ESF to recruit from a competitor or customer has behaved appropriately. By employing a third party to search for the "best candidate," the searching firm distances itself from the social aspects of the market, and appeals instead to the more normatively acceptable idea of a "free market."[34] To quote a director of a firm that had hired the CEO of one of its competitors, "It is not us [the firm searching for a CEO] that is making an overture to a competitor's CEO, but rather a third party [the ESF] who is only trying to fulfill their contractual obligation to a client to find the best candidate possible for the position." For their part, candidates, as we have seen, believe that taking a call from an executive search consultant is more acceptable than taking a call from a competitor about a job. As one recent CEO candidate puts it, "There is no harm done in taking a call from a search firm. You don't know who the company is and you are not giving away any company secrets. It is purely informational."

The other audience to which the hiring of an ESF signals legitimacy consists of constituents who have an interest in the process and the outcome but who are not direct participants in the exchange. From such a constituent's perspective, the employment of an ESF during a CEO search grants legitimacy to what is otherwise an opaque process. The use of an ESF tells external stakeholders such as stockholders that the company is engaging in a thorough and exhaustive process. As one director puts it, "These days, when institutional investors are monitoring your every move, it is very important that the process appear to be a fair process and not a political process." It is because this pressure to demonstrate a fair process is so prevalent that ESFs are often employed even when a known insider is considered the best candidate for a vacant CEO position.

The ESF's legitimating function for both participants and external constituents in external CEO search arises from the perception that ESFs are equally concerned about the interests of all the direct and indirect participants in the exchange. Most of these participants believe that the ESF is not attached by any interest of its own to the subjective interests of either the firm or the candidates.[35] Rather, both of the latter are thought to be important to the ESF in the conduct of a successful search. Therefore, the theory continues, it is in the ESF's interest to carefully consider both the common positions and the diverging interests of the candidates, the firm, and the external constituents whose approval both parties directly involved in the transaction seek. This combination of distance from the candidates' and firms' immediate interests with concern for the external audience gives the ESF's participation its apparently objective quality, and therefore brings legitimacy to the CEO search.[36]

The role of the ESF in providing legitimacy to the external CEO search calls our attention to, among other things, the essentially theatrical nature of the search process. To call external CEO search "theatrical" is not to disparage it as "merely for show," for much of human behavior—however earnestly the players are pursuing their goals—is theatre in the sense of being directed at an audience.[37] So it is with the role of ESFs, which are eager to seize attention for their clients, deflect criticism from themselves and the board, and create attitudes about external CEO search. The theatrical nature of their actions becomes problematic only when other participants in the process fail to understand it as such. For example, directors who later discover that they have chosen the wrong CEO often exploit the marginal status of search consultants to blame them for the unsuccessful outcome. In so doing, they fail to realize that the ESF is in no way instrumental to bringing about that result.

By scapegoating their search consultants, of course, directors seek to avoid blame for their failure in their own role in an external CEO search. That failure, in turn, consists in the way that directors allow themselves to fall under the spell of the star performer in the drama, the charismatic candidate. That directors themselves ultimately invest the charismatic candidate with his or her star power is yet another ironic dimension of the theatrical spectacle that is external CEO search. The final step in our investigation of the external search process is to see how and why this investiture takes place.

CHAPTER 6

CROWNING NAPOLEON: THE MAKING
OF THE CHARISMATIC CANDIDATE

IN 1999 AND 2000, respectively, Lew Platt of Hewlett-Packard and Michael Hawley of Gillette joined the ranks of CEOs from *Fortune* 500 companies forced out of their positions. They were only the newest additions to a nearly decade-old club whose founding members included John Akers of IBM, Paul Lego of Westinghouse, Robert Stempel of General Motors, and Kay Whitmore of Kodak. Hawley and Platt, like many of the other CEOs who had been forced out since the early 1990s, would subsequently be replaced by outsider successors. Like their counterparts on so many other *Fortune* 500 boards in the era of investor capitalism, the directors of Gillette and H-P turned to outsider CEOs in hopes of restoring firm performance and regaining the confidence of investors, Wall Street analysts, and the business media—each of which had unceasingly criticized their respective companies.

Hawley and Platt, despite their positions at the top of two of America's most celebrated companies, were hardly well known. This is not surprising, because neither was a media figure. They were never on TV flogging their companies' products in the way that some CEOs now do. They did not hire ghostwriters to produce self-congratulatory autobiographies. Their pictures did not appear on many magazine covers. More than a few employees in their companies didn't recognize them when they saw them. Yet they were loyal company men. Both—like their predecessors—had spent almost their entire professional careers with the companies they would lead. Both were flagged early in their careers by their companies' human resources departments as individuals with executive potential. Their supervisors were able to observe them in a variety of situations, and on the basis of these observations, they were promoted to positions of ever-increasing responsibility and scope. They were trustworthy subordinates. They waited for their time to come, and when it did, they were promoted to the CEO position. In short, Hawley and Platt both epitomized the post–World War II career executive—which proved to be their downfall when changing times appeared to demand a different kind of corporate chieftain.

In the cases of both Gillette and H-P, the boards of directors believed that what was needed to improve firm performance was not Hawley or Platt's tested and proven managerial skills, but something else. What this "something else" was is not easily defined. The head of H-P's search committee said that the board was looking for someone with "tremendous leadership ability" and "the power to bring urgency to an organization." A director at Gillette remarked that he and his colleagues were looking for someone to "revitalize the organization" and "restore confidence and order."

When directors, search consultants, and influential outsiders (such as analysts and business journalists) try to describe the elusive quality that more and more large corporations now seek in a CEO, they often use the word *charisma*. In its ordinary usage, by scholars as well as by participants in the CEO search process, the term has become a synonym for a variety of other traits now associated with corporate leadership. Today, it has become common to speak of the qualifications for the CEO position in relation not to any specific managerial tasks but rather to the ability of certain individuals to rouse others. What is now considered the all-important quality of "leadership" is all about being able to energize people who are lethargic or skeptical. It is about increasing the self-confidence of employees when the company is collectively anxious. It is about unifying an organization's constituencies when self-interest and political alignments divide them from one another. The corporate leader's job is thought to consist, above all, in helping the organization face up to a crisis situation and then taking it into the future with a guiding and motivating vision. To be able to carry out this defining task, it is now almost universally believed, a CEO must have "charisma."

While the concept of charisma has proven seductive for business school professors, consultants, and the business press, it is, in its ordinary usage today, an elusive and imprecise way of discussing leadership. Although biographers and journalists have devoted many a page to measuring the "charisma" of figures such as Jack Welch, Steve Jobs, and Lee Iacocca, the word, as generally used, is as difficult to define as "love" or "art," and few who use it succeed in conveying what they mean by it. Corporate directors and search consultants, for their part, use their own kind of shorthand to describe a candidate's charisma. The words they employ again and again include "chemistry," "executive presence," "articulation," "stature," and "change agent." Like the specification sheets examined in chapter 4, these overworked terms underscore how difficult directors find it to think in anything but the most conventional terms, even while supposedly seeking a CEO who will overthrow convention. Directors elevate the individuals with whom they associate these charismatic qualities, however vague they may be, and discount those who do not possess them, often citing the lack of one or more of these characteristics as their reason for rejecting a candidate. They also tend to believe that the charisma that they seek in candidates is something that comes through inheritance and early formative experiences and cannot be learned or acquired later in life.

To see these perceptions and judgments in action, consider the situation at a large insurance company in which the CEO search had been narrowed to three candidates, two insiders and one outsider. One director described the criteria he had used to evaluate the candidates by saying, "[I] would look at how they verbalized their thoughts, conceptual abilities, ability to express themselves clearly, talk about other people, how they rationalize their actions, their posture, mannerisms, and way of dress." The search consultant leading the search explained his preference for one candidate in similar terms, while also citing breeding and sex appeal as key factors:

> I liked the subtleties of his presence, his inflections, and how he talked to others. I also liked how he was raised. He had good parents, tremendous genetics. All the right things were present: responsibility at early ages . . . commitment to community. . . . I also noticed how secretaries blushed and seemed so genuinely glad to see this person, unlike the other . . . candidates.

When I asked another director at the same firm why the runner-up candidate was not selected, he stated:

> A top executive must have stature and poise. Someone needs to move with focus, crisply and gracefully. They need to make the first move to shake hands (two strong shakes). I know if they are listening if they lean forward when they sit. They should be able to lead with small talk, but quickly get into the heart of the matter. They can't appear to be easily flustered. . . . I have to have the impression that someone else—a secretary or assistant—is handling the details of their life. . . . [David] did not display any of this, so he was off my list.

Given their own individual personalities and tastes, members of the same board do differ from one another, of course, when describing which attribute or attributes of a particular candidate they find charismatic. Considering the existence of these individual differences, we might also expect that different board members would exhibit preferences for different candidates. It may therefore seem surprising that directors involved in a given search show a strong tendency to zero in on the same candidate. Yet this tendency toward consensus contains an important clue to the true nature of charisma. For it suggests that the charismatic power that directors attribute to a particular candidate is derived only in part from the individual responses of directors, and to a much greater extent is a social product—that is, a creation of the social expectations vested in the candidate (although not consciously) by the directors acting as a group.

It is common in many human activities for some individuals to command more attention than others, even at the same apparent level of competence. Historians, journalists, and other observers often write about personal traits that distinguish such persons from others in a given field, but their accounts can be unconvincing. The celebrity of many movie stars and pop musicians, for example, is attributable not to their dramatic or musical skills or accomplishments but rather to the fact that audiences are excited when they appear on the stage.[1] Similarly, in the CEO labor market, stories, gossip, and legends about some executives travel farther than those about others, irrespective of various individuals' abilities or accomplishments.

Indeed, in the case of CEOs, it would sometimes be difficult to maintain the charisma of the leader if the focus were on his or her actions on the job. Whereas, in the past, charisma was attributed to a particular individual because of his or her deeds, this becomes problematic when those deeds include, say, firing tens of thousands of people while reaping multi-million-dollar bonuses. In today's corporate folklore (which mirrors the psychologizing of public language in American society generally), charisma is often found to be rooted not so much in specific actions and accomplishments as in an individual's ability to overcome some personal handicap. Thus, for example, Jack Welch's biographers prominently note that their subject had to overcome a stutter as a young boy, an achievement that supposedly gave him what it takes to run a giant corporation.[2] John Chambers's biographers observe that this future CEO had to conquer dyslexia and claim that his ability to do so is, in part, what enabled him to build Cisco Systems.[3]

Of course in a society in which any celebrity worthy of the name eventually wants the public to know about some previously unsuspected personal adversity, trauma, weakness, or vice, such tales reveal much more about the audiences that are swayed by them than they do about their protagonists. Charisma, in short, is almost completely in the eyes of the beholders, who fasten on certain leaders out of deeply felt, socially shared needs. Just as the roles of directors and executive search firms in the external CEO search turn out to be comprehensible only when these actors are viewed in relation to the social structures and systems of belief within which they operate, so too with the charismatic candidates who become (or are already) society's charismatic CEOs. To understand the way that the role of CEO candidates is socially constructed, we need to look more closely at the loosely interpreted, often misunderstood concept of charisma.

The Social and Cultural Dimensions of "Charisma"

The economist John Maynard Keynes once wrote: "The ideas of economists and political philosophers, both when they are right and when they are wrong, are more powerful than is commonly understood. Indeed the world is ruled by little else. Practical men, who believe themselves to be quite exempt from any intellectual influences, are usually the slaves of some defunct economist. Madmen in authority, who hear voices in the air, are distilling their frenzy from some academic scribbler of a few years back."[4] Keynes's statement is applicable to the concept of charisma, which over the course of a century has gradually found its way from the works of thinkers such as Max Weber and Sigmund Freud into our common lexicon. As noted in chapter 3, Weber transferred the term—whose root meaning is "the gift of grace"—from its religious context into politics. He described charisma as the ability of some individuals to evoke in others feelings of devotion, confidence, illumination, and heroism. He also contrasted charismatic leadership with leadership based on custom and tradition, or on competence related to "rationally created" rules of law. The charismatic leader is thus one whose right to rule is legitimated by neither tradition nor rules but rather by his apparent endowment with superior powers for solving particular problems.[5]

Weber argued that the charismatic leader, in his purest form, is viewed uncritically by his followers, being regarded as all powerful, all wise, and morally perfect. Yet this ideal type is unlikely to be found in actual situations. Weber also argued that traditional societies were most vulnerable to episodes of charismatic authority. In a liberal democracy such as the United States, society is believed to exist for the sake of the individual, not the other way around. Over time, democratic individualism drives the members of such societies toward ever more radical declarations of independence, thus reducing their susceptibility to charismatic authority. Weber did suggest, however, that in rare historical circumstances even advanced democratic societies could be subject to eruptions of charismatic authority. (He might have been surprised at his own extrapolative powers, had he lived only a few years longer and seen the rise of Hitler in his native Germany.) In the context of business organizations, then, the question is how this type of leadership could have appeared in the contemporary corporation. To begin answering this question, we must first briefly discuss Weber's insights into the nature of control and legitimacy as they apply to organizations.

One of Weber's basic arguments was that all organizations are dependent on some type of controlling authority. Ultimately, any controlling authority must be seen as legitimate to keep itself intact. In the organizational context, traditional authority is exemplified by nineteenth-century business organizations, in which it was not uncommon for the heir of the founding entrepreneur to take over the company on the latter's death or retirement.[6] Charismatic authority in business organizations originally manifested itself in the person of the founders of entrepreneurial firms: whereas Weber offered prophets, visionaries, saints, and revolutionary leaders as examples of charismatic leaders, Henry Ford or Andrew Carnegie would be the earliest examples of such charismatics in a business setting. Legal or rational authority—which rests on the appeal of the propriety and efficiency of formally enacted rules and statutes—is in turn exemplified in a business context by CEOs in the era of managerial capitalism. For our purposes, the contemporary shift from rational authority to charismatic authority in business is of particular interest.

While "charisma," in everyday usage, has come to be viewed as a characteristic inherent in certain types of individuals, to seize on this particular aspect of Weber's definition of it is to miss his most important insights. After all, Weber's distinction among traditional, charismatic, and rational authority suggests that each is a product of a very particular set of social and political circumstances. Indeed, Weber recognized that charisma was mostly defined by its social context, that it was, at its roots, a social phenomenon.[7] He argued, to be more precise, that much of society's faith in a charismatic leader is derived not from any personal characteristics of the individual, but rather from a particular set of social relations and the cultural context within which those relations are embedded.

One key fact about the social relations supporting charismatic leadership is that, although a leader's claim to obedience from his or her followers is formally described as a duty, it is always subject to validation by those followers.[8] In other words, Weber argued, a leader could not be said to be charismatic unless others recognized the claim to authority. Moreover, the leader's charismatic claims are in need of constant reaffirmation by his followers. If charismatic leaders do not bring benefits to their followers, or if their special abilities appear to desert them, their charismatic claims and legitimacy disappear. Once the leader's "magic" is assumed to be gone, power over the followers ceases to exist.[9]

A second essential aspect of charisma is that it is dependent on the cultural context. Elaborating on Weber's basic idea that charisma is partially grounded in the cultural context, literary scholar Leo Braudy has noted that, in the centuries of ecclesiastical and aristocratic power, charisma was often a byproduct of status or of some overt demonstration that one was in the service either of God or of some higher purpose. As society became more secularized and free from aristocratic pretensions, however, charisma came to be regarded as an individual property.[10]

The changes in the social and political environment to which Braudy refers obviously had important consequences for the unique brand of capitalism that would develop in the United States. One of the tenets of the new economic individualism that came to flourish in America was that success was a product of individual effort. As Weber noted in his masterpiece *The Protestant Ethic and the Spirit of Capitalism*, this popular philosophy was rooted in a maxim from *Poor Richard's Almanac*: "God helps those who help themselves."[11] With the rise of charismatic empire-builders such as Carnegie and Rockefeller, the personal virtue supposedly evidenced by the accumulation of wealth was elevated as a sign of charisma in the sense of "the gift of grace." Paeans to the industry, determination, and other such qualities of the self-made man became a staple of business biographies and autobiographies. These same books, however, offered few specifics when it came to business advice: success was spiritual, not achieved through such crass means as building monopolies or breaking unions.[12]

The aura of the charismatic business leader began to fade somewhat during the Great Depression, a process that continued through the end of the Second World War. Cracks had first begun to appear in the myths of Rockefeller and Carnegie during the recessions of the 1890s and the Progressive Era of the early twentieth century, when it became clear that their fortunes were rooted as much in their ruthless competitive behavior as in their exemplification of Protestant virtue.[13] Moreover, as the swashbuckling, founder-led enterprises of Carnegie and Rockefeller began to give way to the more faceless, professionally managed corporations that followed in their wake, it was harder to find such prominent examples of self-help and individual motivation as the surest way to success. By the end of World War II, as Europe and America surveyed the devastation wrought by charismatic personalities such as Hitler and Mussolini, most Western nations had become wary of the charismatic leader. Meanwhile, more and more critical scholarly work in history and sociology was finding that the myth of the self-made individual was more of a social-control mechanism than an inspiring reality—a way to keep hope alive as opportunities increasingly closed to those lacking educational or other such credentials.[14]

Although the myth of the self-made man survives in American business culture (even if most of the heroic entrepreneurs of the Information Age—e.g., Bill Gates, a Harvard dropout and the son of a successful lawyer—have not exactly risen from humble backgrounds), the arrival of the era of investor capitalism in the 1980s, as we saw in chapter 3, gave rise to a new species of charismatic business leader: the outsider CEO hired by a beleaguered board of directors to save a troubled company. We have also seen how, even as important transformations in the ownership and control of large American corporations have put an ever greater focus on the CEO, a new definition of the effective CEO has emerged in conjunction with a new ideology of business itself, as corporations have begun trying to create ties of identification, commitment, and loyalty on the part of employees in ways that have made business increasingly resemble a secularized religion. This new ideology has created the need for CEOs who can advance the contemporary corporation's attempt to impart to work relations a type of pseudo-community, one whose informal structure can be contrasted with the sharp distinctions in formal authority and fine-grained division of labor found in organizations during the era of managerial capitalism.[15]

Yet despite the importance of cultural influences and how they interact with the mutually dependent social relationship between leaders and followers to bolster the authority of the charismatic CEO, consideration of such phenomena can take us only so far in understanding why and how charismatic authority has arisen to replace rational authority in America's great corporations. To gain a fuller understanding of this in many ways baffling change, we need to shift our focus from society and culture to the level of the firm itself, where Weber's theory of charismatic authority also proves instructive.

The Structural Antecedents to Charismatic Succession

Besides discussing the social relations and cultural context that underpin charismatic authority, Weber emphasized the structural conditions under which a society or organization is more likely to adopt a charismatic orientation in selecting its leaders. Weber understood that the orientation toward charismatic authority, while part of the human condition, was especially prone to emerge under what he called "extraordinary" social circumstances. In particular, Weber noted that charismatic leaders tend to arise in the midst of acute social disruptions. However, given his sweeping theoretical concerns, Weber's discussion of the particular mechanism through which changes in structural context give rise to charismatic authority remains very general. This generality, in part, has resulted in the misappropriation of the concept of charisma to explain the success or failure of leaders with little regard to the conditions that brought them to power in the first place.

The political anthropologists Doug Madsen and Peter Snow present one of the most compelling discussions in the scholarly literature to date of how disruptions to a social institution can give rise to charismatic authority. They write:

> The collapse of a great social enterprise, such as a polity or an economy, brings with it for many (but not all) of those involved a collapse of their own personal worlds. Expectations are dashed and hopes ruined. Fundamental assumptions are undermined. Social arrangements and economic structures disintegrate. Often "understanding" is lost and with it, the sense of being able to cope.

Under such stressful conditions, Madsen and Snow point out, people not only want to affiliate with others but also prefer to be members of groups with strong leaders.[16] Although the collapse of a polity or an economy may offer an extreme example of social disruption, the same principle can be seen at work in the corporate world when we consider the structural factors leading to charismatic succession.

The adoption of a charismatic succession process—by which I mean one in which candidates are evaluated on their personal characteristics, rather than on a set of predefined skills or other attributes aligned with the strategic requirements of the position and capable of being objectively assessed—represents a radical departure from CEO succession as it has historically been conducted. That charismatic succession can be found in large, complex organizations is even more surprising, because scholars would predict that it would be precisely in such institutions that charismatic succession would be least likely to take place. Since the 1920s, many scholars and practitioners alike have regarded charisma as an obstacle to rational organizational processes. To the extent that charismatic leaders existed in business, they were believed to be associated only with entrepreneurial enterprises.[17] In his work documenting the rise of the large business firm, Alfred Chandler viewed the shift away from charismatic succession and toward a more rational process as one of the most significant consequences of the managerial revolution that had led to the modern business organization.[18]

In contrast to the traditional and charismatic succession practices that had preceded it, the emergence of the large corporation brought with it a revolutionary concept. Individuals would now be hired and promoted on the basis of their training and abilities, not simply because they had founded the organization or had been sired by the founder. Executive careers would therefore begin not at the top, but at an entry-level position. The CEOs of large corporations all had similar career paths that usually started with being hired as management trainees. These new hires would then work their way up the job ladder as the consequence of internal promotions. External hiring would be rare and limited to a small number of specific entry points.[19] Salaries would also be determined via an administrative process, such as job evaluation, in which the relative importance of particular positions to the objectives of the enterprise was ascertained through technical analysis. The path to the top of the organization would entail the accumulation of both seniority and administrative expertise obtained through lateral and vertical promotions.

Today, most scholars continue to believe that CEO succession has been rationalized and depersonalized in America's large corporations. How and why, then, has charismatic succession reemerged there? Two factors in particular seem to have been catalysts in moving directors away from the rational succession process. The first is that, for any given organization, the external search represents a break from tradition or routine, just as it has been for organizations generally. Second, an external CEO search often takes place in the context of poor organizational performance.

EXTERNAL SUCCESSION AS BREAK FROM ROUTINE

While CEO succession has always had the potential to disrupt the activities of an organization, over the last century large companies had taken concrete steps to mitigate this disruption. In particular, these firms adopted explicit and implicit rules to ensure a more orderly succession process than had once prevailed. Many of these rules were intended to depersonalize the succession process. Exceptions to such policies were rare and, typically, required the approval of a firm's board and shareholders. Boards saw these rules and routines governing CEO selection and succession as providing order and predictability in succession decisions. Walter Salmon, a director of several *Fortune* 500 firms, describes the orderly succession process that obtained at Quaker Oats in the 1970s and '80s:

> We had a rigorous process of management development. The field for selection was broad so that we had at least two or three good choices for successor CEO. Moreover, the board had gotten to know these individuals over the years and the needs of the company and the strengths of the individuals being considered were identified. . . . The board had experience with the . . . insider. They go from a process of being an unofficial successor, then officially identified as a successor and then, finally anointed. This gives us [the board] time to get to know the person from board presentations as well as validating the CEO's recommendation. The sitting CEO takes the primary role or leadership role in this process. He educates the board over a period of time on his selection.

The process at Quaker Oats was typical of that of most large companies in the post–World War II years.[20] These companies invested heavily in their human resource departments and management development programs to ensure a steady supply of executive talent for the various organizational positions. This reliance on internal labor markets for CEO succession has been, historically, a central defining characteristic of large U.S. corporations. In one company I examined, for example, the board of directors has created what it calls "depth charts" of its major executives. These depth charts have the names of three or more potential CEO successors whose performance the board reviews each December. The charts summarize a manager's strengths, weaknesses, and corporate experience. People on the depth chart know who they are, and their supervisors work with them to build their capabilities.

The adoption of fixed CEO succession rules for recruiting from the internal market provided a set of prepackaged solutions to what historically had been a difficult transition for firms, the transfer of formal leadership from one individual to another. The emergence of stable rules to guide CEO succession signaled to organizational constituents that an organization's activities would continue uninterrupted during a leadership transition. The legitimacy of the new CEO's power depended on the belief that the appropriate rules and procedures had been followed when making the decision.

When firms decide to search for a CEO from outside their own ranks, however, the rules and procedures that previously guided CEO successions are not very useful. Consider the case of American Express in the early 1990s, a situation that while unique in its particulars, illustrates the general point of how disruptive CEO search becomes when it departs from a company's institutionalized process. In the late 1980s and early 1990s, problems in American Express's core travel-card operation and its Shearson Lehman brokerage had begun to cut significantly into earnings. Yet CEO James Robinson III, nicknamed by the press the "Teflon executive," had deftly avoided blame for the firm's poor performance and strategic missteps throughout the 1980s, always managing to hang on despite challenges to his leadership over the years.[21] (As further evidence for how closed the CEO labor market is, consider that Robinson's two biggest challengers for the position were Sandy Weill and Lou Gerstner). Yet as the company's dismal performance continued into the early 1990s, the press and the company's shareholders began to subject Robinson's monarch-like control over American Express to increased scrutiny. In the fall of 1992, after much cajoling from investors, a small group of board members finally called for Robinson to step down and for the board to initiate a search for an outsider CEO. Robinson acquiesced, announcing that he would step down within a few weeks. In what was taken as a sign of good faith, he also took the responsibility for leading the search for American Express's next CEO.

Because of the chaos that had erupted after dissident directors had called for Robinson's exit, the American Express board was "largely paralyzed," according to one knowledgeable insider. "The American Express board had never searched for an outsider CEO before," says this observer.

> It was your standard showcase board and read like a who's who of celebrity CEOs and former political dignitaries—Henry Kissinger, George Fisher of Motorola, et cetera. . . . They collected their fees, rode on the corporate jets, had access to numerous clubs and corporate apartments. . . . They had always relied on the process of the old CEO retiring and appointing his successor. There was never much else to do.

When Robinson took charge of the search, he did his best to ensure that this tradition would continue. One source intimately familiar with the details reported that anytime the board interviewed a viable candidate for the position, Robinson's wife—a top New York public relations executive—leaked the name to the press. Since the most acceptable candidates were already actively employed, the result was that the most sought-after candidates publicly declared that they were not interested in being considered for the position. According to another source familiar with the search, "Had Robinson not interfered with the search process, the board would have surely appointed an outsider. Given the scrutiny they were under, it was the best way to restore credibility."

Meanwhile, over the course of two months in which the external search was supposedly going on, Robinson convinced a majority of the board to vote to keep him on as chairman of American Express. The board also finally approved his handpicked successor, insider Harvey Golub, as chief executive. During this period, moreover, Robinson managed to force the resignation of the three directors who had been most active in calling for his resignation, as well as to demote the son of one of the dissident directors. Only amid newly reported losses at Shearson, which provoked fury from the largest shareholders and most influential business media, did the American Express board take action and ask for Robinson's full resignation.

The break from routine that finding a successor for Robinson came to be for American Express was captured in a Harvard Business School case:

On September 20 [1992], the meeting of outside directors began when Robinson [the existing CEO] stepped outside the room. [Former Mobil Corp. CEO and American Express director Rawleigh] Warner rose and asked for permission to address the group. . . . He then proceeded to deliver an extensive catalogue of Robinson's mistakes. . . . After finishing his presentation [sic] the board asked what Warner would propose they should do; Warner replied that the board should ask Robinson to step down immediately and should replace him with a board member as acting CEO. . . . As the board began to discuss the proposal, it became clear that board sentiment ran strongly against Warner's plan. A number of directors reportedly vociferously objecting [sic] to simply deposing Robinson in such a manner, and the proposal was rejected, with only a few directors supporting it.

The board did agree, however, that more active succession talks should get underway. Robinson was asked to come up with a plan to be discussed at the board meeting the next day. . . . [A search committee was formed with Robinson as the head of the committee. This was unusual since Robinson would be identifying the successor that would result in his forced dismissal.]

In December, the news that Robinson was leaving was revealed for the first time in a *Fortune* article. The article suggested that a "coup" had taken place, with Warner leading the charge, an assertion which brought prompt denials from Robinson and Warner. . . . Robinson and Warner were never able to convince skeptical journalists and commentators that a coup had not taken place. Indeed, several publications seemed to delight in [Robinson's] downfall, with such story titles as "The Toppling of King James III" and "A Quiet Coup at American Express."

The [*Fortune*] article and the attendant scrutiny of the firm put additional pressure on the succession committee to work quickly. . . . Robinson also began to defend his record, to both the media and to his directors. In phone calls to directors, he argued his side of the story. . . .

The company's stock arose $1.40 the day after the announcement that Robinson would leave his position and Robinson endorsed [Harvey] Golub, but some directors harbored doubts about Golub. These doubts, exposed in a series of press leaks . . . belied an increasing division of the board between those who supported Robinson and his choice of a successor, and those who opposed Robinson and wanted outside candidates to be considered more seriously. [Some board members objected] to Golub's brusque style. Some board members were concerned that he did not fit into the genteel American Express culture. Finally, a few board members were allegedly opposed to Golub merely because he was Robinson's candidate. Drew Lewis, a Robinson loyalist, made the following statement: "Take Howard Clark Sr., and Rawleigh Warner. They're out to get Harvey as an extension of Jim. They're out to scalp him." . . .

The press speculation concerning the CEO was becoming quite unbearable and morale at American Express was reportedly dropping as uncertainty about the company's future surfaced. Also, it was clear that the board was sharply divided on the question of who should lead American Express. . . . [22]

The break from routine succession, with all of its potential for such disruption, and the orientation toward charismatic succession are closely linked. Under the kinds of circumstances that cause a board to consider breaking from its routine succession process, the board is usually under pressure to announce a successor quickly. If the board does not act quickly enough, one director told me, it will be perceived either that no single insider has the full backing of the board or that the company is having difficulty attracting a good CEO because of the depth of its problems. This pressure moves boards away from an objective, measured process geared to evaluating the needs of the firm and the strengths and weaknesses of the candidates. Instead, the search becomes more particularistic, overtly political, improvisational, and undisciplined. Because few firms have a set of established policies and procedures guiding external succession, directors are more likely to look for someone who can restore order to the firm. One search committee chair leading a search for a factionalized board described his and his colleagues' thinking thus:

We were divided on the board. The company had two distinct cultures that needed to be brought together. We needed someone who could bring us back together. Someone whose force of personality could take a chaotic situation and make us a unified whole. . . . The disruption from [X's] departure and the resulting chaos and disorientation pushed us to find that strong personality, that strong person, who could bring us together and restore stability to the situation.

The disposition to charismatic succession is intimately related to this need for order. Candidates who are already CEOs, who come from high-performing firms, or who are associated with companies and individuals that are representative of the directors' ideals for their own firm—in other words, those who meet the criteria behind the social matching process described in chapter 4—have a distinct advantage in these situations because, appearing to the directors to be known quantities, they quell directors' own anxieties about an external search in a way that makes them seem to possess charismatic qualities.

THE EFFECTS OF POOR PERFORMANCE

Whether a firm is performing well or poorly affects whether the board is more oriented toward rational or charismatic succession. When the firm is performing well and the organization's environment is stable, boards will follow the traditional process of allowing the outgoing CEO to choose a successor. By contrast, when the firm's performance is poor, directors are more apt to look for a charismatic outsider to improve it.

A number of comparative studies of charismatic leaders that have sought to quantify factors favoring the emergence of charisma have confirmed the high correlation between crisis and the turn toward charismatic leadership.[23] Organizational crisis can, of course, take a number of different forms, but the most prevalent is poor performance and the discontent that accompanies it. Performance crises in organizations create a level of frustration and impose a set of demands that are different from those in normal situations. They also induce feelings of insecurity and anxiety among board members.

The usual interpretation of the connection between charisma and organizational crisis is that charismatic leaders gain a following by articulating a vision that is perceived as addressing the organization's problems, then motivating people to act on the vision. Alternatively, through their articulation of an organizational mission, they may draw attention to critical situations of which their subsequent followers were only dimly aware. Of course the mission that the charismatic leader articulates may turn out to be disastrously wrong, as in the case of a retailing CEO who came from a high-end department store chain, moved to a middle-market one, and tried to carry out his vision of the organization becoming an upscale, high-margin retailer. After nearly bankrupting the company, he was replaced by another high-profile outsider who thought that the organization needed to "return to its roots as a middle-income retailer." Such failures only point to why large corporations once eschewed charismatic leadership in favor of rational authority.

More than the "vision" that they sometimes provide, however, charismatic outsiders offer organizations in crisis the hope that they engender by their very status as outsiders. Although it can arise under other circumstances, belief in the salvific capacities of the charismatic outsider becomes particularly potent when coupled with a sustained period of declining performance caused by structural changes in an industry. Polaroid, for example, has for some time been dying a slow death, as instant film has been replaced by the digital camera. Meanwhile, AT&T—with the majority of its revenue and almost all of its profits coming from long-distance service—has foreseen its impending demise as an analog company in a digital world and has tried to change its business models, albeit with little success to date.[24] The problem in both cases is not managerial but structural. In such circumstances, the research in organizational strategy and ecology suggests that the best thing to do would be either to scale back expectations and return the profits of the organization to shareholders, or to shut the enterprise down altogether. Yet in business, such courses of action, however rational they might be, are seldom considered viable options. One is supposed to find a heroic solution to every problem. And what solution could be simpler than to hire some omnipotent outsider, a can-do executive with charismatic qualities? He may (like John Walter, the president, COO, and CEO-designate of AT&T for less than nine months before the board changed its mind about making him CEO—only to turn around and hire another outsider, C. Michael Armstrong) have no relevant industry experience. Yet the outsider or "stranger," as Georg Simmel notes, offers hope and promise.[25] His presence, at least temporarily, creates the illusion of possibility, far more than would the promotion of an inside executive. Insiders are associated with the losing team. They are, as one director puts it, "too pessimistic about the future." The outsider who knows little about the firm's particular problems naturally finds it much easier to be optimistic.

This particular link between poor performance and the turn to charismatic succession is confirmed by a comparison of statistics for forced and natural turnovers, which reveals that poorly performing firms are most likely to fire their CEOs (see table 4.2, pp. 88–89). Correspondingly, these same firms are likely to see an individual as the solution to their performance problems. To the extent that directors also believe that firm performance cannot be restored by relying on past approaches, they are apt to believe that the organization must be transformed by an omnipotent outsider. Disruptions in technology, changes in regulation, or other situations that make old processes and rules less useful, create conditions in which companies tend to turn to charismatic succession. Evan Lindsay, an executive recruiter specializing in search in the insurance industry, makes explicit this link between environmentally induced poor performance and the search for charismatic leadership when he discusses the widespread problem of stagnant insiders in the ranks of insurance executives:

> The insurance industry, almost since its birth, did not require anyone good. There was no need for anyone with leadership qualities or people who had vision, strategy, and the ability to enact change. The primary determinants of who would be CEO prior to the late 1980s was [sic] "age and service." The biggest problem, given the dramatic regulatory changes in the financial services industry, is the need to make the transition from manager to general manager. Most insurance executives could not make this dramatic change. As boards . . . began to look for successors they were unhappy with their internal labor markets.

Performance crises so heighten the apparent need for change that even poor performance that cannot be attributed to the CEO often induces boards to seek a new leader—even though such action may be mostly symbolic and the range of plausible actions that a new CEO can take constrained.[26] Performance crises often discredit past decisions and past authorities in the organization. They also seem to call for strong leaders. Some of the literature on small groups finds that a crisis in confidence among problem-solving groups has the effect of concentrating influence in fewer hands.[27] In the case of CEO succession, when directors feel that they have lost their way and are looking for a solution to their problems, group structure changes to favor the selection of strong leaders. In other words, it creates conditions for the abdication of responsibility and transfer of control to others.

Under conditions of poor performance, moreover, the imagined solutions to complex problems often wear the reduced features of iconic individuals. Evan Lindsay describes exactly such a situation at a large insurance company in the South that had experienced a severe performance decline. Although many of the problems of the company arose from a complicated set of changes in the regulatory environment, the board felt that although "the company was in a deep hole, [it] could be saved with the right guy, like a Jack Welch or Lou Gerstner of insurance." In describing potential CEO candidates to directors, executive search consultants sometimes say, "He is a lot like Lou Gerstner" or "He has had experiences similar to Jack Welch's." The names of these individuals easily convey an image to directors: Lou Gerstner stands for turning around corporations. Jack Welch emblematizes trimming corporate fat and constantly reinventing the most valued corporation in the world. Yet when directors find themselves, in the latter stages of the external search process, looking not at Jack Welch or Lou Gerstner but rather at three or four somewhat less godlike candidates who, at least on the surface, appear quite similar to one another, what do they do? How is one of these candidates designated the charismatic leader? It is time to look more closely at the candidates in the external CEO search process, and at how and why particular candidates are chosen for the role of charismatic CEO.

The Construction of Executive Charisma

We noted earlier in this chapter that directors on a given board show a strong propensity for zeroing in on the same candidate among the three or four who end up as finalists in the typical CEO search, and that this tendency can be explained by the fact that charisma is much more of a social product than an attribute possessed by individuals. Earlier sociological analysis of charisma has emphasized the contextual conditions that increase the susceptibility of individuals, groups, and even societies to charismatic authority—conditions such as break from routine and poor performance, which we have just seen as key elements in the turn to charismatic CEO succession. While contextual conditions are important, my own conception of charismatic attribution differs from that of previous scholars in suggesting that individuals' evaluations of someone else's charisma are in large part generated by the social characteristics—and, to some extent, by the socially valued individual attributes—of the individuals being evaluated. For example, nothing predisposes directors to belief in the charisma of a particular candidate so much as the admiration that flows from that candidate's association with a firm of high repute.

As an example of this tendency, consider the 1996–97 CEO search at Stanley Works, a tool manufacturer in Connecticut. The firm had been performing poorly for several years, while Wall Street analysts and directors alike had described it as lacking a clear strategy for improving performance. Many directors felt that the lack of a clear strategy resulted from the CEO's lack of vision and failure to define the organization's purpose. In my interviews with Stanley's directors, there was almost no discussion of the fact that the firm was in an industry that had experienced little growth over the past decade. Nor was there discussion about how mega-retailers, such as Wal-Mart and Home Depot, had been demanding lower prices from Stanley than did the traditional mom-and-pop hardware stores that were fast being driven out of business by this new competition. Little reference was made to increased global competition, in the face of which low-cost, high-quality tools from Asia had gained significant market share in the United States. Stanley's directors simply felt, according to two different board members, that if they hired the right CEO, "he would introduce and formulate the right strategy" for the firm.

After conducting an extensive search, the Stanley Works board hired John Trani, the former president of GE Medical Systems. When I asked different Stanley directors to explain their reasons for hiring Trani, the most often-discussed factor was that he had come from General Electric and worked for Jack Welch. Directors discussed GE's track record in developing executives. All of them pointed out that there were other former GE executives who were now leading U.S. companies and had improved their performance. None of these directors, however, made any explicit link between Trani's specific experiences at GE and the problems facing Stanley. Nor did directors entertain the possibility that the reason Trani was willing to change jobs was because he knew it was unlikely that he would ever be promoted to CEO at GE, a firm of much higher status than Stanley.[28]

GE's performance also influenced the Stanley Works directors' evaluation of Trani. One Stanley director described the board's logic:

> Although I believed [sic] there were three or four candidates that we had identified that could do this job, the other committee members were set on this individual. John Trani was seen as superior by an order of magnitude. The personal chemistry that the board had with him was remarkable and he had, after all, come from GE, which by any measure has performed remarkably well during Jack Welch's tenure. I can't think of a company of comparable size that has created more value than GE during Welch's tenure.

Comments from analysts following the Stanley Works search only reinforced this faulty logic: for example, Nick Heymann, an analyst with NatWest securities, said, "[Trani] was one of the top ten executives at GE, which means he's probably one of the top ten executives in the world. [Stanley Works investors] have good reason to be optimistic."[29] As of this writing, both the board's and the analysts' initial optimism about Trani has proven costly, as John Trani's vision of transforming Stanley into the "Coca-Cola of hardware" has seemed to be more of a hallucination than a sound strategy, and the firm has continued to flounder.[30]

The remarks by Stanley's board members suggest that a board's perceptions of a candidate's charisma depend, at least in part, on the status of the prior employer, the performance of the prior employer, and whatever affiliation a candidate might have with another executive of high repute. (These external attributes should be considered illustrative rather than as an exhaustive list of external criteria that create perceptions of charisma.) The attribution of charisma to a particular individual by means of such criteria has obvious parallels to the social matching process that is used to sort candidates into the categories of eligible and ineligible. Like social matching, the process by which charisma is attributed to one particular candidate is inherently social at its root. However, one subtle but key difference separates the social matching process used at an earlier stage of a CEO search from the attribution of charisma to one of a handful of final candidates. This difference can be explained using the sociological concept of the "other-directed." Social matching, at its root, is an "other-directed" process. In social actions that are "other-directed," actors pay close attention to the expectations and evaluations of others in determining their own actions. The evaluations and expectations of these others, in fact, become the standards of what is considered legitimate and appropriate.

In the context of external CEO succession, directors' efforts to produce a set of candidates that outsiders will consider legitimate causes them to adhere to a set of widely held expectations about what characteristics a qualified CEO candidate should display. Over time, the widespread adoption of and adherence to these criteria by large numbers of organizations has given them a "taken for granted" or "rule like" status that seems to require little or no justification. One benefit to boards of relying on the social matching process is that it produces outcomes that are easily defended. (Recall the old adage "Nobody ever got fired for buying IBM.") In the external CEO labor market, the primary reason that the social matching process is adhered to is uncertainty about how the chosen candidate will perform once hired. Because the performance of any CEO candidate cannot be known in advance, social matching produces a set of defensible candidates who, even if they fail, will obviate criticism to the effect that the board did not choose a candidate with the appropriate characteristics. Social matching helps explain why most outsider CEO candidates appear virtually indistinguishable from one another across many observable criteria.

In contrast to the social matching process that produces a final list of candidates, however, the attribution of charisma to a particular candidate is driven not by mere defensiveness but by admiration on the part of directors for the affiliations that candidates possess or—to take a somewhat more complex case—for qualities that directors have been socially conditioned to admire. At the simplest level, charismatic attribution seems to be a response to an individual per se; when directors speak of an individual's leadership capabilities, they seem to be saying that the commanding presence of a particular individual evokes in them a desire to follow (and indeed a hope that the leader will solve the company's problems himself, thereby relieving his followers of responsibility for making decisions). For example, when asked why Jamie Dimon was selected as CEO of Bank One over the internal candidate, Verne Istock (who, at least on the surface, had more experience in commercial banking than did Dimon, and who had been running day-to-day operations at the bank since the departure of John McCoy), one Bank One director replied:

> We selected Jamie Dimon because he was clearly the real leader among the candidates. Jamie came in as such a strong leader. He was quick on his feet, very logical, and very persuasive. . . . He would not waste time getting stability and consensus, but instead do what it took to make us the number one bank. . . . Istock, on the other hand, was more consensus-oriented. He felt that the bank needed to be stabilized and the executives needed a rest from the turmoil that had resulted from the merger and McCoy's departure.

In most cases, of course, people do not try to understand why they find some individuals more charismatic than others; they feel the need only to ascertain their reactions to these individuals. As we saw in chapter 3, however, definitions of what corporate CEOs should be like, and the characteristics that are valued in them, are historically dependent and have been transformed over time. Thus the Bank One director's response to Dimon's apparent charisma was not merely individual or subjective, but was in fact generated by, and acquired through, a social process that teaches directors to value or respect people who are "quick," "logical," and "persuasive," and to discount those who are perceived to be oriented toward "stability" and "consensus."

Directors' attempts to evaluate candidates' leadership abilities through their personal reactions to individuals become even more problematic when one considers the highly suspect context of the typical interview. Many directors describe themselves as being able to discern a person's leadership qualities in the course of a very brief encounter; in my interviews with them, several directors commented to me about their ability to discern the true leadership ability of an individual within a few minutes of meeting him or her. Yet although directors believe themselves to be good judges of the character of individuals based on observable personal characteristics, in truth they are often making snap judgments about candidates in a very narrow context. Their view of personality as a clue to an individual's likely subsequent behavior is simplistic and misleading. Instead of behaving in a way that is consistent with a single situation, such as an interview, all of us reveal different parts of ourselves to different people in different contexts. We speak differently with people who are perceived to be of higher or lower status than us. We act differently with our intimates than we do with our acquaintances. And in all of these situations, we engage in what Erving Goffman calls "impression management." Impression management is a process in which people seek to control the image that others have of them through their behavioral projection of information about themselves; it includes factors ranging from emphasis and tone to actual disclosures and omissions in what is said. People frequently employ impression management behaviors to achieve objectives and goals. Engaging in impression management does not necessarily involve false pretenses or deception, but rather packaging ourselves so that those with whom we interact will draw the conclusions about us that we prefer.[31]

In view of the elementary fact that human beings engage in impression management, the idea that a candidate's leadership abilities can be determined in the course of a single, brief encounter appears as one more highly irrational aspect of the external CEO search process. Yet a single, brief encounter is, in fact, the only one that board members who do not already know a candidate will get in the course of the search. In the external search process, moreover, the interview on the basis of which the final decision is made is designed not to test the mettle of a candidate and learn more about his or her qualifications for the CEO position, but rather to meet a whole other set of in some sense extraneous requirements dictated by the peculiar nature of the external CEO labor market. Given this fact, it is difficult to ascertain how directors can make sound judgments about candidates' integrity, maturity, interpersonal acumen, motivation, and in-depth understanding of a company on the basis of what they are able to observe in a CEO interview. Yet this no-win situation arises inexorably from the tortuous logic of the external CEO selection process.

At every point in the external search process up till now, we have seen behaviors that seem surprising and even irrational if one assumes that the process is geared to considering the widest possible range of candidates and evaluating them on a set of objective measures defined by the strategic situation of the firm, the specific managerial tasks that the CEO is called upon to perform, and so forth. We have seen, for example, how directors themselves perform the roles usually assumed to be performed by executive search firms—that is, drawing up a list of candidates and obtaining vital information about them—while neglecting to consider the needs of the firm in identifying and evaluating the candidate pool. We have seen how the role of the executive search firm is not to expand the candidate pool or to provide information about the candidates, but rather to act as an intermediary between directors and candidates in a market where small numbers of buyers and sellers, risk to both, and concerns about legitimacy impose a unique set of constraints on the behavior of both parties to the transaction. In focusing more closely on the role played by candidates in the external CEO succession process, we find ourselves observing yet another apparent anomaly, one in which the final stage of the search becomes not so much a critical evaluation of the candidates as a conferring of power on them— even before one of the candidates is officially elevated to the position of CEO. It is to this climactic ritual of the external CEO search that we must now turn our attention.

THE DEFERENTIAL INTERVIEW

In the traditional CEO succession process, the firm's board, which included its outgoing CEO, exerted great power over the candidates. This power—apparent in Reginald Jones's description (quoted in chapter 3) of the CEO succession process at General Electric that resulted in the selection of Jack Welch—was a function of the fact that the board was making the hiring decision and could choose from a variety of internal candidates, all of whom were actively competing for the position.

The power dynamics of the internal succession process stand in stark contrast to the power relationship between the board and the candidates when a charismatic succession process is adopted. The most fundamental difference can be seen in directors' deferential behavior toward the candidates in charismatic succession. Because the charismatic model of the CEO position casts candidates in the role of hoped-for saviors, directors feel extremely dependent on them. To ensure that the firm does not lose a candidate, directors and their search consultants try, by various means, to minimize the likelihood of misunderstanding and to lessen the negative consequences of any miscommunication that might occur. One way in which they do this is to limit the amount and intensiveness of direct contact between directors and candidates.

We have already discussed the role of the executive search firm as a buffer between candidates and searching firms. Another means by which the necessary buffering is achieved is the common practice—quite surprising in light of the broad responsibilities of the CEO position and the costs of a poor match—of firms' interviewing candidates only once before making a decision. Moreover, even within the already severe limits on contact between candidates and directors imposed by this practice, directors create yet another layer of buffering by the manner in which they conduct the interview. Because the face-to-face interview is a particularly intense exchange, fraught with potential problems that could result in a candidate withdrawing his candidacy, directors' behavior in the interview process is characterized by guarded politeness and extensive impression management. Informality, which can be easily misconstrued, is, for that reason, carefully avoided. Directors also exhibit such universally recognized signs of deference as excessive self-consciousness and downright obsequious behavior. As one bank director observes, "When we are down in the final process, I don't want to be seen as the person who 'lost the candidate.' The last thing we need to do when the process has gone this far is to lose the candidate and have to start again because of a squabble the candidate had with me." Thus directors not only eschew such obviously dangerous behaviors as aggressive or threatening tones of voice but even go so far as to limit the number of questions they ask. As one candidate recalls a CEO interview:

> This was not like a medical school interview. There was not a lot of asking questions. Instead, they spent most of the time selling the company to me. They pointed out all the good things going on in the company and how this is a great opportunity.

Indeed, directors generally go into the interview with little, if any, preparation, training, or strategy for questioning candidates. The questions that they do ask, moreover, are often timid, hypothetical, and oriented to the future rather than designed to explore the candidate's handling of actual jobs and situations in his or her past. This too is surprising, since it is precisely this kind of information that is lacking in an outsider search. The potential consequences of this failure to probe CEO candidates about their past work experiences in a way that is routine in interviews for other positions in American corporations are dramatically illustrated by the case of "Chainsaw" Al Dunlap, the now-disgraced former CEO of both Sunbeam and Scott Paper. By 1996, when Sunbeam hired him for its top job, Dunlap had become a celebrity CEO on the strength of his "turnaround" of Scott Paper (where he served from April 1994 to December 1995) and the ruthless cost-cutting (including the firing of eleven thousand workers) with which he had partially accomplished that feat. (Dunlap had also published an autobiography, *Mean Business*, in which he bragged that he "deserved" the $100 million he had walked away with after engineering the sale of Scott Paper to Kimberly-Clark.) One former Sunbeam director now admits that the board was so enamored of Dunlap and desirous of the immediate boost that his hiring would bring to the company's stock price that it discounted previous criticism of his "mean business" management style as exaggerations by disgruntled former employees. Yet if the board had been willing to probe Dunlap's reputation for unseemly, unprofessional behavior, it might well have uncovered that his abrasive dealings with others had gotten him fired, twenty years before, from a company that later accused him of having overseen much the same kind of accounting fraud that would lead Sunbeam to fire him in 1998.[32]

The avoidance of challenging, potentially discomfiting questions in a CEO interview not only protects candidates and directors from embarrassment but also serves as a symbolic means of conveying the directors' appreciation to a candidate for considering the position. This message has already been communicated by other means at an earlier point in the search process, for by the time a candidate is presented to the board, the search consultant has made specific attestations to this individual concerning how well he or she is regarded by the directors. Steve Scroggins of Russell Reynolds describes the process as a "careful pre-sell to the candidate about the opportunity and why it is right for them [sic] in terms of a next career move." Meanwhile, in an effort to elevate the stature of a particular candidate in the board's eyes, the search consultants will also have let the client know how "hard they worked to convince the candidate to agree to the interview" and how "lucky they [the directors] are that this particular candidate agreed to be interviewed." This advance work—coupled with the directors' awareness that, because the candidate is already employed, they will have to make the job considerably more attractive than his or her current position—typically ensures a smooth interview process. As one search committee chairman comments:

> We want the candidates to be attracted to the firm. We need them to seriously consider the job, so we go out of the way to make sure they see the firm in the best light. . . . As board members, we will be working with them in the future, so they have to like the people they are going to be working with. We are all on our best behaviors. You are not going to insult someone you are trying to attract.

DEFERENCE TO CANDIDATES AS A FUNCTION OF THE MARKET

The attitude of deference that directors show toward CEO candidates is not simply ritualized behavior with only symbolic implications but in fact has substantive consequences for the candidate's role in the external CEO search. Specifically, the deferential treatment that candidates receive increases their bargaining power in the transaction (and, as we shall see momentarily, increases the power of the new CEO vis-à-vis the board). When it comes to the candidate whom the board will ultimately select as its new CEO, it is during the deferential interview that control is actually transferred from the followers to the charismatic leader. The selection of the new CEO then turns out to resemble nothing so much as Napoleon's coronation as Emperor of France, when the new ruler— usurping what was supposed to be the Pope's role—placed the crown on his own head.

If this process sounds irrational, it nevertheless makes sense when we consider that what charismatic succession represents to all organizational constituents is the promise of a better future. In such cases, the hiring of a celebrity CEO is the ultimate asset. In this frantic age of short attention spans, fame has become short-term fortune. The selection of a CEO can, and sometimes does, affect the market value of a firm by billions of dollars in the course of a single day—and businesses have increasingly banked on their ability to boost their stock prices by means of the right choice. The promise may or may not be fulfilled, but even false hope has value, especially to the candidate—for candidates recognize that the directors' deference is readily convertible to more material advantages. As one outsider CEO candidate describes his experience with a company at which he eventually accepted a job:

> They recognized that they were in front of a huge sea change in their business. Half the company was in the traditional [x] business and this business was going digital. They wanted somebody who could handle both the financial and marketing parts of the business and the technological change. I had gotten a good reputation in [y] business and . . . they thought I was the person who could transform a company to where they needed to go. . . . I also knew that they did not have many other alternatives.

Directors generally do not have "many other alternatives" because, as we have seen, the social matching process that boards use introduces an artificial scarcity of sellers into the external CEO market. Because the directors are using a charismatic succession process, moreover, they are comparing candidates not against a particular skill set but rather against one another. With CEO candidates already perceived as in short supply, directors narrow the candidate pool further by focusing on the charisma of the final candidates. Thus the board ends up looking not for someone with the skills of Lou Gerstner but rather for a stand-in for Lou Gerstner himself. By focusing on the individual, directors end up actually restricting their choice to *a single candidate*, thereby further closing the market. By focusing their attention on a single individual, needless to say, directors significantly reduce their bargaining power.

The charismatic candidate's superior bargaining position is rooted not just in the small number of sellers in the external CEO market, and the further narrowing of the candidate field effected by the directors' focus on individuals, but also in the market's other two defining features: risk to participants and concerns about legitimacy. The element of risk to directors comes into play because the candidates, being already employed, feel much less dependent on the outcome of the process than do the directors. As previously noted, moreover, if it becomes known that the directors failed to get their first-choice candidate, this will not bode well for the firm, as any subsequent CEO selected will be seen as the second choice and will therefore have to overcome questions about the appropriateness of his choice and the legitimacy of his succession.

Besides leading to imbalances in power between the directors and the candidates, the deferential treatment of candidates can result in poor matches. This is because excessive deference to candidates on the part of directors further exacerbates the problem of poor information for both sides. From the candidates' perspective, this problem is attested to by the CEO candidate, quoted above, who describes how the board of directors at the firm at which he interviewed attempted to sell the position as a "great opportunity." "I didn't know if it was a good opportunity, however," the candidate recalls. "It is not like this is a completely candid exchange. We are both trying to impress and sell each other. They are putting their best face forward; I am too."

Even in the best of circumstances, the kind of knowledge the directors and candidates are seeking about one another cannot really be gained in an interview. True knowledge of another person is the culmination of a slow process of mutual revelation. It requires the gradual setting aside of interview etiquette and the incremental building of trust, leading to the exchange of personal disclosures. It cannot be rushed. Choosing CEOs from inside the firm used to enable directors to get to know the candidates in this way. Internal labor markets created space as well as time for such a process. They were sanctuaries from the pressure of external observers such as analysts and the business media. Yet when the internal succession process is rejected, the increased pressure to choose a CEO reduces the amount of time available and results in charismatic succession. In this situation, directors rely on the exaggerated reputations of certain individuals without putting these reputations into a more specific context. Consider the case of one diversified consumer products firm that hired a CEO from the much larger Johnson & Johnson and found the decision costly. As one director relates:

> Johnson & Johnson was seen as one of the great ponds for getting managers. It had a reputation in the consumer products field, much like that

of GE. However, in our case, it turned out to be the wrong fish. When [Steve] moved to our company, we didn't have nearly the resources that J&J had. It was not until one year into [Steve's] tenure at a board meeting that I understood the problem. . . . He complained at a board meeting that the reason the firm's performance hadn't improved was that he didn't have an executive team with nearly the same intellectual and analytical power that he had with his colleagues at J&J. They didn't share the same instincts. It was then it dawned on me that part of the reason that [Steve] had been so successful at J&J had less to do with him and more to do with the J&J system and J&J culture, something we could never duplicate or even wanted to create in our own firm. I knew then that [Steve] wasn't likely to work out.

This kind of reliance by directors on the outsized reputations of firms or candidates, as well as the excessive deference toward candidates that it helps to breed, are all the more ironic and needlessly self-defeating in view of the fact that candidates themselves—at least until it becomes clear that they are the board's choice to be the new CEO—do not necessarily feel nearly as powerful as they are in the directors' eyes. Even the most sought-after candidates, after all, are human beings with their own wants and insecurities needing to be assuaged.

For example, CEO candidates may be coming from companies where —perhaps because of the charismatic figure already occupying the CEO suite—the path to promotion to the top job is blocked. Whereas economists often consider individuals in organizations to be unconstrained in their mobility, in the internal promotion process in organizations they are anything but. In organizations where the CEO position is occupied, it cannot be occupied by another individual until the incumbent vacates the position. Because of such constraints, there are numerous instances in which the next-in-line executive is willing to move to another organization. (The two primary reasons leading CEO hopefuls to conclude that the path to promotion is blocked for them are proximity in age to the incumbent and the possession of either direct or indirect information to the effect that he or she is unlikely ever to be appointed CEO.)

Whatever an individual's prospects at his or her current firm, the decision to move to another firm by a candidate who is not currently a

CEO is almost always motivated, at least in part, by the desire to receive the dramatically higher monetary rewards associated with the position. Such candidates, however, also have more complex reasons for wanting to go to another firm. For most executives, being named to the CEO position is an affirmation of one's individual skills. As one CEO candidate said to me, "For most of my career I have been working under a larger-than-life figure. I have done most of the work and very rarely received the credit. I wanted to show everyone that I could do it on my own." To the extent that a CEO believes that the judges who put him in the position are wise critics, he can believe, if just for a moment, in his own excellence. The awarding of the position is no ordinary transaction, for it is done with a public announcement singing the praises of the new CEO. "It [is] all very heady," relays another CEO. "At the moment you are on top of the world, and all the sacrifices you made to get there seem worthwhile."

For candidates who are already CEOs, the opportunity to move to a new firm may represent a chance to enhance one's personal prestige by moving to a higher-status organization. This type of reflected institutional charisma is no different from that associated with having joined a prestigious club or graduated from an elite university. CEOs compete with their peers for admiration, just like everybody else. Two important ways in which they do so are by becoming well regarded and being sought after by other firms. Even if they are already successful in a firm of respectable status, CEOs are continually concerned with the evaluations of others. They are aware of the prestige rankings of their own firms, of other CEOs, and of themselves. As social beings who have all their material wants satisfied, CEOs can and do channel their cravings into the hunt for status, admiration, and sometimes even the envy of their peers. One of the most important consequences of this status system is the flow of CEOs from one firm to another. This process is determined, in part, by the decisions CEOs make about whether moving from one firm to another will enhance, stabilize, or diminish their status. Reputation, in other words, is one of the main currencies in the external CEO market.

Candidates' concern with status, in turn, increases the apprehension with which they approach the prospect of joining a new firm as an outsider CEO. This apprehension then motivates candidates to make full use of the extraordinary bargaining power that the charismatic succession process hands them vis-à-vis the board. Candidates understand that their hiring represents an attempt by the directors to change the fortunes of the organization, and particularly to restore the status it has lost by performing poorly. Candidates are also aware, however, that while their hiring can temporarily affect the status of the organization, changing it permanently is a slow process that requires continually proving oneself. In this respect, candidates are more realistic than either directors or the external constituents, such as the business media and analysts, who expect them to get fast results. Moreover, because candidates recognize that they will be sacrificing their current status, they often demand recompense in the form of prestige, power, and money. As one candidate reveals, "The reality is that when you get far enough along in the process, you can ask for pretty much anything you want. The nightmare scenario for the board at this point is having to restart the process. So you ask. And you get." In some such circumstances, the demands extend beyond pay and severance packages. Several CEO candidates ask for power and authority. In many cases, the candidates demand that they be given both the CEO and chairman positions as well as the right to make some decisions regarding the composition of the board. (Such was the case with Jamie Dimon, who had negotiated with the Bank One board to be able to reduce its size by six members, and then appointed two directors whom he knew well. Dimon's desire to control the Bank One board was understandable given his experience under Sandy Weill at Citibank. A governance expert might suggest, however, that the consequence of such a bargain is weaker monitoring of the CEO by the board.)

In any event, even the opportunity to join a more high-status company does not allay all the anxieties that a new CEO experiences. The initial gain in status may be temporary; if the organization is in very dire straits, this moment of glory may prove to be only a brief prelude to a later failure. Consequently, even the most confident and optimistic CEO must consider the implications of the decision to change firms. At the same time, candidates are hampered in their ability to understand these implications owing to the information problem that affects sellers as well as buyers in the external CEO market. In contrast to the ideal situation (often assumed as reality by economists) in which participants in a market have the relevant data to make informed transactions, CEO candidates, in choosing to move from one firm to another, cannot reliably predict what the costs of such a move will be over time. It is also difficult for them to calculate the potential payoff.[33]

Thus CEO candidates—despite the Napoleonic or even godlike stature that they have in the eyes of directors and others who both influence and are influenced by directors' choices in an external CEO search—turn out in some respects to be ordinary mortals subject to forces beyond their complete control. As Jamie Dimon has remarked to me, "Everybody has a book—a story." And as Dimon and his charismatic cohorts also understand, to be part of a story, even one's own, is to be to some degree at the mercy of the storytellers. Yet for the most part, CEOs and CEO candidates have benefited—often enormously—from the tales that have been told for the last two decades about "leadership," "talent," and "the market." And in the age of the charismatic CEO, it needs to be stressed, both those directly involved in the succession process and others who stand on the outside looking in, are involved in the telling and retelling of these stories. Discerning whose interests are harmed in the process, even as the interests of a small coterie of insiders are advanced, is the final, most critical step in understanding external CEO succession. It may also be the first step in learning what can be done to make the CEO selection process better serve the legitimate interests of both corporate constituents and society in general.

CHAPTER 7

OPEN POSITIONS, CLOSED SHOPS: LEARNING FROM THE EXTERNAL CEO SUCCESSION PROCESS

THE EXTERNAL CEO labor market was born in a burst of rhetoric about wresting control of corporations away from a group of self-interested insiders, as senior managers in the era of managerial capitalism had come to be portrayed. Expanding CEO search beyond the confines of the internal labor market—or so the rationale for the practice supposed—would open the CEO position to a broader group of individuals who would bring greater talents and breadth of "vision" than could be found within any one company, and who had little vested interest in the status quo. The proponents of the external CEO market thus expropriated the principles of the market and the logic of competition. They proposed to take a closed system and crack it open.

As we have seen in the foregoing pages, however, the external CEO succession process as it currently operates is anything but an open, competitive system. While today's CEO labor market is defended as if it were a market in the classical sense, it is in reality nothing of the sort. Far from being the "institution-free" mechanism portrayed by economists and even some sociologists, the external CEO search process is governed at every stage by structural rules and institutions previously thought to be confined to the firm. In the process as it actually unfolds in one large firm after another, external institutions such as socially based categories of eligibility, the evaluations of investors and the media, and third-party intermediaries (i.e., executive search firms), play a central role in controlling access to jobs and facilitating or hindering mobility.

Because the external CEO market deviates in critical ways from the kinds of markets described by neoclassical economics, its outcomes cannot be assumed to be optimal and efficient—as, indeed, they turn out not to be when considered critically. To take just one example: as a result of the influence of external institutions on the external CEO selection process, many individuals who could be CEOs are not even on the radar screens of those who could be tapping them for the position. Thus, the external CEO search process has created a closed ecosystem of top-tier executives for whom the so-called glass ceiling appears perfectly opaque, since it hides those on the lower floors from the view of directors and search firms. This is not only a waste of talent but also, as it turns out, a recipe for returning corporations to the kind of oligarchic control from which external CEO search was supposed to deliver them.

Viewed in the historical context, the rise of the external CEO labor market contains an even keener irony. With the fall of the Soviet empire in the closing years of the last century, markets have come to rule the world, as most alternative systems for organizing an economy have been discredited. Meanwhile, despite a brief period in the 1990s when the Internet and other advances in communications, and the seemingly limitless availability of capital, seemed to threaten the continued dominance of the large, multinational corporation, this form of organization now appears not only safe but, in many ways, more enduring, more potent, and more critical to our wellbeing than at any other time in history. The irony is that in America, the process that determines who will lead these organizations has been walled off, like the East Berlin of old, from the tumultuous discipline of market forces. At the top of the new, supposedly shareholder-centered corporation of today, the organization men of yesteryear have been replaced by a small cadre of individuals insulated from competition by what is, in effect, a closed shop, and now reaping the benefits of an unprecedented transfer of wealth from corporations and their shareholders to CEOs (and ex-CEOs), regardless of the latter's capabilities or performance.

In other words, today's cult of the charismatic CEO and the closed succession process that perpetuates it are more than just historical curiosities. They are developments that threaten serious damage both to corporations themselves and to the society that they increasingly dominate. It is time to examine the consequences of the rise of the charismatic CEO for American corporations and American society, and then to begin thinking about how a more rational system of CEO succession might be put in its place.

Consequences of External CEO Succession for Corporations

In seeking a charismatic outsider to be CEO, boards of directors generally ignore, or seriously underestimate, the risks that outside succession entails. Indeed, considering that an external search often represents a quest for a corporate savior for a firm that is in trouble to begin with, hiring an outside CEO can, in some instances, actually threaten the survival of the organization itself. In companies producing everything from copiers to sugared water, from razor blades to ATM machines, corporate boards are sending more CEOs packing than ever. While these fired CEOs undoubtedly have their egos bruised, they emerge from the ordeal considerably richer than before. Yet the same cannot be said for the damaged organizations they leave behind. Xerox flirted with the bankruptcy courts for several months following the brief but disastrous tenure of outsider Rick Thoman. Sunbeam ended up in Chapter 11 less than five years after its hiring of a hoped-for corporate savior, Al Dunlap. In the winter of 2001–02, it appeared that the financial services firm Conseco, after going outside to hire GE Capital's superstar Gary Wendt and paying him a near-record $45 million signing bonus, was edging toward insolvency.

Part of the risk involved in external succession stems from the fact that boards—having bought into the dominant mythology about the role of the CEO that makes an outside successor seem appealing or even necessary in the first place—feel, and succumb to, pressure to appoint a new CEO as quickly as possible once the position becomes vacant. We have seen numerous examples of the unrelenting pressure that board members feel once firm performance falters. Under this strain, and often with little thought to the consequences, board members cave in, dismiss the CEO, and begin the search for a new CEO who will appease investors, the business media, and Wall Street analysts. Thus directors, as we have seen, rush through a process that ought to be approached with care and deliberation. Search committees are assembled with little thought to their composition. Directors do not stop to ask themselves whether the individuals on the search committee have any deep understanding of the problems facing the company, or whether they might have biases arising from their functional backgrounds or particular interests. Nor, indeed, do they pause to give any serious consideration to the strategic situation and needs of the firm and how these should affect the succession decision. What they focus on, instead, is how analysts and the business media will react to their choice of a new CEO. This approach exemplifies the purely defensive, legitimacy-seeking mentality that characterizes so many business decisions today—even one that directors describe as among the most important that they ever have to make. By allowing themselves to be dominated by the instinct for self-preservation, boards neglect their duty to act in ways that protect the long-term health of the organization.

A second risk inextricably interwoven into external CEO succession arises from the way that the process requires decisions to be based on incomplete and often defective information. The kind of information and knowledge that is critical to making a CEO appointment is not easily transferred across organizational boundaries. Much of it originates in the informal interactions between an executive and his or her peers and subordinates, and circulates through an organization's informal internal channels. This information and the channels through which it flows, however, are not accessible to an outside firm conducting an external search. While directors attempt to use their contacts in other firms to gather such information, its second-hand quality makes it a poor substitute for the kind that is available within the bounds of a given company.

A third risk arising from the external succession process is that in the absence of high-quality information about how an individual has performed and is likely to perform in actual situations, directors rely on a sorting process—one that I have called social matching—that puts a premium on the defensibility of certain candidates and leaves others out of consideration altogether. The result is that boards, from the outset, seriously reduce their chances of finding the best person for the CEO's job.

All of these risks are apparent in the kind of careful consideration of the external search process itself that I have tried to present in this book. Yet some of the most tangible, and ultimately most serious, dangers to companies that opt for external succession become evident only after the board has chosen its new outsider CEO. Chief among these is the danger both to the bottom line and, even more profoundly, to the continued social and moral legitimacy of the corporation itself, represented by one of the great economic scandals of our time, what *Fortune* magazine has recently called "The Great CEO Pay Heist."[1]

CEO PAY: THE SPIRALING COST OF CHARISMA

How much is a charismatic CEO worth? Increasingly, the answer given by boards of directors is whatever he or she has the chutzpah to demand, with no real requirement that pay be tied to "performance" even as conventionally (if questionably) measured in terms of changes to a firm's stock price. Despite the lack of a convincing link between the CEO and corporate performance, firms continue to buy into the mythology that the key to improving long-term firm performance (over and above whatever short-term boost to the stock price they hope to achieve by this means) is hiring an external savior. To defend their actions, boards create complicated pay schemes with elaborate justifications—almost always buried in the footnotes of the annual report—describing how their pay system, often designed by the CEO himself and legitimated by a compliant executive compensation consultant, links the fortunes of the CEO to the fortunes of the shareholder, even though (as we shall see below) the most common arrangements do not achieve even this questionable objective.

Although the curtain is being pulled back on the subject of CEO pay, the facts are sufficiently disturbing to bear repeating. According to an executive pay survey conducted by the *New York Times* for the year 2000, the average CEO of a major corporation received a record-breaking $20 million in total compensation that year, including nearly 50 percent more in stock options and 22 percent more in salary and bonus than in 1999. Compare these figures with others from the Standard & Poor's 500 Index, the primary gauge of the overall stock market, which fell 10 percent in 2000, and the NASDAQ Composite Index, which dropped 39 percent. (During the same year, according to the Department of Labor, the typical hourly worker received a three percent raise, and salaried employees about four percent.) Moreover, the figures for CEO pay in the year 2000 represent but one segment of a significantly longer-term trend. One study that examined CEO pay levels at publicly held corporations found that CEO pay jumped 535 percent in the 1990s, dwarfing the 297 percent rise in the S&P 500, a 116 percent rise in corporate profits, and a 32 percent increase in average worker pay (not adjusted for inflation). To put this into further perspective, this same study found that since 1960 the pay gap between CEOs and the president of the United States has grown from 2:1 to 62:1; if average pay for factory workers had grown at the same rate as it has for CEOs during this boom instead of barely outpacing inflation, their 1999 annual earnings would have been $114,035 instead of $23,753. Finally, if the minimum wage had risen as fast as CEO pay, it would now be $24.13 an hour instead of $5.15, which is less, in real dollars, than it was in 1970.[2]

Closer examination of the issue of CEO pay reveals even more clearly how little connection exists, in practice, between the financial rewards showered on CEOs and the interests of corporations and their shareholders. For example, almost two-thirds of total CEO compensation is now in the form of stock options, which, in turn, currently represent the equivalent of 13 percent of corporate liabilities.[3] These are liabilities because eventually the firm will have to pay the difference between the price of the stock and the price at which the stock option was granted. Enormous grants of stock options to CEOs have been justified on the grounds that they link CEO pay to performance. Yet recent research has shown that one of the first actions that new CEOs typically take is to break this link by exercising their options (and selling their shares) as soon as possible. Indeed, even though the number of option grants to CEOs and other top managers exploded between 1993 and 1995, overall levels of stock ownership by senior executives in their own firms did not increase in these years.[4] Although investor relations departments increasingly explain executives' steady sales of stock in the firm as a "routine diversification" of wealth, this practice would seem explicitly to defeat the purpose for which stock options are said to be granted in the first place. Enron's top executives and directors, for example, apparently reaped over $1 billion from sales of company stock in 2000 and 2001, even as their reckless financing schemes set the stage for disaster.

What is the ultimate cost to corporations and shareholders for the profligacy of directors in compensating CEOs? While boards have, for many years, treated stock options as "costless," economists and others have convincingly argued otherwise (and indeed a Nobel Prize was awarded to the economists who discovered exactly what options of all types do cost by using what is called the Black-Scholes pricing formula[5]). Yet because expensing the cost of options on a company's income statement results in lower earnings, CEOs have fought against any attempt to require corporations to provide a truthful accounting in this regard.[6] The roots of their resistance may well lie in the fact that if companies are required to spell out in clear terms the true costs of executive compensation, executives will stand to make less on their options. This deception, of course, imposes costs on investors generally in the form of the market distortions arising from such faulty information.

In addition to producing misleading earnings reports, stock options also have consequences for the future in the form of diluted ownership. When stock options are exercised, the overall pool of stock in the public market increases, making each share investors own worth a little less than before. One theory that has been used to support the granting of stock options proposes that any loss in terms of dilution is more than compensated for by the growth in the company's stock price as a result of the incentives that options create for executives. Yet even if the incentive value of stock options can be shown to outweigh these costs (despite the emerging evidence that CEOs divest their ownership as soon as possible), the wisdom of concentrating the majority of a firm's options in the hands of a few top executives instead of spreading them more widely round the firm is questionable.

In any event, corporate boards, in their pursuit of charismatic CEOs through the external succession process, have transferred literally billions of dollars from organizations and shareholders to the personal control of CEOs and ex-CEOs—too often with little, nothing, or even less than nothing to show in return.[7] I believe that in the not-too-distant future, we will look back and marvel at the colossal folly of this chapter in American business history. A market in which participants' actions impose costs that are not taken into account is, in economic terms, inefficient. The kind of glaringly inefficient outcomes represented by CEO pay are a direct result, in turn, of the closed nature of the external CEO market.

Although the full story of the relationship between the turn to the external CEO market and the skyrocketing of CEO pay since the 1980s is still emerging, the outlines are becoming sufficiently clear. The perceived shortage of qualified CEO candidates in the external market is certainly one contributing factor. Another is the very model of the charismatic CEO, which views the chief executive's position as somehow qualitatively different from other top management posts. As companies began increasingly to look to the external market to fill the CEO's job, the supposed shortage of qualified candidates, coupled with directors' desire for a corporate savior, encouraged and enabled monopolistic behavior on the part of CEO candidates. As the external CEO market evolved, CEO compensation came to be less and less consistent with the overall internal policies of organizations, especially when external compensation consultants (generally chosen by the CEO candidate himself) entered the picture and introduced the false yardstick of the compensation packages of other CEOs—small numbers of which were hand-picked by the consultant for purposes of comparison. Search consultants and the business media fanned the flames by promulgating the idea that a CEO's compensation was a measure of his personal worthiness. Golden parachutes, golden handcuffs, and the whole panoply of mechanisms for lavishly rewarding CEOs without regard to performance—all of which were unheard of before the age of investor capitalism—became standard features of CEO pay packages.[8]

The assertion that stratospheric CEO compensation levels are the result of a closed market would be disputed by those, like the economists Robert H. Frank and Phillip J. Cook, who—although they are critics of high CEO pay—claim that such outcomes result from the intensity of competition in a market. In their book *The Winner-Take-All Society*, Frank and Cook show how the pay differentials that have long been common in sectors such as entertainment and sports—where a small group of performers walk away with most of the total rewards—have migrated into areas such as law, medicine, and investment banking.

They also argue that the greater the intensity of competition, the greater the propensity toward winner-take-all markets. In the CEO labor market, which Frank and Cook consider a "winner-take-all" market, they maintain that competitive forces stemming from technological and other such changes, coupled with new rules facilitating more open competition, have made the top-performing CEOs that much more valuable.[9] Obviously, this view of the CEO labor market as open and competitive could not be more different from the picture of it that emerges from my own research.

In his discussion of professional pay in his book *The Cost of Talent*, on the other hand, Derek Bok outlines the implications of closed markets for compensation:

> In these circumstances [where uncertainty and the cost of a poor choice are high], vigorous price competition is more the exception than the rule, for price is seldom a prime consideration in deciding which professional to hire. Chief executives do not win their jobs by offering to serve for less than their leading rivals. Nor do surgeons appeal to prospective patients by promising to replace their hips or remove their tumors for lower fees than are customary. Not only is money a secondary matter in choosing such executives and professionals; offering one's services for unusually low rates may signal some sort of weakness and thus repel clients rather than attract them.[10]

As Bok also notes, once there is deviation from the traditional conditions of competitive markets, ordinarily benign market mechanisms can have perverse effects: for example, the effort to publicize CEO pay in the 1980s had the unintended effect of ratcheting it up.[11] While I am sympathetic to Bok's view that spiraling CEO pay is influenced by a variety of market imperfections, his reasoning is still grounded in traditional economic logic in that it attributes the problem to asymmetric information. Bok's perspective is also, then, ultimately quite different from that presented in this book about the roles of structure, culture, and closure in driving the basic processes of the external CEO market.

Still, Bok, Frank, and Cook represent voices of skepticism that have been largely drowned out by the armies of apologists for today's inflated CEO pay packages. Economists in particular—including Michael Jensen, Ed Lazear, Kevin Murphy, and Sherwin Rosen—have been resolute defenders of the status quo, pointing to other highly compensated professionals, such as sports stars, when making the case that some lavishly overpaid individuals are merely receiving what their talents and accomplishments deserve.[12] It is true that one superstar's performance may make all the difference in the fortunes of a basketball or hockey team. Yet the obvious fallacy involved in attributing the performance of any large, complex organization (functioning, as it does, by the interdependent efforts of thousands) to the contribution of any single individual turns the CEO into a kind of demigod compared to mere mortals such as basketball's Michael Jordan. "For God's sake, Clemson has created five billion dollars in shareholder value," people say to defend the compensation awarded to the latest CEO to benefit hugely from this rather simplistic notion of cause and effect. Yet most of what causes a company's share price to double, as we noted in chapter 2, lies far beyond Clemson's, or any CEO's, immediate control.[13] Giving a CEO full credit for his company's stock price is only marginally less ludicrous than giving a president credit for a good economy. In the meantime, however, while defenders of the system present their mathematical models and retrospective analyses purporting to demonstrate that CEOs are worth what they receive because their compensation is set by "the market," the bills presented to shareholders continue to mount rapidly—even when the returns to these investors are stagnant or dwindling. Yet these monetary costs are not the only ones that corporations and their shareholders incur as a result of charismatic succession.

THE NONMONETARY COSTS OF CHARISMATIC SUCCESSION

The turn to charismatic leadership represents an attempt to find an individual who will provide a guiding vision for the organization. Yet the vision of a charismatic leader is a poor organizing principle for contemporary firms, which increasingly depend for their success on the sharing of intelligence and the dispersal of decision-making authority across all levels of the organization. For one thing, charismatic leadership, intentionally or not, necessitates strong centralized rule. Charismatic authority often professes a love of egalitarianism and empowerment, but such noble-sounding declarations—like the dictator's professions of "love" for his people—can, and frequently do, turn out to be self-deluding or manipulative. Even when a firm is fortunate enough to find an individual with a vision that is appropriate for it, the charismatic leader easily founders when it comes to execution. The problem lies in the fact that charismatic authority discourages criticism. Visionary leaders generally do not respond well to questions or complaints about the measures they have taken (including questions such as the one that the philosopher Isaiah Berlin, responding to a famous saying of Lenin's, put to them: how many eggs are you willing to break to make your grand omelet?). Without being able to hear any critical, questioning voices, however, the charismatic leader in a large, complex organization has no way even of knowing whether he or she is being effective.

One of the most serious casualties of the apotheosis of the charismatic CEO is often the dedication and loyalty of other top managers. To presume, as the charismatic succession process implicitly does, that a single individual deserves vastly more attention and rewards than are bestowed on anyone else in the organization ignores the reality that organizational performance is driven by more than one person. This is why the ideas behind the "war for talent," with their emphasis on recruiting and retaining stars and ignoring others in the organization, are so deleterious.[14] As the research of Jeffrey Pfeffer has demonstrated, low expectations amount to a self-fulfilling prophecy.[15] Why might we see such an effect when a CEO is selected from the outside? The external succession process not only places extraordinarily and even excessively high expectations (with commensurate financial rewards) on the incoming CEO but also implicitly devalues the contributions of insiders, who may reasonably conclude that they are not expected to "drive" organizational performance. Seeing the bulk of the rewards for top management going to a single individual not only lowers the commitment of others to the organization but also decreases these individuals' willingness to invest in skills that will help the organization but are not necessarily marketable outside of it. Corporations, for their part, have also invested less in developing their own managers as they have increasingly looked outside to fill the top slots: a senior partner at the executive search firm Russell Reynolds (who asked to remain anonymous) says that the reason the firm's business has grown dramatically in recent years is the failure of companies to invest in and develop managers. Meanwhile, the true monetary cost to firms in terms of knowledge, ex-

TABLE 7.1
CEO Pay and CEO Differences with Top Five Officers in Companies, 1992–1996

	Year				
	1992*	1993	1994	1995	1996
Mean CEO total compensation	1705.314	189.622	2147.903	2398.995	3097.899
Mean gap between CEO total compensation and mean of entire executive team, including CEO	816.8128	894.6207	1056.202	1198.447	1622.514
Mean gap between CEO total compensation and next best paid executive in top 5	657.0173	751.8023	869.5156	1043.772	1476.391
Mean gap between CEO total compensation and mean of entire executive team, excluding CEO	1021.016	118.276	1320.253	1498.058	2028.143

*Note: N is only 648 for 1992; 850 observations for all other years.
Definitional notes:
Total compensation is the sum of salary, bonus, stock options, stock grants, and other income.
Where option values are missing, they are assumed to be zero.
Where CEO dummy data is missing and at least one individual in that year is listed as CEO, its value is assumed to be zero.
All comparisons use the top five executives (by salary) in a corporation in a given year.
Where data exists on fewer than five executives, firms are excluded.
I have used the larger firms by sales in each year. Hence, the exact composition of the list changes across years.
All figures are in inflation-adjusted 1994 dollars.

pertise, and sustainable competitive advantage as executives hop from one company to another, is incalculable.

While eroding the commitment to the organization of senior managers other than the CEO, charismatic succession can also result in weakened corporate governance. In the process of recruiting a savior from outside the firm, boards, as we have seen, often relinquish their own power. Many external CEO searches take place after the board has wrested power from the incumbent CEO—a task that is all the more difficult when, as is so often the case, the CEO also occupies the position of chairman. A chairman and CEO wields a great deal of control over the board's agenda as well as over the information that the board receives regarding the performance of the firm. The chairman also exercises both formal and informal authority in shaping board committees, including the compensation and appointments committees. After a forced CEO turnover (as, for example, in the Bank One board's decision to oust John McCoy), it is common for the board to separate the chairman and CEO positions while conducting a CEO search. However, after making this separation—one applauded by many corporate governance experts—most boards that hire external successors end up combining the positions again at the behest of the incoming CEO. In almost all the cases I examined, in fact, the preferred candidates made it a condition of their accepting the CEO position that they be given both titles.[16] At the same time, a new outsider CEO will often take other steps to build his own power base in ways that may be detrimental to the health of the organization—for example, by removing incumbent executives and replacing them with others whom he already knows. Such consequences of the external succession process are especially perilous in that, as we have seen, once a new CEO has been appointed, the decision is not easily reversed.

For these and other reasons, charismatic CEO succession is a well-paved route to disappointment—and not just for corporations but for CEOs themselves. By creating expectations that cannot be met, and privileging the most myopic demands of investors, analysts, and the business press over the genuine needs of the firm itself, the charismatic succession process sets up many a new CEO for likely failure. These individuals, of course, still walk away with enormous monetary rewards to salve their wounded egos, but they also give up their careers and reputations as part of the exchange. Companies, in the meantime, pay out in several ways for the rapid churning of chief executives that we see today—not just in expensive severance packages but also in turmoil and lost opportunities. For both firms and the individuals who lead them, charismatic succession too often amounts to an exercise in futility and waste.

One potentially even more far-reaching issue remains for corporate directors who are willing to learn from the deep flaws in the charismatic succession process. This concerns not just the profitability of corporations but also their continued social and moral legitimacy in a nation whose citizens, for a growing list of compelling reasons, are increasingly suspicious of corporate power and conduct. As the sociologist Daniel Bell has observed (restating an insight of Max Weber's), "The ultimate support for any social system is the acceptance by the population of a moral justification of authority."[17] The justification for the old system of managerial capitalism lay in its supposed efficiency. When that system broke down and was replaced by the shareholder capitalism that reigns today, the overthrow of the old managerial elite was justified on the grounds that corporations were important social creations that could not be guided solely by a self-interested class of insiders. Yet the new system, presided over by the charismatic CEO, quickly became disconnected from any moral moorings and has adopted an orientation that is incongruent with its original justification. To bring the corporation and its social environment back into alignment, directors—and indeed all corporate stakeholders, which in some sense now includes all citizens—would do well to ponder the effects of external, charismatic succession on American society at large.

Consequences of External CEO Succession for Society

Large private corporations are now a dominant, if not the dominant, force in American life, and indeed are among the most powerful institutions on the planet. As all but their most extreme opponents and defenders must agree, large corporations both confer social benefits and impose social costs through a wide variety of activities. They confer social benefits when they earn profits for a broad base of shareholders, contribute some of those profits to social or humanitarian efforts, pay a fair share of taxes, provide employment for large numbers of people, and create products and services that improve our lives. They impose social costs when, for example, they eliminate jobs in communities that critically depend on them, market sex and violence to youth, damage the natural environment, deceive investors about their financial condition, or purchase the compliance of politicians whose duty it is to mitigate or oppose their harmful acts. These kinds of activities are, or eventually become, more or less visible—unlike the still mostly hidden process by which large, publicly held corporations select their CEOs. Yet the current system of external CEO search, I would argue, imposes social costs just as surely as do many more salient corporate actions.

To begin with, society pays a price when firms allocate to individuals an inordinate amount of resources that could otherwise be distributed to a broader base of shareholders or reinvested in the enterprise itself. A supposedly open society also suffers, socially as well as economically, when the top jobs in its large corporations are allocated on the basis of social attributes rather than demonstrated ability for performing the tasks of the job. Such social costs of external succession are not easy to quantify, but that does not make them any less real. Indeed, the closer we look at just these two consequences of the external succession process—excessive CEO pay and limited mobility into the CEO position—the more serious and potentially far-reaching their implications appear to be.

CEO PAY AND THE DEMISE OF THE PROTESTANT ETHIC

Max Weber, that keen observer of human social systems, once described the uniqueness of America as its ability to restrain itself in the midst of natural abundance and wealth.[18] The Puritans who settled New England expected themselves and one another to be economically self-sufficient, and indeed regarded the material prosperity that many of them achieved as evidence of divine election. Yet even while laboring to store up riches for himself, the Puritan was supposed to subordinate his personal interests to the needs of the community. Moreover, wealth—while a divinely conferred blessing—was also seen as a powerful temptation to the sin of pride. Thus the cardinal virtues in Puritan society were self-denial, delayed gratification, and self-restraint, which eventually came to be viewed as characteristics distinguishing Americans from their decadent cousins in Europe.

Seventy years after Weber published the first version of his classic work *The Protestant Ethic and the Spirit of Capitalism*, Daniel Bell reflected on the demise of the Protestant ethic in the twentieth century in his book *The Cultural Contradictions of Capitalism*. What Bell called the "Puritan temper" in America had been subverted, he said, by the hedonistic, consumption-oriented capitalism that emerged in the 1920s and eventually proved impossible to reconcile with traditional Protestant virtues. Writing in the 1970s, Bell described the "split character" of the "new capitalism" by observing in the present tense that "[capitalism's] values derive from the traditionalist past, and its language is the archaism of the Protestant ethic" (even if, as Bell proceeded to state the contradiction, capitalism's "technology and dynamism . . . derive from the spirit of modernity").[19] It is interesting to note that Bell was making these observations just before the era of shareholder capitalism was born in the 1980s, giving rise to today's charismatic CEOs with their multi-million-dollar compensation and severance packages. For while it is possible to debate whether American capitalist culture today retains any of the values of the "traditionalist past" or pays more than lip service to the Protestant ethic, the rocketing of CEO pay since the early 1990s at least suggests that the leaders of corporate America no longer feel bound to maintain even so much as the appearance of traditional Protestant virtue.

While this phenomenon is arguably an effect of a much larger, more long-term societal crisis, it is also one that generates actual and potential consequences of its own. To bring these consequences into focus, consider a dimension of the problem that has garnered much attention and created justifiable alarm of late: the now-yawning chasm between CEO compensation and the wages of corporate America's lower-paid workers. As most Americans now know, the earnings gap between blue-collar workers and corporate CEOs is at an all-time high. Whereas in 1980 the average CEO made 42 times as much as the average blue-collar worker, by 1990 this same CEO made 85 times more, and by 2000 he was earning (if that is the word) a staggering 531 times the annual wages of a factory worker. Such figures—while sufficiently troubling on their own—also represent a small but symbolically significant part of an even larger, more disturbing story that is also, by now, familiar to all: the growing disparity in wealth between the small number of those at the top of the American economic heap and virtually everyone else.[20]

While the compensation packages for CEOs are only one small contributing factor to the high level of economic inequality in the United States today, they have a symbolic import that, it can be argued, eats away at the very foundations of American society. A century ago, as what was left of Calvinist theology in America was morphing into the equally dark and severe creed of Social Darwinism, the political and social scientist William Graham Sumner opined: "The millionaires are a product of natural selection. . . . They may fairly be regarded as the naturally selected agents of society for certain work. They get high wages and live in luxury, but the bargain is a good one for society."[21] Today, we can find many reasons for questioning whether the "bargain" that Americans have made with CEOs—or rather that CEOs and directors have made with and for themselves—is such a good one for anyone but its immediate beneficiaries. Not the least of these reasons, perhaps, is the way that outsized, unearned rewards for those at the top of the system devalue work itself. In the process, they send a clear message to the rest of society: playing by the rules that have traditionally pertained in America is only for those unable to make up new rules for themselves.

EXTERNAL CEO SEARCH AND THE BLOCKING OF MOBILITY

In a development directly related to growing economic inequality, a profound unease and insecurity dogs the American middle class today. Although we live in a time of unprecedented material prosperity, more and more individuals feel that their own economic circumstances have never been so precarious. The promise of America to every previous generation has been that the lives of one's children would be better than one's own. Yet this may no longer be the case, as the prospect of significantly improving one's economic circumstances seems increasingly to be becoming a monopoly of the few.

One major cause of the economic insecurity of American workers today is a significant change in the social contract between corporations and the workforce with respect to employment. In an illustration of this change, Jack Welch used to say proudly that GE didn't guarantee anyone continued employment, and that the only way for an individual to remain employed in the company was to remain competitive in terms of his or her own skills and performance. (GE still uses a "forced curve" grading system in its performance reviews for employees.)[22] Yet to be hired as CEO in many large corporations today, an executive, as we have seen, need not meet any rigorous standard of skills or performance but only be the right sort of person from the right sort of company. And even though shareholders employ their own grading systems that increasingly cause directors to fire CEOs, these same directors see to it that cashiered chief executives will not be buffeted by economic insecurity.

As in the matter of excessive CEO pay, the system of external CEO succession and the way that it parcels out its rewards to a privileged few serves as a potent symbol, as well as symptom, of a much larger social problem. In 1900, the leaders of American corporations were an extremely homogenous group. They were male, white, mostly native-born Protestants from "good" families. Today, the most recent studies of the social backgrounds of top executives reveal that they are still, for the most part, male, white, native-born Protestants from socially and economically advantaged families. In a survey of work on this topic, the economist Peter Temin has noted that while every study of the social composition of the executive class, ranging back over several decades, has found this same homogeneity, most have also predicted that this situation would not last. Researchers in the 1950s, 1960s, and 1970s, Temin says, "portray [the subjects of] their study as the last generation for which their observations would be true. Conditions have been changing, and the expectations of these various authors may have been rational. But the composition of the American business elite has not changed."[23] Given the dramatic changes in American society in the last century—particularly the integration of women and ethnic minorities into the work force over the last thirty years—the persistent homogeneity of the American corporate elite is troubling.

In this book I have sought to provide an explanation for this phenomenon by focusing on the process by which CEOs are selected in external searches. Imagine for a moment a society that is completely open, one in which an individual's talents and efforts determine that person's station in life. This would be a dynamic society in which competition would determine economic outcomes, and in which an individual's social characteristics have little bearing on his or her present or future. Now imagine the opposite, a society in which an individual's status and prospects are predetermined by a set of well understood and accepted traditions. Our society is supposed to more closely approximate the former condition than the latter, but it is the second, closed type of system that the external CEO labor market most resembles—so much so that when a woman or an African-American becomes a CEO of a *Fortune* 500 company, it is worthy of a cover story in a business magazine. Most people still expect a CEO to be a white male of a certain age and, often, of a certain educational and class background.

American democracy has always drawn its underlying strength from the ethos of meritocracy. The greatness of America that Alexis de Tocqueville remarked upon in the early nineteenth century was a result of the thread of social equality running through every American institution. Because the United States did not have a rigid class system based on birth, it could take full advantage of its people's talents and, at the same time, generate social cohesion across a range of physical space and a variety of ethnicities impossible to hold together in any other country. The progressive-era historian Frederick Jackson Turner argued that the openness of America was what guaranteed the distinctive quality of American society, which was opportunity for all. While America would certainly have inequality, Turner argued, it would be a dynamic inequality, not a static one in which birth rather than merit determined one's place in the social hierarchy. Even Milton Friedman, one of the gurus of today's neoclassical, "free market" economists, has argued that mechanisms that inhibit economic opportunity and social mobility pose a threat to democratic institutions.[24] Meanwhile, at the very pinnacle of corporate America, boards of directors maintain a closed system of CEO succession that restricts access to opportunity based on socially derived criteria and, once again, flies in the face of fundamental American values. That they do not set out consciously to block mobility in this way—an important point to which I will return momentarily—hardly mitigates the corrosive effect of their actions on the traditional American social compact.

SOCIAL CLOSURE AND THE UNDERMINING OF TRUST

The central concept I have used for understanding how the external CEO labor market arrives at results such as excessive CEO pay and the blockage of mobility into the CEO position is that of *closure*. In developing my description of how closure works in external CEO succession, I have built on Max Weber's description of social processes that lead to a restriction to a limited set of individuals of access to resources and opportunities. The social closure process, as Weber describes it, operates by fixing on a certain set of attributes that are intended to justify a focus on a narrow group of individuals.

Previous scholars who have developed the concept of social closure have argued that closure comes about through an intentional act of social exclusion. Aage Sørensen, for example, wrote about the development of labor unions and internal labor markets as intentional means of creating a social closure process to limit the competition for particular jobs.[25] Andrew Abbott writes about the professionalizing of occupations through licensing or accreditation as a means of securing a monopoly over the type of work being performed.[26] In contrast to such approaches, I argue that social closure does not require intentional collective action. Rather, the process works by relying on a set of legitimated criteria that give rise to a social category of eligible individuals.[27] While Weber argued that almost any observed characteristic—race, gender, or social origin, for example—could be seized upon to effect closure, I argue that the attributes fastened on in the CEO labor market are associated with three particular socially defined and legitimated characteristics: previous position, performance of an individual's previous firm, and status of that previous firm. The mechanism through which closure operates at the board level is the social matching process, which results in closure by keeping those who do not fulfill its criteria from being considered for the position. In other words, closure generates an artificial scarcity of candidates who are considered for the CEO job. The function of closure is not only to limit the competitive field in this way but also to set the terms of competition and to assign the rewards for work done in accordance with these limits. It creates the rules of the game, constituting the boundaries by which people will be judged and criticized.

At its core, then, the external CEO labor "market" operates as a circulation of elites within a single, sealed-off system relying on socially legitimated criteria that—contrary to conventional economic wisdom —are not to be confused with relevant skills for the CEO position. Relying on legitimated criteria, meanwhile, has created a new process of stratification that operates even more powerfully than sets of criteria based on, say, property, educational credentials, or inherited titles, because it is legitimated by the larger cultural system (as discrimination based on race, gender, or religion, for example, would not be). Judged against the more optimistic claims for markets and the mobility and fluidity for which they supposedly allow, my findings are a strong reminder of the persistent influence of closure processes in markets. They therefore fundamentally challenge neoclassical economic accounts of the CEO labor market. For precisely this reason, current celebrations of how the "market" has reformed processes of corporate control are, in reality, premature. Restricting the CEO labor market to a select set of candidates and then pretending that the outcomes can be justified as a consequence of the market process is a self-serving conceit.

What is wrong with closed markets? Along with the more particular problems that they create (such as paying some individuals excessive amounts and blocking access to positions for talented potential candidates), closed markets undermine the faith in an *open* market system on which financial markets rest, a faith that would be monumentally expensive for society to replace through enforcement mechanisms. Nor is it just the financial markets whose smooth operation depends on the maintenance of trust in the basic fairness of the market system, but also all of the interlocking economic, social, and political institutions of which our society consists.

While some would argue that closed markets are ultimately unsustainable, my findings about the external CEO market point to a set of factors tending to strongly reinforce and replicate its processes. Moreover, despite the widespread view that corporations are undertaking radical change in their systems of leadership and breaking open their organizational structures, the reality is that such reversals are rare and almost assuredly cannot happen quickly. The face of power may change —a new CEO arrives, only to be replaced two or three years later by another—but the routes of ascent to power remain the same. Nor are the factors inhibiting change confined within the corporation. There are powerful forces in our society dedicated to the perpetuation of a set of myths about the efficacy of the charismatic CEO and the self-regulating capacity of markets, and the ideological commitment of those who subscribe to and promulgate these myths can have an almost religious intensity.[28] Challenging the ideology of the charismatic CEO is thus one step that can be taken to establish the CEO selection process on a more rational basis. Challenging prevalent misconceptions about markets is another.

Opening the External CEO Labor Market

One of the fundamental premises of this book is that the external CEO labor market is a social institution. It is an institution not in the narrow sense of a formal organization, but rather in the broader, sociological sense of a set of socially habituated behaviors that constrain and direct action along a particular trajectory. The external CEO market is a *social* institution because it is in continuous, dynamic interaction with a more comprehensive social system from which it receives its core organizing principles. It is when these core organizing principles are shared and reinforced within a society or group that a market assumes the form of a full-fledged institution. It follows from this that the way we think about the external CEO market is, to a great extent, what accounts for its particular characteristics.

Although the closed nature of the external CEO market suggests that it would be difficult to change, we could, in truth, change it in significant ways by beginning to think differently about critical issues. This is all the more true because of the relatively small size of this market, and because, as I have argued, the perceptions of the actors involved directly affect its operations and outcomes. The first step in reorienting our thinking about CEOs and how they should be chosen is to realize the arbitrariness and even irrationality of many of our current ideas and attitudes. Thus, for example, the assumption that bringing in an outsider as CEO is the best way to bring about change in a faltering organization could be subjected to the critical scrutiny that it has so far largely been spared. Without pretending that it is possible or even desirable to return to the safety and stability of the era of managerial capitalism and the internal CEO succession process that then obtained, we might think about ways that the best features of the old succession system might be adapted so as to combine merit-based competition with the ability to bring in new blood.

Perhaps the most fundamental—and fundamentally irrational—attitude underlying the closed external CEO market is the belief in charismatic authority itself. The attraction of charismatic leaders is that they promise a solution to all of our problems if only we follow the leader with unwavering certitude. Whereas rational authority is logical, temperate, and even-handed in its recognition of the constraints on leaders, charismatic leadership is all about passion and the smashing of limits. Rational authority recognizes that organizational problems are fine-grained and complex, while charismatic authority dissolves particulars and complexities in the blinding light of "vision." Because it is rooted in sentiment rather than reason, charismatic authority is ultimately weak and unsustainable—a truth that has been demonstrated throughout history.

Yet for all of its manifest defects, charismatic authority has always been alluring for the simple reason that it avoids accountability and responsibility for outcomes. So, for example, charismatic authority has proven seductive for boards of directors that prefer to avoid wrestling with the complex interactions of environmental factors and corporate strategies and operations that largely determine a firm's performance. Although outwardly sober citizens, and while being charged in reality with the stewardship of vast conglomerations of society's resources, many corporate directors today discharge—or rather shun—one of their most important duties with what amounts to a belief in magic.

THE RESPONSIBILITY OF CORPORATE BOARDS

The process by which boards hire a new CEO is often directed at finding a charismatic leader and then tailoring the job to his skills. A more deliberative and rational process would entail evaluating the current strategic challenges facing the firm and the skills that a new CEO must have to help the organization meet them. To try to find the "right person" and then adapt the job to him is to put the cart before the horse. This belief that there is one right person for the job is at the core of the whole process of charismatic succession. It is also a dodging of responsibility, an act of evasion that begins with directors' unwillingness to face the fact that choosing a CEO is difficult.

The myth of the charismatic CEO disguises this inconvenient reality. The charismatic illusion is fostered by tales of white knights, lone rangers, and other such heroic figures whose origins lie in the fairy tales that serve a child's need to feel protected from the world's dangers. When we meet this extraordinary man (and it is almost always a man) who is going to save the day, we expect to be able to recognize him. The charismatic leader is easily identified by the feelings of awe that he inspires in others. There is no need to look hard at the leader himself, let alone to question whether he is really right for the task at hand.

Corporate directors today complain more or less incessantly about the seriousness of their organizational problems, the failed strategies of their CEOs, and the difficulties they have in finding adequate "leaders." Sometimes they voice these complaints publicly, at other times anonymously or in whispered conversations with fellow tribesmen. They talk as if their inability to find a CEO who can solve all their organizations' problems is the result of a curse placed on the board. Conversely, one rarely hears directors actually taking responsibility for poor decisions made in hiring a CEO. Instead of facing the possibility that their own flawed search and selection processes are responsible for such failures, most directors seek to avoid the pain this would entail by blaming their poor decisions on bad advice from their search consultants, or on candidates who misled them about their skills, or on circumstances supposedly beyond their control, such as pressure from analysts, investors, and the business media.

The lengths to which boards go to avoid assuming responsibility for choosing a CEO is ironic given that, as noted in chapter 4, many directors describe this as one of their most important decisions. Perhaps the most damaging result of the quest for a corporate savior is the dependency that it creates in directors, who not only surrender inordinate power to charismatic candidates but may even repeat this behavior again and again.[29] This is especially tragic because, as much of the literature on organizations and strategy maintains, CEO turnover potentially offers a unique opportunity to improve an organization's performance. Although boards are unlikely to take advantage of this opportunity if they operate on the assumption that the "talent" of the CEO is the key to competitive success, executive succession can, in fact, create a foundation for organizational renewal. But the first step in making this happen must be for directors to start acknowledging and accepting the complexity and difficulty of the succession decision, and abandoning the search for simple answers.

No single individual can save an organization. One reason that directors cling to the belief in corporate saviors is that, like the rest of us, they find it painful to abandon familiar, long-cherished ideas. Herein lies another major challenge for corporate boards. For if they are to find an alternative to charismatic succession, board members must let go of old beliefs and faulty theories about leadership and organizations. Given the relationship between the structures and beliefs now governing the external CEO succession process and the social systems in which this process is embedded, directors must take a critical attitude toward existing social ideas—including many that are deeply ingrained—about the efficacy of charisma and the nature of "leadership" itself.

There are two commonly followed ways of thinking about organizational leadership. One—which has become dominant in the age of the charismatic CEO—is to say that leaders should be chosen for their personal characteristics and then held personally responsible for their decisions. A second, which was actually practiced in the age of managerial capitalism, is to deny the importance of personality altogether and to attempt to construct impersonal institutions. Yet there is an alternative to this either/or choice, one that recognizes that institutions and the individuals who lead them reflect and influence one another—indeed, that they are inextricably interwoven. As the philosopher Karl Popper wrote in his great work *The Open Society and Its Enemies*, "The principle of leadership does not replace institutional problems by problems of personnel, it only creates new institutional problems. . . . [I]t even burdens the institutions with a task which goes beyond what can be reasonably demanded from a mere institution, namely, with *the task of selecting the future leaders*."[30]

The latter observation points to one of the key contradictions within the idea of charismatic organizational leadership. For even granting for the sake of argument the validity of the whole notion, it is impossible to devise institutional processes for finding leaders who will really "break the mold" in the way that all CEOs are now, at least in theory, supposed to. As Popper pointed out, institutional processes for selecting leaders—whether they be formal or informal, explicit or implicit—never work well because they "always tend to eliminate initiative and originality, and, more generally, qualities which are unusual and unexpected." It is simply not efficacious, he went on to observe, to "burden" institutions with the "impossible task of selecting the best."[31] Such an approach to succession also transforms the process into a race or contest, thus turning the system into one that emphasizes individual gain at the expense of organizational excellence.

The futility of trying to use institutional processes for selecting "leaders" (as opposed to managers) is well illustrated by the process of social matching that lies at the heart of external CEO succession. Although there is no demonstrable validity to the categories used in the social matching process to sort candidates for the job of CEO, directors continue using them, to a great extent because they are legitimated by society at large, thus offering a path of least resistance when difficult decisions might otherwise have to be made. It will thus take no small measure of intellectual independence and courage for directors to begin examining their received ideas about who is qualified to be a CEO, and then to stand up to outsiders—particularly analysts, investors, and business journalists—who stand ready to demand that the new CEO conform to their favored image.

The fiercest resistance to change, however, that any directors bold enough to question the conventional wisdom will have to face will come from their own peers in the boardroom. After all, as everyone knows, most corporate directors are CEOs themselves, and thus the direct beneficiaries of a way of thinking that creates an artificial scarcity of "talent" and thereby justifies paying CEOs with boundless extravagance. Being only human, directors naturally use the rules of the social institutions within which they operate to pursue their own advantage. For this reason, it is incumbent on the rest of society to own up to its own role in maintaining the various fictions on which the reign of the charismatic CEO depends, and to face its own responsibility for introducing some rationality into the way that CEOs are chosen, evaluated, and rewarded.

INSTITUTIONAL INVESTORS, BUSINESS SCHOOLS, AND THE BUSINESS PRESS

If phenomena such as the closed nature of the external CEO labor market and today's excessive CEO pay packages truly represent, as I believe they do, the breakdown of a system, the good news is that this failure presents a genuine opportunity to create a better one—not by tearing down structures in the vain hope that a "free" market will spontaneously emerge in their place and rectify the situation, but rather by reforming underlying structures and altering beliefs. So, for example, because the vast majority of corporate equity is held by institutions acting as the agents of individual shareholders, investors have significant leverage in pushing for reform. And because the external CEO market, as a socially constructed institution, is constituted to a great extent by widely shared beliefs, its present way of operating could be changed by bringing those beliefs into greater congruence with observable social and organizational reality. The more the present system and its underpinnings are questioned, the more susceptible to change it will become—although, as sociology tells us, it is no small undertaking to induce people to question the kinds of fundamental beliefs that create and support such institutions.

For society at large, as well as for corporate directors, unquestioning belief in the desirability of charismatic authority itself is one of the key obstacles to reforming the present system of CEO search. In the age of investor capitalism, faith in charismatic authority has become an increasingly crucial element in the subjugation of critical thinking. Within many organizations, the shift from rational to charismatic succession has come to be taken for granted so that nobody now remembers that succession was ever handled in any other way. In the larger society, as we have noted, faith in the efficacy of charismatic authority is bound up with the sacrosanct individualism that characterizes American culture. So strong are the beliefs that sustain the existing external CEO labor market that the bizarre processes by which many CEOs are now selected and compensated have come to appear part of the natural order of things. To question such beliefs is to leave oneself open to the suspicion that one is a dangerous radical, or simply mad.

Ultimately, then, long-term change in the CEO labor market will require overturning the current consensus among professional investors and the public at large about the validity of the charismatic CEO model. Institutional investors, in particular, will need to be educated about the organizational realities hidden or distorted by popular myths about heroic corporate saviors. (One of the potential silver linings to the Enron disaster is investors' new awareness of how seriously they can be, and have been, misled by the spirit of an uncritical age and the blandishments of charismatic corporate leaders.) Organizational theory points to two institutions that can play a role in affecting the support and legitimacy that the charismatic CEO model now commands: professional business education and the business media. In their present forms, these two institutions tacitly support the orientation toward charismatic leadership on the part of executives, investors, and other corporate constituents by the way that they shape and reinforce existing thought and discourse on the relationship between the CEO and firm performance. Without changes to these institutions, I believe that any changes to the existing order will likely be incremental and have little substantive impact.

Business education has come to exercise enormous influence as business itself has become thoroughly dependent on professionally trained individuals—so much so that it is increasingly rare to find a management consultant, professional director, investment banker, analyst, venture capitalist, or executive who does not have some professional business training through either an MBA or an executive education program. The formal educational process in business schools is one powerful means through which new ideas are promulgated, legitimated, and diffused throughout organizations. The professional networks that this process produces as a second-order effect are another. Thus both the content of business education and the networks that it creates and maintains can be used to dislodge prevalent misconceptions about the role of the CEO in affecting corporate performance.[32]

The purpose of business education is to train and develop professionals with the skills to analyze and deal effectively with the complex problems of business. Professional business education ultimately seeks to inculcate both an understanding of the fundamentals of business and the ability to respond to the demands of actual business situations. The case method of instruction is central to this objective. In the case method—rooted in the Socratic tradition of active discussion—learning occurs not just through the students' mastery of the substantive content of a case but also through an interaction in which students and instructor explore the full complexity of the case situation. The power of effective case instruction is well known. The emotional drama that develops when those with differing perspectives seek both to advance their ideas and to better understand the ideas of others creates a powerful learning experience.

To understand the relevance of the case method to what business school students learn about the role of the CEO, it is important to note that the case approach puts students in the shoes of a protagonist facing a complex, multifaceted, real-life business problem. In recent years, the field of organizational behavior has used this aspect of the case method quite effectively to teach students about leadership. In contrast to research that has muted the importance of individual agency and indirectly encouraged other-directed leadership behaviors, we have made significant strides in encouraging students to be more inner-directed and to rely on their own individual talents, intuitions, skills, and experiences to become more effective organizational actors. We have provided students with a number of frameworks for understanding how those in leadership positions can better motivate others and align the interests of organizational members with those of the organization. We have taught them that they do not have to accept the status quo and can be active in changing their companies' environments. We have provided them with a set of tools, grounded in our understanding of how to affect human behavior, that lets them tap into the basic drives of human beings to acquire material goods, do well at their jobs, and feel that their lives are purposeful and meaningful.

Yet despite these achievements, the leadership model currently taught in business schools stands in need of further development. Written from the point of view of a single CEO protagonist—as are many leadership cases with which I am familiar—our pedagogical tools can subtly reinforce the charismatic orientation that dominates contemporary discussions of leadership, particularly the assumptions that leadership exists primarily at the CEO level and that individual corporate leaders, especially those at the top of the organizational hierarchy, exercise more control over organizational outcomes than they actually do. Students, understandably, have an easier time identifying with an individual's perspective on a situation than gaining a more comprehensive view of it. (An increased emphasis on cases involving non-CEO leaders, and drawing on the perspectives of multiple protagonists, might be one way of counteracting the idea that a single individual's actions can solve the complex problems with which leaders are usually faced.) Yet they need to learn not just about the possibilities but also about the constraints facing organizational leaders.

By pointing out that leaders are constrained in their decision-making by many stubborn factors, we can teach our students that these individuals often find themselves in positions in which they have only limited control over events.[33] As Michael Cohen and James March have argued, we do our leaders a disservice when we overemphasize their power to affect their situations and downplay the limitations placed on them by the force of circumstance.[34] We put competent people in untenable positions when their constituents tend to assume that a leader has the power to do whatever he or she chooses simply by virtue of holding a formal office. By expanding our teaching of leadership to consider the constraints that leaders face, we can not only help them to do their jobs better but also reduce the temptation for them to attribute all good outcomes to themselves. If we can teach future leaders to think of themselves less as heroes and more as people who face difficult decisions, and to recognize the tradeoffs involved in making their choices, we will be more likely to see them ask for help from others and seek social support for their judgment rather than feeling as if they must have all the answers all the time.[35]

While the business education process and the networks it creates have a profound impact on how members of the business elite think about the role of the CEO, another influential institution—the contemporary business press—has driven a trend toward the popularization of management theories. In the last decade, mass media, especially newspapers and magazines, have increased their coverage of both management ideas and business firms. Yet the business media's role has come to extend beyond simply conveying information and opinion. The business press is now a kind of stepchild of the business education establishment, having itself become a producer and legitimator of management ideas. Because most corporate managers have an aversion to management "theory," especially when it is described as such, many of their ideas about business are increasingly influenced by what they read in the daily newspapers, management magazines, and industry journals as well as by what they watch on CNN and CNBC. Whether individual journalists acknowledge it or not, the business media have become a critical power broker in the construction of management ideas. Like the Internet (once it had evolved from an obscure communications protocol into a phenomenon sui generis), the loose-jointed business press of today is all the more powerful because its influence is pervasive, indirect, and atmospheric. In this new form, it occupies an important intermediary role among investors, board members, analysts, the general public, and the firm. It has become part of the very process by which these actors understand and interpret reality, telling people both what to think about and how to think about it in the realm of business.

Management scholars who study the role of the media in business have uncovered a general pattern through which the business press has become a source of new management theories. These scholars find that what often start out as nuanced academic ideas are turned into fads once they have been filtered through the mass media, which ground these often complex concepts in ideology, rhetoric, symbols, and illustrations that endow them with popular appeal. Through their expertise in storytelling and adroit use of symbolic tools such as dramatization, the media have even begun to influence the very way that people make inferences about cause and effect. As Robert Eccles and Nitin Nohria have shown in *Beyond the Hype*, the ability to convey an idea through a dramatic story increases the legitimacy of the idea and the rapidity with which it is diffused.[36] The political scientist James Barber, for his part, describes journalists as the mythmakers of our age:

> The painters of those [journalistic] pictures, when they can get them believed, exercise a power that is nothing less than the power to set a course of civilization. In modern politics, lacking grander visions, we make do with glimpses of possibility and shades of meaning—a kaleidoscope of fact and metaphor and judgment. Journalism, our composite Homer, delivers those partial sightings, which substitute for heroic myth. If it is the default of the political parties that burdens journalism with sorting out candidates, it is the default of the contemporary intellectuals that leaves to journalists the task of composing our ruling ideas.[37]

While Barber's focus is on the role of the media in contemporary electoral politics, his ideas have important implications for the phenomenon of the charismatic CEO. As we have seen, the relationship between CEOs and firms is often constructed in the form of legends and myths about the spectacular (positive or negative) effects a CEO can have on firm performance. Dramatizations of the impact that a "good" CEO like Jack Welch can have on a firm create a powerful narrative that serves to reinforce the cult of the charismatic CEO. Even boards of directors, as we have also noted, are often guided in their strategic decision-making by the legends of successful CEOs, frequently related by the business press in coarse-grained, over-simplified stories that attribute far too much influence to individuals than is warranted by any realistic view of large organizations in complex environments.[38]

While the business media have participated in the construction and legitimization of the charismatic CEO model, this same institution can also help to change that model. Because the media can focus attention on a subject and put it on the public agenda, they can actively shape a more balanced account of the role of CEOs in corporations, educating directors, investors, analysts, and the lay public about the main factors affecting firm performance. Journalists need to focus less on the personality of the individual CEO and more on questions of strategy, industry conditions, and other real determinants of corporate success or failure. They also need to become more skeptical. The steep rise and spectacular fall of Enron and its onetime CEO, Jeffrey Skilling, offers a particularly telling illustration of the dangers of shining the spotlight on a charismatic CEO while neglecting to subject his more visionary claims to careful scrutiny. It at least seems plausible that more hard-headed coverage of Enron by the business press might have raised some red flags before belated revelations about the company's finances abruptly shattered investors' trust and sent the firm into a tailspin.

FAREWELL TO OZ: EXTERNAL CEO SEARCH AND THE MYTH OF THE SELF-REGULATING MARKET

While a more realistic view of the nature of, and requirements for, the CEO position would go a long way toward opening up the closed process that external CEO succession has become, this particular shift in viewpoint is not all that is needed. The problem is more recalcitrant than that. All closed social systems are difficult to break open because the breakdown of closure creates strain. This strain is most evident in situations where the privileges conferred by closure begin to disappear, as illustrated, for example, by the birth of the civil rights movement or the end of apartheid in South Africa. The closed society resists opening. To its ruling members, caste and the distinction between leaders and followers are natural in the sense of being both taken for granted and unquestionable. When a social system begins to open up, this certitude disappears. Those who benefit from the system fight to maintain their privileges amid the turmoil that arises as previously submerged problems of class and social status come to the surface.

In the modern world, one of the most powerful forces for breaking down closed social and political systems has been the capitalist economic system, at least in those times and places where capitalism has been introduced in such a way as to foster genuine competition. Real competition tends to undermine the privileges of closure; conversely, closure is effectively the restraint of competition. Examining the relevance of these truths to the closed system that is the external CEO labor market today, we arrive at the supreme irony that—to the extent that capitalism is a system based on openness and competition—corporate directors, when they come to choose a new CEO, can be some of the fiercest opponents of capitalism anywhere. How can we have been so slow to perceive such a gigantic contradiction?

In all human societies, from the most primitive to the most advanced, magical or otherwise irrational attitudes toward the customs of social life endow these customs with the robustness that they need to survive and reproduce themselves. No one has discussed this phenomenon more perceptively than the sociologist Emile Durkheim, who showed how societies attempt to erase the distinction between the customary or conventional regularities of social life and the regularities found in the natural world. Often this is accomplished through the belief that both social customs and natural laws are enforced by a larger, supernatural will. Taboos then serve to protect customs, institutions, and ideas from becoming objects of critical consideration. As actors assume their postures and play their roles, the entire social spectacle takes on an appearance of objectivity, thereby gaining the complicity of a society's members. Society is thus, in Durkheim's words, a sui generis. All the subsystems of a society, such as its economic and cultural elements, are part of a structurally interrelated whole, unified by a set of inner rules and principles. For Durkheim, the governing principle at the heart of society was the sacred and the unspoken. For Marx—and, ironically, for most of today's economic conservatives—it is the system of economic relations that determines everything else.

For most traditional societies, it is true, the larger, supernatural will believed to govern the visible world and establish its customs has been that of a god or godlike figure. In today's secular societies, this supernatural will is increasingly conceived of as the "invisible hand" of the market. In economic terms, certainly nothing represents the ethos of American society over the last two decades so well as the belief in open, competitive markets and the related conviction that, as part of the natural order, markets are not to be subjected to human manipulation. There is, indeed, much to be said for competition. As the economist Friedrich von Hayek noted, there are few systems for organizing an economy so effectively as the competitive market and pricing system. The disadvantages of closed and bureaucratically organized economic activity have been demonstrated clearly in numerous experiments conducted around the world. If competition is so effective a way of ordering a process of allocation, however, why is there so little of it in the external CEO labor market? How can a closed market persist in the very citadels of American capitalism, the boardrooms and CEO suites of the nation's largest corporations? To a great extent, this is because of the claim—made despite all evidence to the contrary—that the external CEO market is open and competitive. In our society, primary responsibility for this form of mystification can be laid directly at the feet of the practitioners of today's neoclassical economics, a school of thought that, during the twenty-year period that has seen the rise of investor capitalism and of the charismatic CEO, has in many ways assumed the character of a charismatic discipline.

Markets—as the case of the external CEO market makes clear—are not natural phenomena. They are constituted, set in motion, and reproduced by the interaction of social and cultural values and structures, which can and do severely limit their self-regulating capacities. These values and structures, however, are not even of empirical interest to any but a relative handful of economists.[39] For mainstream practitioners of economics, society and culture are (to borrow W. B. Yeats's summary of the Platonic view of nature) "but a spume that plays / Upon a ghostly paradigm of things." Moreover, just as charismatic CEO candidates dazzle corporate directors by their affiliations and status rather than their abilities, neoclassical economics derives much of its power and mystique from similarly extraneous sources.[40]

When contemplating such phenomena as the intellectual hegemony of neoclassical economics or the flawed economic and social outcomes that the ideology of the self-regulating market is used to explain and justify, it is always tempting to blame them on conspiracies. Indeed, the way that sociologists and other students of society have traditionally sought to explain how certain individuals, groups, and organizations maintain their privileged positions is to talk about how they manipulate the social structure for their own advantage. While such uses of power are a fact of social life, conspiracy theories offer little hope of doing anything to restrain them. Besides being frequently difficult to prove, conspiracy hypotheses ignore the fact that members of groups can and do cooperate with one another to preserve their own advantages without having designed (or even reflected on) the social structure as a whole. Moreover, to the extent that flawed social structures are maintained by ideas and beliefs, we all help keep them in place by refusing responsibility for thinking critically about the world around us.

This is not a new or particularly radical idea in America. In one of the most enduringly popular expressions of the traditional American ideals of self-reliance and self-determination, *The Wizard of Oz*, we are taught an important lesson: by pulling back the veil with which power masks its inner workings, we learn not only how the illusions that dominate us are manufactured but also how their maintenance depends on our ignorance of our own powers and abdication of responsibility for ourselves. Along with much else that can be said about them, the cult of the charismatic CEO, the succession process that keeps it going, and the cultural beliefs that contribute to both, all depend on mystifications fully equal in their power to enchant to any of the wonders of Oz. We need to start looking behind the veil to become a more mature, self-aware, and responsible society.

Research Design, Methods, and Sample

When I began the research that became *Searching for a Corporate Savior*, I did not expect to learn what I have written about in the foregoing pages. As a doctoral student trying to describe the CEO labor market in terms of existing economic and sociological theory, I expected to find that the external CEO market was much like any other managerial labor market. For example, when I began my research on executive search firms, I believed that they would prove to be market brokers in the classical sense of the term—that is, parties that connected firms and potential candidates who were unknown to one another. I went into executive search firms seeking evidence to confirm this hypothesis. However, after several months of interviewing consultants and working with their research departments hoping to understand how a search firm uses its networks to find CEO candidates, while also extensively observing how directors and candidates behaved in the search process, I realized that the role of executive search firms was very different from what was commonly understood. It could not be adequately described with concepts such as matching supply with demand or filling structural holes. Something else was clearly at work in this and many other aspects of the external CEO search process.

What that "something else" proved to be is broadly illustrated by an interview with a corporate director that I conducted not long after completing my doctoral dissertation on CEO turnover in 1998, by which point I had already begun to suspect that the external CEO market was indeed (as I have put it in the title of chapter 2) "a different kind of market." For many of the same social and cultural dynamics evident in the course of this single, relatively short encounter play themselves out on a larger stage when large corporations today go into the external market in search of a new CEO.

It was still dark when early one December morning I left my parents' home in Ridgefield, Connecticut, where I had driven from Massachusetts the night before, to catch the 5:39 Metro-North train to New York City. The train arrived at Grand Central Station at 6:32, leaving me plenty of time before my 7:30 breakfast meeting. I walked from the station to the Waldorf Astoria Hotel, which—even though I grew up in New York City (albeit in Queens, which people from Manhattan will tell you is not really New York)—I had never set foot in before.

I was meeting with a director of three large, publicly held corporations who had agreed to be interviewed on the topic of CEO succession. I had been able to make an appointment with this individual through two contacts—one with a search consultant whose firm I had been researching, and another with a director whom I had recently interviewed. (The director who had referred me to the individual I was about to meet was someone I had met through a professor at the Harvard Business School.) Without these initial personal introductions, I would have never been able to secure my present appointment.

The director I was going to have breakfast with—whom I will refer to as John—was in New York on board business. Although I had never met John, I immediately recognized him when he walked into the Peacock Alley (the restaurant, now closed, that was then located just off the hotel lobby). His face was familiar to me from the annual reports and business magazine articles I had studied before our meeting. We sat down for breakfast. John, who had enough of a paunch to suggest that he probably enjoyed a good meal, nevertheless ordered a fruit salad with cottage cheese. I ordered the same, although I would have preferred eggs. In these kinds of situations, I had learned, it was best to follow the lead of the interviewee.

John's persona exuded the kind of confidence one would expect from a person in his position. He looked directly at me when speaking. His voice was deep and assertive. He seemed like someone who had probably played football in college. And although it was December in New York City, he sported a healthy tan. We engaged in some social conversation. John was in town for a board meeting, but would be returning to his vacation home in Palm Springs later in the day. He already knew some things about me. Obviously, he had spoken to his director colleague, who had provided him with some background on my research. Most importantly, John told me that the referring director had described me as a "good guy." In a social ritual with which I was becoming familiar, we then began trying to identify other people we both knew. John named a couple of the directors of the company I had worked for before graduate school in an attempt to identify a common acquaintance. I knew the names, but admitted that I had been at a level of the organization where I would not have been known to these individuals. We then spoke briefly about the director who had referred me to John. After a moment or two of discussion, we both agreed that he was a "really good guy." Then, without missing a beat, John shifted the conversation to the matter at hand. "You are interested in CEO succession," he said. "Let's talk CEO succession."

We spoke for nearly ninety minutes. During this time, John described to me the CEO successions he had been involved in, offering perspectives from both sides of the transaction. John himself had once been an outside candidate for the CEO position at a major corporation, a position he eventually was offered, accepted, and had recently retired from. One of the search firms I had been working with had placed him in this job. As a director of several large public corporations, he was now on the "demand side," no longer a "supply-sider," he joked. Having not only served on boards and search committees engaged in external CEO searches but also having headed a search committee, he had some significant understanding of the CEO firing and hiring processes. For the purposes of this interview, I tried to steer the conversation toward CEO hiring, especially outsider CEO hiring.

John's descriptions of the searches he had been involved in were detailed. He began by pointing out that forced CEO successions were rare events but becoming more common. He discussed the pressures exerted on boards by Wall Street analysts and the business media, the "short-term" perspectives of analysts and institutional investors, and how boards often responded to the demands of these constituents by firing the CEO. He then described the difficulty of finding "real leaders." There was "a shortage of real leaders" inside most firms, John assured me. Moreover, getting one of the few "real leaders" in the corporate world to change jobs was both difficult and expensive. In discussing one of the searches he had been involved in, John described how directors "almost always already had some names in mind" for the position. The "big question" was whether these individuals would be interested in the position. In describing how boards learned which potential candidates were available and which were not, John spoke of the search consultants he had worked with in ways that were colorful, funny, and subtly scornful of the search profession in general. Finally, he described the process by which the board focused on the few final candidates, and why it eventually chose one candidate over the others.

Toward the end of our conversation, I asked John whether the process he was describing for selecting candidates identified the best person for the job. (I had not yet begun to form any opinion about this myself.) Obviously irritated by the question, he replied, "Of course it does." Perhaps the fact that he had reached the CEO suite by means of this very process determined his response. At any rate, my question prompted him to reiterate the points he had made at the start of our discussion. CEO succession was a rare event, but the decision about who to appoint as CEO was the most important one that a board ever made. It was a decision that affected a number of constituencies, and their reactions to it had to be anticipated. John argued that the process was very dependent on individuals' judgments, and therefore that much hinged on the quality of the judges. A board, he assured me, did not take this task lightly and was vigorous in pursuing any and all information about a candidate it could gather.

I took careful notes while John recapitulated many, if not most, of the points that I was beginning to see illustrated again and again the more I studied external CEO searches. Yet some of what I was learning had to do not just with what he and other directors I was meeting (along with candidates and search consultants relating their own sides of the story) were telling me but also with the social codes, behaviors, and rituals that I both observed and participated in during the course of our interview. The same kinds of rules that both enabled and shaped my encounter with John—rules about matters such as presentation of self, status and hierarchy, and what kinds of shared affiliations established a presumption of common values and permitted a measure of self-revelation—were, I was beginning to realize, absolutely essential to the functioning of the external CEO market. I didn't know what kind of market it was or if it even *was* a market, but I was coming to believe that it deviated in profound and significant ways from existing theory and popular accounts.

Field Data Sources

Elites are notoriously difficult individuals to get access to. To get started with my field research, I relied on faculty members at the Harvard Business School to introduce me to search consultants and directors. Many Harvard Business School faculty are board members, and several of them offered to introduce me to fellow directors. I then used these initial connections to get access to other directors.

The forty directors I interviewed ranged in age from fifty-seven to seventy-two. Eighteen of them were either active or retired CEOs of *Fortune* 500 companies. Most were currently active members of the boards of large, publicly held companies. Many had also served on several other boards over the years. Several of these directors served on boards together. My estimates suggest that, via such director interlocks, I had indirect access to about one-fifth of the *Fortune* 1000 firms.

To prepare myself for the director interviews, I analyzed various documents about the firms with which these directors were associated. Among the most important were annual reports, 10Ks and 10Qs, and reports in the business press, especially from the *Wall Street Journal*, the *New York Times*, *Fortune*, and *Business Week*.

Typically, interviews with directors lasted from one to two hours. I tried to focus the interviewees on successions they had been involved in between 1990 and 2002. In total, forty separate succession events across fifty-five companies between 1990 and 2001 were discussed in depth.

When discussing CEO succession with directors, I found that the use of executive search firms came up in every discussion. I realized that I knew very little about search firms, and so soon after my first interviews with directors I began to look for an entry into this industry. Serendipitously, a Harvard Business School MBA classmate had done a summer internship at one of the large search firms and offered to introduce me to her executive sponsor there. At the same time, I was able to make contact with two other search firms. After several visits and phone calls, two of the largest search firms agreed to let me study their work in depth. Working with my search firm executive sponsors, I arranged meetings with the search consultants who focused on CEO searches for large corporations. While most of my meetings were in New York City, I also interviewed search consultants based in other locations including Atlanta, Chicago, and Palo Alto.

My interviews with search consultants typically lasted from ninety minutes to three hours. At the conclusion of the interview process, I had conducted thirty interviews with consultants and developed scores of mini-cases on CEO searches.[1] In addition, I conducted follow-up phone and e-mail exchanges with several consultants to clarify issues as my knowledge of the industry and of the search process increased.

I experimented with tape recording and not tape recording interviews. Ultimately, my impression was that recorded interviews were more self-conscious and uncomfortable for the interviewee. I also found that by taking notes I was more involved and attentive to the interviewee. I took extensive notes during each of the interviews, which I typically transcribed within two days.

The interview guide I developed for studying both directors and executive search firms focused on three key areas: (1) the factors surrounding CEO succession, (2) the directors' and search consultants' exact roles during the CEO search, and (3) why a particular candidate eventually was selected. I encouraged the interviewees to talk about specific cases, not in generalities, when discussing the search process. In an attempt to capture as much detail about the search process as possible, I asked the interview subjects to focus on CEO searches since 1990 (about which their memories were likely to be better than about searches conducted before that date). I relied on an open-ended interviewing technique to discuss the CEO succession and selection process. With all my subjects, my approach was to carry on a partially guided conversation that elicited rich, contextual detail that could be used for analysis.

I supplemented my interview data with data from several other sources. I spent fifty hours conducting field observations of actual CEO and director searches. Some consultants allowed me to listen in on phone conversations with candidates and clients. Here I became informed about the perceptions of the various participants concerning the market and how well a particular search was proceeding. I was also permitted to directly observe and communicate with the search firm research staffs working on particular searches.

Field Data Analysis

For two years after completing my dissertation, I gathered additional field data on directors, candidates, search firms, external CEO successions, and the CEO labor market while also studying sources such as archival data and case files. I simultaneously began the process of reanalyzing my data with the goal of understanding the external CEO market using more general concepts. My approach was to separate what I had studied into two elements, content and form. I saw content as the interests and motives behind the actions of the participants in the market, and form as the specific process through which the interests and motives of the various participants were pursued. In reality, as several social theorists have noted, the two terms are inseparable and the distinction is only analytical (Simmel 1902; Weber, Roth, and Wittich 1978).

To get at the form of the phenomenon I mostly used techniques suggested by Strauss and Corbin (1990) to identify the phases common to all the searches I was studying. Based on the mini-case files I had compiled (see below), I wrote narratives summarizing each of the specific searches studied. I then broadly open-coded the various manifestations of participants' understanding of the CEO labor market. I looked for shared sentiments, references, and perceptions in the interviews that extended beyond the specific cases being discussed. Then, when I found disagreement in, for example, search consultants' descriptions of the process, I sought to understand the reasons for this deviation. Through this process of reconciling the general tendencies with the exceptional cases, theoretical concepts emerged through continued analysis as I sifted and resifted through my field notes, followed up with consultants, and acquired additional information about particular firms. It was during this time that I started to become aware of the form of the external CEO market with its defining features of small numbers of buyers and sellers, risk to participants, and concerns about legitimacy.

Next I began to identify the content of the interactions in the external CEO market. I analyzed the accounts given by interviewees regarding their activities during the search and the reasons given for these activities. In this analysis I took an iterative approach, going back and forth between the interview data and presenting my impressions and developing understanding of the process to colleagues. Further, during periodic updates about the progress of my research, I discussed my findings and thoughts with my executive sponsors from the search firms and with directors.

Statistical Data

DATA AND METHODS

Sample. The statistical data used in this book consists of the *Fortune* 500 for 1980 plus the 100 largest commercial banks, 100 largest financial services firms, 100 largest retail firms, and 50 largest transportation firms. I follow each of these firms through 1996. Executive compensation data was collected from 1991 to 2000. While the selection of large corporations limits the generalizability of my results, I decided on these firms because they are widely followed in the business media, which in turn offers more complete information on company events than is available for smaller firms.

Exhaustive data on the CEO changes within these firms was collected for the period between 1980 and 1996. These successions include all successions between 1980 and 1996 that satisfy the following criteria: (1) the incumbent and successor both can be identified, (2) the *Wall Street Journal*, *New York Times*, or *Business Week* reported the succession announcement, (3) characteristics of the CEO's tenure with the firm and in the position could be collected, and (4) the succession was not directly related to a takeover. These criteria were met in all cases.

Forbes' annual *Executive Survey*, Dun and Bradstreet's *Reference Book of Corporate Management*, Standard and Poor's *Register of Corporations*, and firm proxy statements (10Q and 10K) are used to collect information on CEO tenure, years with the firm, and age. The exact date of and reason for each succession is obtained from the media announcements.

Financial data for the firms was collected from Standard and Poor's COMPUSTAT database.

Board of director data was compiled from Dun and Bradstreet's *Reference Book of Corporate Management*, Standard and Poor's *Register of Corporations*, and firm proxy statements (10Qs and 10Ks).

Executive compensation data was collected from Standard and Poor's Execucomp database.

DEPENDENT VARIABLES AND METHODS

CEO *Firing.* For the analysis of CEO dismissals presented in figure 3.3, I studied the event of forced dismissal. I created two discrete categories of turnover: natural turnover (coded 1) and forced turnover (coded 2). The baseline was no turnover. Therefore I used a multiple-destination event-history model. Forced turnover includes cases in which a CEO departs before age sixty-one and does not leave for an equivalent position at another firm. Natural turnover consists of cases in which a CEO departs for another job or leaves because of retirement, illness, or death.

The logic of the model assumes three possible outcomes for CEO changes: (1) CEOs who do not change their jobs; (2) CEOs who voluntarily move to another job or reach the retirement age; and (3) CEOs who involuntarily leave their positions. The different destination states for CEO transitions require us to model these CEO events as competing risks:

$$T_{vt} = (T_{vt}^*)[f_{vt}(r_{vt})]$$

$$T_{it} = (T_{it}^*)[f_{it}(r_{it})]$$

where v and i refer to voluntary and involuntary turnover, and where each transition (T) is modeled conditional on the competing event not having occurred (Blossfeld and Rohwer 1995). Each of these competing events involves a discrete change of state. These changes can occur at any point in time and the model suggests that there are both time-constant and time-varying factors influencing these events.

The type of analysis used to model the competing events given both changing and constant independent variables is continuous-time transition rate analysis with time-varying co-variates. Effects on the transition rate are estimated by maximum-likelihood procedures that model the probability that a CEO moves out of a job given a set of co-variates. In other words, transition rates are conditional probabilities for the occurrence of the discrete events of interest (the rates of voluntary and involuntary turnover). My main interest lies in how dependent these events are on the set of independent variables I have identified.

As Tuma and Hannan (1984) point out, a number of different continuous-time stochastic models can be specified for the transition equations specified above. I used the log-logistic distribution to model the time dependence of the CEO transition process since this model explicitly models CEO changes in terms of waiting times. To examine the appropriateness of this model, I compared the maximized log-likelihoods assuming this model against those for the exponential, Weibull, and log-normal models; I found that the log-logistic model provided a better fit to the data (significant $<.01$). A visual and regression test of the parametric assumptions suggests that the log-logistic model provides the best linear transformation. A regression test of the parametric assumptions suggests no substantive difference between either the log-normal model or the log-likelihood. The fully specified model with its logarithmic time-dependence is specified as:

$$r_{jk}(t) = \frac{b_{jk}(a_{jk}t)^{bjk-1}}{1+(a_{jk}t)^{bjk}}$$

$$a_{jk} = \exp\{A^{(jk)}a^{(jk)}\}, b_{jk} = \exp\{B^{(jk)}b^{(jk)}\}$$

where r is the transition rate from origin state j to destination states k. The associated co-variates, $a^{(jk)}$ and $b^{(jk)}$ are the model parameters to be estimated.

Outsider Succession. An outside CEO appointment is defined as one in which the new CEO assumes the CEO title within one year of the date that he or she joins the firm. I classify CEOs who join the firm as long as one year before their appointment as outsiders because new CEOs who have been employed at the firm for only one year are likely to have been hired with the expectation that they would eventually be appointed to the CEO position. Hiring an executive before the CEO succession allows him or her to obtain additional specific human capital necessary for the position. The above definition of outside CEOs is consistent with the wide range of definitions used in other studies. For instance, Reinganum (1985) classifies executives who join the firm at the time of the succession as outsiders, while Vancil (1987) includes all executives who have been employed at the firm for five years or less. In my sample, 27 percent of the successions involve outsiders.

To study the probability of outsider succession, I use both logit and multinomial logit estimations for analyses of the turnovers. I use logit modeling to understand the factors that affect the selection of insider versus outsider CEO candidates. I use multinomial logit modeling because I have a dependent variable that can take on more than two discrete outcomes and these outcomes have no natural ordering (i.e., no turnover, insider selection, outsider selection).[2] Both models are estimated as:

$$\text{Prob}(Y = j) \frac{e^{\beta_j' x_i}}{1 + \sum_{k=1}^{J} e^{\beta_j' x_i}}$$

where j is the number of outcomes and x is the estimator(s). If there are only two outcomes ($j = 2$), estimates are identical to those produced by logit modeling (Greene 1993: chap. 21).

INDEPENDENT VARIABLES

Tenure. CEO tenure is dated from the year the individual at the firm under consideration took the CEO position. Tenure was determined as the difference between the last year a CEO occupied the position and the start year, plus one. If the CEO continued to occupy the position in 1996, the observation was treated as censored. To avoid left-hand censoring, I coded the original start years of all the CEOs as of 1980. For example, Lee Iacocca, CEO of Chrysler in 1980, was originally appointed in 1978. Consequently, his start date is coded as 1978. As a result, I was able to measure the tenure of each CEO in the sample and, therefore, avoid the potential issue of survivor bias for subsequent CEO appointments. Tenure serves as the time clock for the event-history tables—that is, a CEO's tenure defines a "spell."

Firm Performance. I use annual operating returns of the firm to proxy the CEO's performance. The annual operating return for a firm is defined as the ratio of operating income before depreciation and taxes to operating assets. Because operating income does not include taxes, royalties, dividends, interest income received, or any dividends paid to stockholders, it is considered a robust measure of the operating performance of an organization (Smith 1990).

Founder. I coded a dichotomous variable to indicate firms in which the CEO is also the founder of the company. Founder CEOs are coded as 1, non-founder CEOs as 0. This variable proxies for the power that founder CEOs derive from their close identification with the company.

Separation of Chairman/CEO Positions. I coded a dichotomous variable to indicate firms in which the CEO and chairman positions are separate. The separation of the positions proxies for the relative control the CEO can exercise over the board's access to information and resources. Firms in which the positions are separate are coded as 1. Firms in which the two positions are held by the same person are coded as 0.

Year of Hire. Dummy variables for the period during which the CEO was hired are included in the model. These dummy variables capture both the effects of the social conditions during the period within which the CEO was hired and the effects of tenure. For the firing analysis, three categories were used: CEOs appointed before 1980, and CEOs appointed after 1985. The omitted category consists of those CEOs appointed between those two periods.

Director Composition and Interlocks. I compiled data on board of director composition and board interlocks. Inside board members were those directors identified as current or former executives of the firm. Insiders were coded as 1, outsiders as 0. I created two measures from this data.

First, I measured the total number of directors. I also created a percent-insiders measure to capture the relative strength of outside directors.

The "centrality" of a firm's board members to other firms is used to measure the embeddedness of the board within the interlocking directorate. When defining a network it is best to be as inclusive as possible in determining which elements of the network to include, particularly when the diffusion of information and practices among contacts is at issue; thus, I compiled board data for all firms required to report board composition to the SEC. This includes all firms in the sample. Inside board members are those directors identified as executives, former executives, or others financially connected (e.g., affiliated law firm or consultant) to the firm.

Board interlocks are defined as the sum of all ties a firm's board had to all other boards in this sample, that is, the total number of other boards each director sat on, summed across all directors (minus any redundant ties). As discussed in chapter 4, both directors and search consultants believe that the board of directors is a primary source of specific information on potential candidates. In a direct attempt to more closely operationalize the concept of how some boards would have better information than others, I asked interviewees, "How could this be known?" Both the search consultants and directors consistently responded that the ability of the board to access other directors who could provide more detailed information about the candidate mattered. In particular, the directors and other CEOs they knew from board connections were important.

Because the interviewees suggest that the type of information necessary to make a CEO hiring decision is confidential and emerges from director connections, I include two measures of centrality. The first measure used is degree centrality, which is simply the number of interlocks minus any redundant ties. It considers the direct connections a firm has to other firms (Davis 1991; Haunschild 1993).

The absolute number of firm interlocks has been used to operationalize several concepts in the organizational literature. As discussed earlier, Davis (1991) and Haunschild (1993) have used number of interlocks as a measure of normative and mimetic influence, respectively, on a firm's board. Others have used it as a general information measure (Useem 1984). This measure has also been used by organizational economists to argue that heavily interlocked boards are often too busy to govern effectively. Core, Holthausen, and Larcker (1997, 16–17), for example, argue that large numbers of interlocks reduce a board's ability to attend to its duties because of time constraints and thereby reduce board effectiveness.

A number of criticisms, however, have been directed at relying on this measure alone in director interlock studies. First, it is a proxy for several network concepts and, therefore, limited in its explanatory power for any single concept (Mizruchi and Bunting 1981). Second, the measure ignores the variance in the number of directors per company and, consequently, the potential of a firm to establish connections (Bonacich 1987). Finally, it weighs all interlocks equally and assumes a linear relationship between interlocks and other organizational characteristics, such as size (Mizruchi and Bunting 1981).

Thus, to isolate the information effects of director interlocks suggested by the field research, I use a second measure that has become more prominent in the network research to capture the prominence and depth of involvement of actors in relations with other actors—the Bonacich centrality measure. This captures the centrality of an actor by considering not only direct or adjacent ties of a firm's directorate but also indirect paths involving intermediaries. Thus, the Bonacich measure would capture the difference between a firm's being connected to IBM (a computer firm with many ties to other firms) versus connected to Grand Union (a supermarket chain with only one tie to other firms). The Bonacich measure includes this possibility by incorporating a parameter that reflects the extent to which an actor's centrality is a function of the centrality of actors to whom the actor is tied. This measure can be considered as an information indicator (Bonacich 1987; Hansen 1996). That is, better information is likely to be obtained from directors who are in contact with prominent or central directors who themselves are in contact with many other directors. The strength of this measure for the study of director interlocks has been described in several methodological reviews and empirical studies (Mintz and Schwartz 1981; Mizruchi 1982; Mizruchi and Bunting 1981). Formally,

$$C_i \approx \frac{1}{\lambda} \sum_{j=1}^{N} r_{ij} C_j$$

where N = number of organizations linked with i, rij equals the number of connections with the particular link, Cj equals the centrality of the organizations linked with i, and j is the largest eigenvector of the matrix r.

Because the two measures of centrality and Bonacich power are highly correlated and potentially likely to bias the standard errors, I use the residuals of Bonacich power as the measure.[3] This involves formalizing the relationship to model the overlap between the two centrality measures and using the residuals as the predictor. This measure separates out the degree-centrality effects from the information-centrality effects. This is a standard technique when correcting for multi-colinearity (Kennedy 1992). The assumption here is that multi-colinearity arises from an actual approximate linear relationship among some of the regressors, which in the case of the Bonacich measure and number of interlocks is mathematically true. Consequently, this relationship is formalized and the estimation then proceeds in the context of a simultaneous equation-estimation problem.

Chapter One: *"Everyone Knew He Was Brilliant"*

1. The source for much of the background information on Bank One is Hart and Utyerhoven (1996) "Banc One—1993."
2. Weber (2000) "The Mess at Bank One."
3. Hart and Utyerhoven (1996) "Banc One—1993."
4. In addition to my own interviews with Bank One executives, directors, and the search consultants, I relied extensively on an article by John Engen for *Corporate Board Member* magazine to corroborate my interviews and enrich the description of this case. See Engen (2000) "Hiring a Celebrity CEO."
5. Weber (2000) "The Mess at Bank One."
6. Ibid.
7. Cahill (1999) "CEO McCoy Quits a Flagging Bank One."
8. Ibid.
9. One director from the former First Chicago described Bank One's senior management as "those cowboys from Columbus, trying to take over an institution that almost single-handedly financed the growth of Chicago."
10. Wahl (2000b) "Bank One's Problems Go Deeper than Ailing Credit-Card Division."
11. Weber (2000) "The Mess at Bank One."
12. Ibid.
13. Cahill (1999) "CEO McCoy Quits a Flagging Bank One."
14. According to a report in *Barron's* that appeared months after the search was concluded, one Bank One investor, Bill Miller of Legg Mason Value Trust, submitted his own list of CEO candidates to the search committee, with the eventually successful candidate, Jamie Dimon, at the top of the list. See Laing (2000) "Fixer-Upper."
15. Engen (2000) "Hiring a Celebrity CEO."
16. Ibid.

17. Scism, Raghavan, and Siconolfi (1997) "Lost Trust"; and Anonymous (1998) "Finance and Economics: Fall Guy."

18. Lowenstein (2000) "Alone At The Top."

19. In addition to newspaper articles and interviews with several of the protagonists, Lowenstein (2000) "Alone at the Top" is the primary source of the background information on Citigroup, Sandy Weill, and the merger between Travelers and Citibank.

20. Ibid.

21. Ibid.

22. Ibid.

23. Ibid.

24. Ibid.

25. Ibid.

26. Ibid.

27. Scism, Raghavan, and Siconolfi (1997) "Lost Trust."

28. Lowenstein (2000) "Alone At The Top."

29. Ibid.

30. Ibid.

31. Scism, Raghavan, and Siconolfi (1997) "Lost Trust."

32. Lowenstein (2000) "Alone At The Top."

33. Ibid.

34. Ibid.

35. Ibid.

36. Ibid.

37. In my interviews with him, I also found Reed to be studied and precise in his remarks and discussions.

38. Lowenstein (2000) "Alone At The Top."

39. Ibid.

40. Ibid.

41. Silverman and Nathans Spiro (1999) "Is This Marriage Working?"

42. When Dimon was fired at Citigroup, its stock sank nearly $11 billion. See Loomis (2000) "Dimon Finds His 'Fat Pitch'; One Bank that Needs Saving."

43. Beckett and Raghavan (1999) "Former Citigroup President Dimon Gets $30 Million Separation Package."

44. Engen (2000) "Hiring a Celebrity CEO."

45. Raghavan (1999) "Deals & Deal Makers"; and Raghavan and Beckett (1999) "Companies Want Dimon To Become 'Mr. dot.com'."

46. Interview.

47. Interview.

48. Interview.
49. Interview.
50. Interview; and Engen (2000) "Hiring a Celebrity CEO."
51. Ibid.
52. Ibid.
53. As reported by ibid. and confirmed to me by Dimon.
54. Ibid.
55. Ibid. Dimon's employment agreement is available online (as of this writing) at http://tckrs.thecorporatelibrary.net/contracts/ceo_one.htm.
56. Engen (2000) "Hiring a Celebrity CEO"; and http://tckrs.thecorporatelibrary.net/contracts/ceo_one.htm.
57. Feldman (2000) "Has Bank One Found its Savior?"
58. Wahl (2000a) "Bank One Gains Wall Street Credibility."
59. Hintz (2000) "Boy Wonder."
60. Fitch (2000) "Dimon Dose a Shot in Arm."
61. Weiss (2000) "Jamie Dimon: The Wrong Man for the Bank One Job?"
62. Laing (2000) "Fixer-Upper."
63. In the account of Dimon's appointment that it published in March, the *Wall Street Journal* also reported that Dimon had wanted Istock to step down then instead of staying on as president, as the latter did until September 2000. See Raghavan and Sapsford (2000) "Jamie Dimon Takes Top Spot At Bank One."
64. Brunswick and Hayes (2000) "Dimon in the Rough."
65. Popper (2001) "Bank One Shares May Be Floating on Thin Air." The analyst Popper quotes is Tom McCandless of CIBC World Markets.

Chapter Two: A Different Kind of Market

1. Child (1972) "Organizational Structure, Environment and Performance," finds that the strategic decisions of top executives can have a substantial impact on firm performance. Lawrence and Lorsch (1967) *Organization and Environment*, study executive decisions about adapting particular organizational structures in response to changes in the technological environment and find that the adoption of the appropriate structures led to improved firm performance. Four more studies—Kotter (1988) *The Leadership Factor*, Kotter (1990) *A Force for Change*, Tedlow (2002) *Giants of Enterprise*, and Tedlow and John (1986) *Managing Big Business*—also provide well-documented examples of how executives can shape the success and failure of individual firms and even industries. A critique of the scholarship that relies on case-based or small-

sample approaches to understanding organizational births and organizational changes can be found in Hannan and Freeman (1989) *Organizational Ecology*.

2. Resource-dependence scholars argue that much of what affects a firm's performance is outside the control of the CEO; see, for example, Pfeffer and Salancik (1978) *The External Control of Organizations*. Population ecologists find that the structure of a firm's industry, the competitive intensity in that industry, a company's culture, and sunk investments in existing assets, predict firm performance much more reliably than do managerial intent or actions; see, for example, Hannan and Freeman (1989) *Organizational Ecology*. Some scholars argue that CEOs take advantage of the fact that a firm's performance is mostly predicted by external factors when they negotiate pay packages that reflect positive industry trends and protect themselves against negative industry trends; see Bertrand and Mullainathan (2000) "Do CEOs Set Their Own Pay?"

3. For a review of the scores of studies from this perspective on various industries, see Carroll and Hannan (2000) *The Demography of Corporations and Industries*; and Hannan and Freeman (1989) *Organizational Ecology*.

4. Carroll and Hannan (2000) *The Demography of Corporations and Industries*, 6–7.

5. Wasserman, Anand, and Nohria (2001) "When Does Leadership Matter?"; and Hambrick and Finkelstein (1987) "Managerial Discretion."

6. For two recent examples of how Greenspan has been treated as personally responsible for the recent success of the American economy, see Woodward (2000) *Maestro*, and Martin (2000) *Greenspan*. One of the most interesting facets of these works is the considerable attention they give to seemingly trivial details about Greenspan's personal habits, such as how heavy his briefcase appears when he is walking into a Federal Reserve meeting, or his love of jazz. Perhaps this is because Greenspan's public utterances are so jargon-laden and contradictory that even professional economists have difficulty decoding what he is saying, so that those who would interpret the man must resort to chewing on more easily digestible details.

7. The mechanism underlying performance-cue effects, in turn, is what social psychologists call the fundamental attribution error, which presents itself when people: (1) underestimate the power of a situation in explaining events; (2) overestimate the impact of a person; (3) attribute personality traits based on an observation of behavior, even in a strong situation. For a review of the concept, see Brown (1986) *Social Psychology*.

8. Brunswick and Hayes (2000) "Dimon in the Rough."

9. Eccles and Crane (1988) *Doing Deals*, 214–221.

10. Ibid.

11. Groysberg (2001) "Can They Take It with Them?"

12. Khurana and Nohria (1996) "Substance and Symbol."

13. Many corporate governance experts frown on this practice, arguing that it gives the CEO too much control over the agenda of board meetings and over directors' access to information. Research has also shown that when the CEO and chairman positions are combined, boards are less likely to dismiss poorly performing CEOs. Zelleke (2001) "The British 'Non-executive' Chairman" nicely summarizes the point:

> The central purpose of corporate governance is to ensure that management is *accountable* to the proper constituencies, however these may be identified in a particular national context. Boards of directors are charged with monitoring management to ensure that accountability. On that basis alone, an 'efficient' governance structure would seem to require that boards be free of the conflict of interest inherent in the board being chaired—and often, in practice, dominated—by the firm's top manager. The same logic suggests that boards composed of relatively few members of management would be more objective, and therefore effective, as monitors.

14. Merrick (2000) "Bank One Decides to Trim its Board." In my own research (Khurana 1998) I have found that, contrary to popular belief, larger boards are more likely to dismiss CEOs when performance is poor.

15. See Brunswick and Hayes (2000) "Dimon in the Rough." While there is nothing extraordinary, after all, about a CEO having power to dismiss members of his team, in this case the dismissals could be interpreted as self-protective or self-indulgent rather than in the best interests of the firm. When John Reed was selected CEO at Citigroup after a heated race with another executive, one of his first actions was to make peace with executives who had supported the other candidate.

16. As we shall see in chapter 4, it is principally on the supply side that scarcity in the external CEO labor market would appear to be artificially created.

17. Crystal (1992) *In Search of Excess;* and Bok (1993) *The Cost of Talent.*

18. To pay one's CEO at or below the median is to implicitly acknowledge that one has, at best, only an average CEO. Rather than admitting that their firms are run by "average" CEOs, most directors simply pay new CEOs as if they were above average. This phenomenon is what Graef Crystal (1992) has referred to as the "Lake Wobegon effect" in executive compensation.

19. Ibid., 222.

20. Marsden (1983) "Restricted Access in Networks and Models of Power."

21. Baker (1984) "The Social Structure of a National Securities Market."

22. Swedberg (1994) "Markets as Social Structures."

23. The 1993 CEO search at the financial services firm American Express (discussed in greater detail in chapter 6) also illustrates some of the more damaging things that can happen when the confidentiality of such a search is breached. Because of news leaks about potential outsider replacements for departing CEO James Robinson, the most desirable candidates for the American Express job publicly disavowed any interest in it. Moreover, the leaks exposed the various factions on the American Express board, each of which was backing a different candidate.

24. The basic idea of adverse selection is laid out in Akerlof's (1970) classic discussion of lemons in the used car market, "The Market for 'Lemons': Qualitative Uncertainty and the Market Mechanism."

25. For an excellent overview of the literature on agency theory, see Pratt and Zeckhauser (1991) "The Agency Relationship."

26. Fama and Jensen (1983) "Separation of Ownership and Control."

27. Jensen (1993) "The Modern Industrial Revolution, Exit, and the Failure of Internal Control Systems"; and Baker and Smith (1998) *The New Financial Capitalists*.

28. Lorsch and MacIver (1989) *Pawns and Potentates*.

29. Indeed, under such conditions transaction-cost theory predicts that such transactions will take place within the boundaries of the firm; see Williamson (1975) *Markets and Hierarchies*.

30. There has been a trend, of late, of CEOs refusing to accept a guaranteed bonus when the firm underperforms. Directors often respond to this gesture by granting the CEO more stock options. For a discussion of the unacknowledged liabilities imposed on firms by the practice of making large grants of stock options to senior executives, see chapter 7.

31. Scott (1995) *Institutions and Organizations*, 170. Most of the contemporary discussion of the issue of legitimacy is contained in institutional theory. In addition to the nice summary of the field contained in Scott, a variety of essays on the topic can be found in Powell and Dimaggio (1983) *The New Institutionalism of Organizational Analysis*.

32. This situation represents an extreme example, for in most cases the candidate is able to pretty much dictate the compensation terms. The complexity of the negotiation, however, extends to issues such as power-sharing arrangements between the board and the incoming CEO, the provision of a company driver, purchase of a currently owned house, and so on.

33. Viviana Zelizer explores in great detail the importance of this issue in the market for insurance (1978), and how changes in the legal and political structures governing insurance affected the economic value of children (1981).

34. Meyer and Rowan (1977) "Institutionalized Organizations"; and Fligstein (1990) *The Transformation of Corporate Control*.

35. Fligstein (1990) *The Transformation of Corporate Control*. For a theoretical overview of the concept of organizational fields, see Scott (1995) *Institutions and Organizations*.

36. I have found parallels to this aspect of the CEO candidate selection process in both the nonprofit and the public sectors. For a discussion of the importance of legitimacy considerations in the process of presidential candidate selection in public universities, see McLaughlin (1996) *Leadership Transitions;* and McLaughlin and Riesman (1990) *Choosing a College President*. For interesting non-fictional and fictional looks, respectively, at the role of legitimacy in selection, see Cramer (1992) *What It Takes*, and Warren (1946) *All the King's Men*.

37. McLaughlin (1985) "From Secrecy to Sunshine."

38. Zuckerman (1999) "The Categorical Imperative."

39. The majority of examples in which neoclassical assumptions inform the analysis of the CEO labor market can be found in the CEO compensation literature. See, for example, Jensen and Murphy (1990a) "CEO Incentives," Jensen and Murphy (1990b) "Performance Pay and Top Management Incentives," Murphy (1986) "Top Executives Are Worth Every Nickel They Get," and Rosen (1982) "Contracts and the Market for Executives." For an excellent review of the research outlining the debate between economists and behavioral social scientists on whether the CEO labor market is efficient, see Murphy (1998) "Executive Compensation."

40. There are several works of note to cite in this area, and some of them have already been cited. Many of them are built on the foundational theoretical work of Polanyi (1957) *The Great Transformation*. They include Granovetter (1974) *Getting a Job*, Granovetter (1985) "Economic Action and Social Structure," Burt (1992) *Structural Holes*, and Podolny (1994) "Market Uncertainty and the Social Character of Economic Exchange."

41. The term *social construction of reality* was coined by theorists Peter Berger and Thomas Luckmann (1967) in *The Social Construction of Reality*. Working within the subfield of the sociology of knowledge, Berger and Luckmann addressed the issue of how reality can be known:

> It is important to keep in mind that the objectivity of the institutional world, however massive it may appear to the individual, is a humanly produced, constructed objectivity. The process by which the externalized products of human activity attain the character of objectivity is objectivation. The institutional world is objectivated human activity, and so is every single institution. In other

words despite the objectivity that marks the social world in human experience, it does not thereby acquire an ontological status apart from the human activity that produced it. The paradox that man is capable of producing a world that he then experiences as something other than a human product will concern us later on. At the moment, it is important to emphasize that the relationship between man, the producer, and the social world, his product, is and remains a dialectical one. That is, man (not of course, in isolation but in his collectivities) and his social world interact with each other. The product acts back upon the producer. Externalization and objectivation are moments in a continuing dialectical process. The third moment in this process, which is internalization (by which the objectivated social world is retrojected into consciousness in the course of socialization), will occupy us in considerable detail later on. It is already possible, however, to see the fundamental relationship of these three dialectical moments in social reality. Each of them corresponds to an essential characterization of the social world. *Society is a human product. Society is an objective reality. Man is a social product.*

42. McGuire, Granovetter, and Schwartz (1991) "Thomas Edison and the Social Construction of the Early Electricity Industry in America."

43. Zelizer (1983) *Morals and Markets.*

44. See Douglas (1986) *How Institutions Think.*

Any institution that is going to keep its shape needs to gain its legitimacy . . . then [the institution] starts to control the memory of its members; it causes them to forget experiences incompatible with its righteous image, and it brings to their minds events which sustain the view of nature complementary to itself. It provides the categories of their thought, sets the terms for self-knowledge, and fixes identities. (112)

These ideas have also been developed by Charles Tilly (1998), who shows how socially constructed categories can be used to create and maintain inequality in a society. His ideas tie directly back to the concept of the social construction of reality.

45. Powell and Dimaggio (1983) *The New Institutionalism of Organizational Analysis.*

46. See Goffman (1963a) *Behavior in Public Places* and (1963b) *The Presentation of Self in Everyday Life.*

47. White (2002) *Markets from Networks.*

48. Granovetter (1985) "Economic Action and Social Structure."

49. I am attempting to summarize a diverse and deep stream of ideas in economic sociology here. For a useful review of this work, see Smelser and Swedberg (1994) *The Handbook of Economic Sociology.*

50. Logue and Naert (1970) "A Theory of Conglomerate Mergers."

51. Weston, J. F. (1970a) "Diversification and Merger Trends" and (1970b) "The Nature and Significance of Conglomerate Firms."

52. Amihud and Lev (1981) "Risk Reduction as a Managerial Motive for Conglomerate Mergers."

53. Williamson (1975) *Markets and Hierarchies;* and Rosen (1986) "Prizes and Incentives in Elimination Tournaments."

54. An exact percentage of outsider CEOs is difficult to report since researchers define outsider CEOs differently. For example, Richard Vancil (1987) defines outsider CEOs as having been with the firm two years or less. For the purposes of this book, I will define outsiders as having no prior affiliation with the firm at all, a more conservative measure. Recent studies suggest that between 20 and 29 percent of CEO successions at large publicly held corporations are outsider successions. Borkovich, Parrino, and Trapani (1996) examine CEO successions from 1969 to 1988 and find that 20 percent of them during this period were outsider successions. Worrell, Davidson, and Glascock (1993), using a 1963–1987 dataset, code 29 percent of all CEO successions as outsider appointments. The panel analysis of 850 firms from 1980 to 1996 used in my own research for this book finds that 27 percent of CEO successions during this period involved outsiders.

55. Williamson (1975) *Markets and Hierarchies,* and (1981) "The Economics of Organization."

56. Burt (1992) *Structural Holes,* 238–251.

57. Weber, Roth, and Wittich (1978) *Economy and Society,* 341–43.

58. There are several sociologists who have built on the concept of social closure. In particular, Parkin (1974) and Sørensen (1983a) have independently explored Weber's ideas about closure in trying to explain the processes by which inequality is generated in modern society. Suffice it to say here that my conceptualization of closure is different in some important ways from that of these predecessors—a subject to which I will return in chapter 7.

59. Sørensen (1983b) "Sociological Research on the Labor Market," and (1998) "Theoretical Mechanisms and the Empirical Study of Social Processes."

60. Dumont (1980) *Homo Hierarchicus.*

Chapter Three: The Rise of the Charismatic CEO

1. Berle and Means (1932) *The Modern Corporation and Private Property.*

2. Chandler (1977) *The Visible Hand.*

3. Ibid.

4. Ibid.

5. Brandeis, Fraenkel, and Lewis (1965) *The Curse of Bigness*; Brandeis, Lief, and the U.S. Supreme Court (1930) *The Social and Economic Views of Mr. Justice Brandeis*; and Brandeis and Poole (1914) *Business—A Profession*.

6. Fukuyama (1992) *The End of History and the Last Man*.

7. Chandler was not the first to focus on the link between organizational structure and organizational effectiveness. As his introductory text and references make clear, the topic is one that has interested scholars going back at least to Adam Smith. More recent predecessors to Chandler would include Werner Sombart, James Burnham, Ronald Coase, Douglass North, and Oliver Williamson. But all of these dealt with the problem as part of larger agendas. It was Chandler who, focusing on the explicit links among organizational form, the environment, and organizational performance, in effect created two significant subfields: I/O economics and business history.

8. Fligstein (1990) *The Transformation of Corporate Control*.

9. Baker and Smith (1998) *The New Financial Capitalists*. Also see the brief discussion of agency theory in chapter 2.

10. As described by ibid.

11. Burrough and Helyar's bestseller *Barbarians at the Gate* (1990) likely dispelled any remaining romantic notions of CEOs as altruistic statesmen in the service of the public good.

12. Baker and Smith (1998) *The New Financial Capitalists*; and Burrough and Helyar (1990) *Barbarians at the Gate*.

13. Burrough and Helyar (1990) *Barbarians at the Gate*.

14. In the era of deregulation, begun under President Jimmy Carter and accelerated under Ronald Reagan, the legal environment regulating pensions, retirement funds, and endowments changed dramatically. The most important of these changes was the elimination of state and federal laws that had previously prevented these funds from investing more than 5 or 10 percent of their capital in equities. As the regulations eased, an increasing number of firms shifted their investments away from fixed-income investments, such as government and corporate bonds, to equity indexes. For a description of this transformation, see Useem (1993) *Executive Defense*, 33–43, which details the legal and political changes that made possible the collective mobilization of institutional shareholders. Useem also describes the political process that led to a weakening of the SEC rules on joint actions. In particular, several onerous procedures and requirements for jointly voting securities owned by shareholders who controlled more than 5 percent of shares were reduced and/or no longer actively enforced. Useem further notes that by working through LBO funds,

institutional investors were able to circumvent most legal and administrative constraints on coordinating their action against particular firms.

15. Much of this discussion of the new role of institutional investors is based on Useem's (1993) *Executive Defense*.

16. See, for instance, Boyle (2001) "The Dirty Half-Dozen."

17. Brown and Swoboda (1992) "Stempel Steps Down As Chairman of GM."

18. *Business Week* magazine's John Byrne (1993), 32, captured the ferocity with which activist investors now went after the CEOs of underperforming companies when he described the newest weapon of institutional shareholders as "humiliation of the hot, blinding variety."

19. Buffett's firm, Berkshire Hathaway (of which he owns 31 percent), controlled about 200 million shares, or 8.1 percent of Coca-Cola. Money manager Herbert Allen controlled about 9 million shares. Together, Buffett and Allen, the board's two most powerful directors, told CEO Douglas Ivester that they had reached an irreversible conclusion: he was no longer the man who should be running Coke. Ivester could conceivably have decided to fight, but it is unlikely that he would have won in the new environment. It is important to note that unlike GM, which had experienced significant losses, Coca-Cola was performing relatively well at the time. Its return on shareholders' equity was 35 percent, down from the previous year's figure of 42 percent, but still an enviable level of performance by most financial standards. See Watkins, Knoop, and Reavis (2000) "The Coca-Cola Company (A)"; and Sellers (2000) "What Really Happened at Coke."

20. The CEO search at Gillette that identified Hawley was supposedly a broad outside search. Conducted as Al Zeien was preparing to step down as CEO in early 1999, it ended where it had begun, with the designation of Michael Hawley, Zeien's own choice, as the new CEO.

Hawley's dismissal was summarized in the *Boston Globe*. Faced with slower than anticipated growth (the firm's earnings were no longer growing at the double-digit levels that they had since the late 1980s), the board dismissed Hawley in October 2000. Kravis, described by an insider as the "silent assassin," had good reason to lead the ouster of Hawley. His buyout company, Kohlberg Kravis Roberts & Co. of New York, is one of Gillette's largest shareholders, a stake that came with the sale of Duracell International, the battery maker, to Gillette in 1996. At the time of Hawley's firing, Kravis's 51 million shares of Gillette were down $1.5 billion off their 1999 highs. Ousted after thirty-nine years at the Boston-based razor maker, Hawley is another example of the role that institutional investors have played in enforcing unforgiving standards of performance (Reidy [2000] "Gillette Ousts CEO Hawley after 18 Months").

21. As I have found in my own research (see chapter 2, note 54), 27 percent of CEO successions at large corporations in 1980–1996 were outsider successions. This is a large number, especially since outsider CEOs were virtually unheard of before this period. Moreover, internal labor market theory—still the dominant paradigm for studies of CEO succession—would predict close to zero outsider CEOs because of requirements for firm-specific skills and information asymmetries with regard to the productivity of individuals. Meanwhile, the search firm Challenger, Gray estimates that close to 50 percent of all CEOs in large, publicly held companies in the year 2000 are outsiders (Challenger, Gray, and Christmas [2001] *Annual CEO Turnover Report*).

22. "Look at the insiders who have turned around ailing companies and you'll find that they are, in a sense, outsiders. Jack Welch, who transformed the culture at GE, grew up not in the company's old line businesses but in plastics, a young, iconoclastic division" (Dumaine [1993] "What's So Hot about Outsiders?").

Another example of an insider CEO constructed by the business press and others as an outsider is former Ford Motor Company CEO Jacques Nasser, who was explicitly compared with Welch in a *Harvard Business Review* article that appeared shortly after Nasser assumed the CEO position at Ford in January 1999 (Wetlaufer [1999] "Driving Change"). Consider also this passage from a *Business Week* article later that year: "[The CEO position is] a pretty heady place to be for a restless, Lebanese-born ousider. Since starting as a young manager in Australia 31 years ago, he has spent nearly all of his career in the far reaches of the Ford empire. . . . Nasser early on showed the impatience with Ford's bureaucratic fiefdoms that still fuels him today" (Kerwin with Naughton [1999] "Remaking Ford").

23. For two examples of such studies, see Pfeffer and Salancik (1978) *The External Control of Organizations* and Hannan and Freeman (1989) *Organizational Ecology*.

24. Harvard Business School (1982) "Reginald Jones"; and transcription by Vancil (1987) *Passing the Baton*.

25. Rosen (1986) and Lazear's (1995) tournament theory paints executive promotion as a hotbed of competition. Critics have argued that the tournament model ignores that most organizations cannot afford costly executive tournaments in which the losers depart. Moreover, most organizations require a great deal of cooperation between executives, which such "tournaments" would short-circuit. See O'Reilly, Main, and Crystal (1988) "CEO Compensation as Tournament and Social Comparison."

26. GE continues to use this practice to this day, as illustrated by the process leading to Jeffrey Immelt's appointment as Jack Welch's successor.

27. In keeping with this example, several large sample studies have demonstrated a positive effect on a firm's stock price when an outsider CEO is announced. See, for instance, Hudson, Parrino, and Stark (1997) "The Effectiveness of Internal Monitoring Mechanisms"; and Worrell, Davidson, and Glascock (1993) "Stockholder Reactions to Departures and Appointments of Key Executives Attributable to Firings."

28. Colvin (1999) "We Hate to Say We Told You So, but . . ."; and Burrows and Elstrom (1999) "The Boss."

29. Shivdasani and Yermack (1998) "CEO Involvement in the Selection of New Board Members."

30. For a discussion of the existing research on the relationship between CEOs and firm performance, see chapter 2.

31. For a discussion of the fallacy behind claims that stock options link the CEO's compensation to firm performance, see chapter 7.

32. The most saccharine of these press releases recounting a sudden CEO departure was the one announcing John Akers's forced exit from IBM in 1992, a declaration that was so positive that the word "resignation" did not even appear in it. The euphemism employed was that the board of directors had "accepted [Akers's] recommendation to begin the process of selecting a new chief executive officer for the company." Later in the same press release, a board member was quoted as saying, somewhat schizophrenically, that "IBM could not have had more effective leadership in these turbulent times" (PR Newswire [1993a] "IBM Chairman John F. Akers Announces CEO Search"). In the press release announcing the resignation of James Robinson III as CEO and chairman of American Express a year later (after shareholders had rebelled against his continuing in the position and Robinson had finally capitulated), the defeated executive came across as a martyr for the AmEx cause. Both Robinson himself and his successor, Harvey Golub, mentioned the departing CEO's overwhelming devotion to the good of the company as the cause of his act of self-sacrifice (for which Robinson had been paid tens of millions of dollars so that he could continue to live in a company-provided Fifth Avenue apartment and travel on corporate jets) (BusinessWire [1993] "Golub Elected Chief Executive Officer of American Express Company; Robinson to Continue as Chairman, Will also Head Shearson Lehman"; Bleakley, Pae, and Siconolfi [1993] "Robinson Quits At American Express Co.; As Board Support Unravels, Chairman Resigns Post; Successor to Be Named"). Westinghouse Electric's press release about Paul Lego's 1993 dismissal was the most typical. After stating that Lego had "elected to retire," the company "express[ed] its gratitude for Lego's 37 years of dedicated service" and thanked him for agreeing to serve as a consultant (PR Newswire [1993b] "Westinghouse Chairman Paul Lego to Retire").

33. PR Newswire (2000) "Lucent Technologies' Board of Directors Names Henry Schacht Chairman and CEO."

34. Fligstein (1990) *The Transformation of Corporate Control*.

35. Mills (1956) *The Power Elite*; Riesman (1956) *The Lonely Crowd*; and Whyte (1956) *The Organization Man*.

36. Porter (1990) *The Competitive Advantage of Nations*; and Thurow (1992) *Head to Head*.

37. The CEOs of the era of managerial capitalism had attached extreme importance to keeping both physical and social distance from the factory workers. They dressed differently and spoke differently. They magnified their social distinctions and credentials. Today, by putting on the image of "everyday" people—for instance, by donning casual clothing during the workweek, riding motorcycles, and so on—many CEOs attempt to present themselves as natural leaders who have arisen from among the ordinary employees.

38. For a review, see Glassman and Swatos (1986) *Charisma, History, and Social Structure*.

39. Shils (1982) "Charisma, Order, and Status." In this essay, Shils redefines charisma for secular societies, which had traditionally been considered mostly free from charismatic authority, except for the occasionally disruptive personality. In so doing, he makes an explicit connection between the charismatic personality and a society's cultural values. For Shils, charismatic individuals are those who exercise authority and express the values that are of greatest importance in the society. Thus, in societies in which rational-legal authority is viewed as sacred, those closest to this authority are viewed as charismatic and command deference—for example, Supreme Court justices, other high government officials, and those heading corporate bodies.

40. http://www.philipmorrisusa.com, September 1, 2001.

41. http://www.dupont.com/corp/overview/glance/vision/index.html, September 1, 2001.

42. http://www.fastcompany.com/partners/, September 1, 2001.

43. Pfeffer (1998) *Human Equation*, 298.

44. O'Reilly and Pfeffer (2000) *Hidden Value*, and Pfeffer (1994) *Competitive Advantage*, are examples of management texts that advocate this new human-resource-centered view of organizations. They offer excellent examples of companies that have built competitive advantage through people.

45. Brooks (2000) *Bobos in Paradise*.

46. There are several examples in these publications, the most recent being a special *Harvard Business Review* issue dedicated solely to the topic of leadership. According to an editor from the *Review*, the December 2001 special issue on "Breakthrough Leadership" was the best-selling issue in the publication's history.

47. Nohria and Green (2002) "Chrysler: Lee Iacocca's Legacy."

48. One executive search consultant I interviewed described in glowing terms a CEO who could "sell a drink of water to a fish." This approving attitude is becoming increasingly prevalent in a culture where, it is scarcely an exaggeration to say, CEOs have become the equivalent of rock stars. (The cover of the September 4, 2000, issue of *Business Week* features Compaq CEO Mike Capellas dressed in jeans, a guitar slung over his shoulder.) Certainly their celebrity (measured by cover stories in business magazines and visibility in the pages of daily newspapers) and personal wealth confirm our society's willingness to reward them extravagantly for what used to be considered merely a job, not a role as a cultural icon.

49. Byrne (1999) *Chainsaw*.

50. In retrospect, questions about the "leadership" abilities of a now notorious "out of the box" thinker, former Enron CEO Jeffrey Skilling, should have been raised by Skilling's behavior toward a fund manager who, in April 2001— six months before Enron began to collapse under the weight of questions about its use of off-the-balance-sheet partnerships to disguise debt and inflate earnings—asked in a conference call between Skilling and Enron investors to see the company's balance sheet, only to be answered with what he took to be an evasion. "You're the only financial institution that can't come up with balance sheet or cash flow statement [sic] after earnings," the fund manager then said. Skilling replied, "Well, thank you very much, we appreciate that. Asshole" (Hull [2001]).

51. Shiller (2000) *Irrational Exuberance*, 35.

52. Serwer (2000) "There's Something About Cisco." Serwer (2001) later confessed to having fallen under Chambers's spell in what he called, referring to the piece quoted here, "a remarkably imperceptive story."

53. Mehta (2001) "Cisco Fractures Its Own Fairy Tale."

54. Shiller (2000) *Irrational Exuberance*.

55. Expectations about future earnings, rather than past performance, largely account for companies' stock prices. These expectations on the part of shareholders are now the product mostly of *analysts'* expectations.

56. Strauss (2000) "There's No Magic." "A world class executive," said Goldman Sachs's Jack Kelly. He continued: "We certainly think he has the ability to solve Kodak's problems. He's also the right age. He's got lots of vim and vigor left and I think it's going to work out well" (Jones, Randall, and Hillkirk [1993] "Kodak Snaps Up Chief from Motorola").

57. By early 1997, Kodak's stock price had risen 110 percent above its value just before Fisher's appointment. Yet what analysts and investors counting on Fisher to save the company failed to recognize is that Kodak faced fundamen-

tal problems—a technological shift from chemical to digital photography, and a fierce low-cost competitor in Japan—that had very little to do with its executive leadership. Indeed, in the decade before Fisher was brought in, Kodak had been described as having one of the most effective executive teams in corporate America. Today, Kodak stock trades at half of what it did at the time of Fisher's coronation. Fisher himself, meanwhile, has not fared so poorly, having managed to hang on to the chairman position while allowing others to sit in the CEO hot seat.

58. Strauss (2000) "There's No Magic." See chapter 4 for an account of the AT&T succession that resulted in Armstrong's appointment and the company's unsuccessful attempts to come to terms with its new industry environment ever since. Meanwhile, two other examples of analysts' fixation on CEOs seem especially worth noting in light of more recent events. In 1996, when Al Dunlap's appointment as the new outsider CEO of Sunbeam was announced, a Paine Webber analyst was unusually (though perhaps unwittingly) frank about the wishful thinking involved in this perspective when he wrote, "Al Dunlap is the perfect announcement [sic] to give the Street, because the Street *wants to believe* he can do for Sunbeam what he did with Scott Paper" (Strauss [2000] "There's No Magic," italics added). After news of Dunlap's selection to lead Sunbeam was announced, the company's stock jumped 50 percent. Not until later did the world learn how much of Dunlap's apparent success in his previous positions was owing to accounting trickery. And even when, in 1997, Sunbeam's receivables began to increase in ways that should have provided an indication that the firm was pushing inventory on its buyers in an effort to demonstrate rapid revenue growth, few analysts were willing to concede that something was amiss, and most remained unwilling to do so until the bitter end. In light of this failure of judgment, it is also interesting to note the reaction of a Prudential Securities analyst to the announcement of Jeffrey Skilling's appointment as CEO of Enron in December 2000: "This should satisfy any investors who might have been worried that [Skilling] might go elsewhere. . . . There is a huge premium in Enron's stock related to management quality and Jeff is at the helm" (Davis [2000], "No Ordinary Jeff").

The attitude toward charismatic CEOs exhibited here has also no doubt played a part in analysts' reluctance to question the ability of America's most lionized CEO of recent times, Jack Welch of General Electric, to produce uncannily consistent earnings growth for GE year after year over a period of two decades, even though several financial analysts believe that a critical examination of GE's accounting practices reveals that Welch often used gains and losses from certain businesses to offset gains and losses in others, whether these were reported for the right quarter or not (see Birger [2000] "Glowing Numbers"; and Kahn [2001] "Accounting in Wonderland"). Also before the Enron debacle focused attention on how little understood many large public companies are by the stock market analysts who cover them, the business journal *Barron's* complained that analysts no longer conduct broad and deep research offering proprietary insights into industry fundamentals but instead focus on individual companies and anecdotes about them. As the *Barron's* writer put it, these stories tell investors about "the ship, the crew, the [share] price—but they don't let you know whether it's in shallow water or is about to be hit by a tidal wave" (Santoli [2001] "The Whole Truth").

59. Dowd (2001) "Seven Ways to Attract Analysts and Investors."

60. Mathisen (2001) "What I Look for in a TV Guest."

Chapter Four: Board Games

1. Hambrick and Jackson (1999) "Outside Directors With a Stake."

2. Core, Holthausen, and Larcker (1997) "Corporate Governance, CEO Compensation, and Firm Performance," 32.

3. There are several papers on this topic. For a review, see Mizruchi (1996) "What Do Interlocks Do?" Davis and Greve (1997) "Corporate Elite Networks and Governance Changes in the 1980s" show how directors who reside and work close to one another are more likely to adopt similar anti-takeover defenses. Galaskiewicz and Wasserman (1990) demonstrate the importance of geography and cross-cutting social ties with respect to predicting similarity in corporate behaviors. The original research on this topic was conducted by Michael Useem (1984) and C. Wright Mills (1956).

4. See Geertz (1973) *The Interpretation of Cultures*, and Kanter (1973) *Communes*, as separate examples of work describing the social perspectives of small, closed communities.

5. Roethlisberger (1947) *Management and the Worker*.

6. Whyte (1951) "Small Groups and Large Organizations."

7. Mills (1956) *The Power Elite*.

8. Out of the 6,064 board seats in the *Fortune* 500 in 1998, 671 were held by 471 women (see Catalyst [1998]). Age and occupation data was obtained from the 1999 *Directorship* database. Class is inferred from the occupational and educational background of the directors, also included in the *Directorship* data. The status and class finding is one of the most robust in research on elites.

9. The French social theorist Edmond Goblot wrote about how shared work (exemplified by the way that members of the broader community of corporate directors share the same occupation) helps create a sense of group identity:

"Nothing stamps a man as much as his occupation. Daily work determines the mode of life; even more than the organs of the body, it constrains our ideas, feelings, and tastes. Habits of the body and mind and habits of language combine to give each one of us his occupational type. People of the same occupation know one another—by necessity and by choice. Consequently, each imitates the other" (Goblot [1925] *La Barriére et le Nieveau,* chap. III, 38–59).

10. Useem (1984) *The Inner Circle.* Useem's work suggests that the primary information that flows through the interlocking directorate is about "the practices and concerns of most large companies, companies that are operating in virtually all major sectors of the economy. . . . The information pursued is generic information about common business practices and the environment" (56). For a similar argument, see also Mizruchi (1982) *The American Corporate Network 1904–1974* and (1992a) *The Structure of Corporate Political Action.*

Mizruchi (1996) "What Do Interlocks Do?" provides an excellent review of the flourishing research on director interlocks. Davis (1991) "Agents without Principles?" furnishes a good example. Building on an agency perspective suggesting that managers would be inclined to adopt anti-takeover defenses in an effort to save their jobs, Davis found that the network position of a firm's board predicted the likelihood that a firm would adopt a particular type of anti-takeover defense. Director interlocks have also been shown to predict acquisition behaviors (Haunschild [1993] "Interorganizational Imitation"), corporate giving (Galaskiewicz and Wasserman [1990] "Mimetic and Normative Processes"), corporate financing (Stearns and Mizruchi [1993] "Corporate Financing"), and political lobbying (Mizruchi [1992] *The Structure of Corporate Political Action*).

11. Useem (1984) *The Inner Circle.*

12. See Chandler (1977) *The Visible Hand,* and (1962) *Strategy and Structure.*

13. Vancil (1987) *Passing the Baton.*

14. Ocasio (1999) "Institutionalized Action and Corporate Governance."

15. Fromson (1990) "The Big Owners Roar."

16. Russell Reynolds Associates (2001) "CEO Turnover in a Global Economy."

17. Ocasio (1999) "Institutionalized Action and Corporate Governance."

18. Festinger (1954) "A Theory of Social Comparison Processes."

19. Mukul (1997) "Behind the Shuffle at AT&T."

20. Hopkins, Defterios, and Young (1997) "New AT&T Presidential Search Begins."

21. AT&T's market value increased $4 billion on the day of the announcement of Armstrong's appointment. As of this writing, it is trading at one-third

the value it did when John Walters was still president and slotted to be the next CEO.

22. Colvin (2001a) "Changing of the Guard."

23. Useem (1984) *The Inner Circle*; and Vancil (1987) *Passing the Baton.*

24. March and March (1977, 1978) introduced the term *social matching* to describe the process by which credentials and signals are relied on to sort candidates. Using data on one state's school superintendents, they found that most of the superintendents were nearly indistinguishable across a range of criteria, including behaviors, career paths, credentials, and prior performance evaluations. Drawing on social psychological research on decision-making under uncertainty, the researchers explained this lack of variation by postulating that when matching individuals to jobs, organizational decision-makers relied on socially defined criteria, or "social matches," such as certification or adherence to an institutionally legitimate career path. Although I have adopted the Marches' term, my use of it differs from theirs in some subtle but important ways, since I see legitimacy and defensibility, as well as uncertainty, as important motivators of the social matching process.

25. Douglas (1986) *How Institutions Think.*

26. Mills (1956) *The Power Elite*, 127.

27. Young (2001) "Lucent Could Cut Jobs, Take Big Charge."

28. In conducting my research for this book, I quickly learned not even to raise this issue in conversations with directors. For in the case of three board members whom I interviewed in the early stages of this study, I lost credibility after referring in a casual manner to the sociological school that regards the CEO's role as largely symbolic, and pointing out that most empirical studies have shown that CEOs have little control over firm performance.

29. Merton (1957) *Social Theory and Social Structure*, 475–90.

30. Durkheim and Mauss (1963) *Primitive Classification.*

31. To study the workings of status matching here, I adapted the techniques of mobility analysis of Blau and Duncan (1967), which rely on the use of mobility tables to show the origin and destination states and how people move from one to another. To operationalize firm status I relied on network centrality as measured by firm sales (Mizruchi, Mariolis, Schwartz, and Mintz [1986] "Techniques for Disaggregating Centrality Scores in Social Networks").

32. Veblen (1973) *The Theory of the Leisure Class.*

33. Podolny (1994) "Market Uncertainty and the Social Character of Economic Exchange."

34. Stuart, Hoang, and Hybels (1999) "Interorganizational Endorsements."

35. Strauss (2000) "There's No Magic." The same story can be repeated for Xerox, Eastman Kodak, and Hewlett-Packard, all companies that hired

high-status outsider CEOs in recent years only to see their market valuations drop significantly. Although it would be a mistake to hold the CEOs individually responsible for the drop in their company's stock prices in these cases, the directors who hired them clearly got much less than what they bargained for.

36. For research highlighting the demographic homogeneity of CEOs, see Temin (1997) "The American Business Elite in Historical Perspective," and (1998) "The Stability of the American Business Elite."

Chapter Five: The Go-Betweens

1. Revenue figures on the executive search industry are courtesy of *Executive Recruiter News* and its editor Joseph Daniel McCool. I am referring here only to retained search, not contingency-based search. In retained search, the search firm is paid a fee regardless of whether the position is filled.

2. Russell Reynolds Associates (1994) "Reflections."

3. Baron, Dobbin, and Jennings (1986) "War and Peace."

4. Byrne (1986) *The Headhunters*, 23.

5. Whyte (1956) *The Organization Man*.

6. Vancil (1987) *Passing the Baton*.

7. Margolies (1978) "International Paper Says Du Pont's Gee Will Become Firm's President on April 1." While Gee was initially appointed president of International Paper, the company made it clear that he would be given the CEO title within a few months.

8. Grover (1980) "Outsider Chief at International Paper Vows to Develop Inside Succession Line"; and Metz (1979) "International Paper's Profit Outlook Is Rosy But Some Analysts Are Ambivalent on Stock."

9. Walsh (2001) "Luring the Best in an Unsettled Time."

10. Russell Reynolds Associates (1994) "Reflections," 34–35

11. Ibid., 16 (italics original).

12. Ibid., 50–51.

13. Byrne (1986) *The Headhunters*, 200–2. I am also grateful to John Byrne for sharing his experiences in researching the industry as well as for providing a sounding board for many of the ideas in this chapter early in my research.

14. Ghemawat (2000) "Egon Zehnder International," 1

15. Byrne (1986) *The Headhunters*, discusses job-hopping among search consultants, while Yoshino, Knoop, and Reavis (1998) "Egon Zehnder International: Implementing Practice Groups," 22, note that Egon Zehnder is alone among executive search firms in not hiring consultants from other firms.

16. Byrne (1986) *The Headhunters*, 207.

17. The idea of people who accept the values of a group still having marginal status in relation to it is different from what Merton's discussion of reference-group theory would predict; see Merton (1957) *Social Theory and Social Structure*, 319. While search consultants adopt the values of a group to which they aspire to belong, this mimetic behavior does not aid them in attaining membership in that group. Indeed, there is no anticipatory socialization, for few search consultants become members of the executive elite.

18. There are some parallels in the plight of search consultants and other such middlemen to Merton's discussions of the "marginal man." However, Merton did not discuss the high correlation between marginal status and middleman status (Ibid., 324). The theoretical linkage between the two was developed by Blalock (1967) *Toward a Theory of Minority Group Relations*.

19. Coughlin (1976) *Double Identity*; Desai (1963) *Indian Immigrants in Britain*.

20. Mahajani (1960) *The Role of Indian Minorities in Burma and Malaya*.

21. Bonacich (1973) "A Theory of Middleman Minorities."

22. Podolny (1993) "A Status-Based Model of Market Competition"; and Eccles and Crane (1988) *Doing Deals: Investment Banks at Work*.

23. This is an interesting fact since there are four major firms with the size and prestige to garner most of the business in the field of CEO search. One explanation of the practice of including only three in the shootout might be that there is only enough time to consider three firms. Yet perhaps inviting all of the Big Four to participate would only emphasize that they constitute a kind of cartel, while choosing from among three enhances the appearance of genuine differentiation among the major search firms, with the added benefit of making the shootout look like a real competition.

24. Russell Reynolds Associates Web site.

25. Spencer Stuart Web site.

26. Russell Reynolds Associates Web site.

27. Spencer Stuart Web site.

28. Burt (1992) *Structural Holes*; Granovetter (1974) *Getting a Job*; and Granovetter and Tilly (1988) "Inequality and Labor Processes."

29. Nohria (1992) "Information and Search in the Creation of New Business Ventures."

30. Geertz (1973) *The Interpretation of Cultures*.

31. Simmel (1902) *The Sociology of Georg Simmel*, and (1955) *The Web of Group Affiliations*.

32. Goffman (1963a) *Behavior in Public Places*, 96.

33. Ibid., 106

34. One result of this appropriation of the concept of the free market in the external search process was noted by New York Times reporter Judith Dobryzynski (1996) in writing about the 1996 CEO search at AT&T that resulted in the appointment of outsider John Walter. In the new dispensation, Dobryzynski observed, "every executive in the land becomes fair game, thus reinforcing a trend that is turning executives, like professional athletes, into free agents."

35. The reality is that executive search firms are not necessarily so impartial. In CEO searches where both inside and outside candidates are being considered, the ESFs—which charge retainer-based fees while also receiving the equivalent of one-third of the successful candidate's negotiated annual cash compensation—are motivated to usher in outsider CEOs for two reasons. First, judging from the cases I studied, compensation is usually higher for outsider CEOs than for insiders. Second, the real returns for the search firm come in subsequent retained searches as the outsider CEO brings in his new, outside management team.

36. The idea that ESFs play a crucial role in signaling the legitimacy of external CEO search to various constituents would not be surprising to researchers studying mediated markets. For example, Ezra Zuckerman (1999) once noted that the legitimating role of securities analysts in financial markets has a significant influence on investors' demand for a firm's securities. Zuckerman found that investors look toward analysts' determinations regarding the legitimacy of a particular firm's security offerings: those securities that do not obtain recognition for their full industrial participation in a particular sector are discounted by analysts and, as a result, trade at a lower price. Similar observations have been made about other mediated markets in which the underlying quality of the product is uncertain and the process of selection is opaque.

37. Goffman (1967) Interaction Ritual.

Chapter Six: Crowning Napoleon

1. Goode (1978) The Celebration of Heroes, chap. 1.
2. This psychologizing of the CEO's leadership abilities is evident in this excerpt from a 1998 Business Week article about Welch:

> It had taken him 21 hard years and a bruising succession battle to make it to the top. But finally, in 1981, Jack Welch achieved his greatest ambition. At 45, the long-shot candidate became the youngest chief executive in General Electric Co.'s (GE) history. The climax to his ascension was his first shareholders' meet-

ing in Phoenix. After holding forth for two hours, the triumphant Welch walked offstage, his blue eyes moist with tears. "I wish my mother had been here," he whispered to GE director and friend Silas S. Cathcart.

Jack Welch, sentimental? In time, he become known as Neutron Jack, the man who cut GE's workforce by more than 100,000 employees in his first five years as CEO. But that moniker suggested a one-dimensional character, failing to shed light on a far more complex and private individual. Welch has always been more: a dutiful son who worshiped an adoring Irish mother, a loyal friend who still returns to Salem, Mass., for high school reunions, and a witty, self-deprecating husband and father of four.

Growing up in Salem, Welch was as he is today: unpretentious, demanding, and feisty, quick to use obscene language when his temper flares, but also remarkably compassionate and caring. His decisions to lay off employees to sharpen GE's competitiveness, say insiders, were painful and anguished.

His force of will in the game of business was just as strong in the scrappy games of hockey and baseball he played as a teenager. "Most people change when they go to work for a big company," says George W. Ryan, a longtime friend and high-school buddy. "They are forced to conform to survive. Not Jack. He forced the company to change."

His mother, Grace, whom he strongly resembles, gave him the confidence to refuse to conform. Welch learned much from her—including pure persistence. It took 16 years before she and husband John Sr. saw the birth of their only child on Nov. 19, 1935, in Peabody, Mass. John Sr., a Boston & Maine train conductor and union leader, worked long hours, often leaving for work at 5:30 a.m. and not returning until 7:30 at night.

Welch and his mother would drive to the train station together, sit in the car in the dark, and talk while waiting for his dad to arrive. She convinced him that he didn't speak with a stutter, even though he did. She told him to aim for the sky. She took him to Fenway Park and helped cultivate his near lifelong passion for the Boston Red Sox. She nurtured his competitive instincts in games of black-jack and gin rummy around the kitchen table. And when she beat him, Welch recalls, she'd slam the cards on the table and shout "Gin!" in the loudest voice possible. "I had a pal in my mom, you know," he says. "We had a great relationship. It was a powerful, unique, wonderful, reinforcing experience" (Byrne [1998] "I Had a Pal in My Mom").

3. The following passage from a 2000 profile of Chambers is representative:

John Chambers is the company's third CEO, but today's Cisco bears his indelible stamp. Born and raised in Charleston, WV, the son of two doctors, Chambers and his two sisters [sic] grew up in a tightly knit family. He sang in the church choir, enjoyed fishing with his now retired gynecologist father, Jack, and fondly remembers family vacations spent on Carolina beaches. Chambers married his high school sweetheart, Elaine Prater and dotes on his two children—son, John, Jr. and daughter, Lindsay. He graduated second in his class at high school despite having mild dyslexia, a learning disability he persevered to overcome through working harder and tutoring. Even to this day he dislikes lengthy written memos, preferring to communicate verbally. His presentations are almost thoroughly memorized and dynamically delivered underscoring the preacher-like flair with which he addresses audiences. As a West Virginia University undergraduate he played basketball, still his favorite sport—notably an intensive team spirited one, and later earned a law degree from West Virginia and an M.B.A from Indiana University (Donlon [2000] "Why John Chambers Is the CEO of the Future").

4. Keynes (1973) *The General Theory of Employment, Interest, and Money*, 383–84.

5. The basic source for my whole discussion of Weber, here and below, is Weber (1947) *Economy and Society*.

6. While this is much less common today among large corporations, it is not totally unheard of. Ford Motor Company, Anheuser-Busch, and Motorola are all currently run by heirs of their respective founders.

7. Weber's own use of the word "extraordinary" to describe the powers of the charismatic figure has proven to be something of a red herring, as it has focused attention not only on the charismatic individual himself but also on the most subjective and elusive aspects of charisma. Despite decades of research by psychologists that has sought to determine the personal factors associated with charisma, little progress has been made in this area. See the introduction to Glassman and Swatos (1986) *Charisma, History, and Social Structure*, for a review of this work. Scholars who have done comparative work have studied everything from physical appearances to rhetorical skills to work habits in an attempt find some characteristics that are commonly associated with charismatic personalities. In the end, however, they have had little success in identifying these special qualities. Few personality traits are more subjectively perceived and resistant to precision than those ordinarily thought to give a person charisma. To be charismatic, after all, is to be thought to possess something elusive and mysterious that cannot easily be either explained or defined. What *can* be defined more precisely—and what Weber and others *have* defined—are the social processes by which charisma is conferred on or attributed to individuals.

8. "Its [charisma's] bearer seizes the task for which he is destined and demands that others obey and follow him by virtue of his mission. If those to whom he feels sent do not recognize him, his claim collapses; if they recognize

it, he is their master as long as he 'proves' himself" (Weber [1947] *Economy and Society*, 1113).

9. "He [the charismatic] gains and retains [power] solely by proving his powers in practice. He must work miracles, if he wants to be a prophet. He must perform heroic deeds, if he wants to be a warlord. Most of all, his divine mission must prove itself by *bringing well-being* to his faithful followers; if they do not fare well, he obviously is not the god-sent master" (Ibid., 1114, italics original).

10. Braudy (1986) *The Frenzy of Renown*. To understand the role of charisma in a broader sense than it was described in chapter 3, we need to see its connection to the history of Western ideas about the relationship between the individual and society. Braudy argues that the idea of charisma is inseparable from the historical and social circumstances within which it is embedded. In traditional societies, the charisma of Julius Caesar and Alexander the Great provided standards by which monarchs were measured for centuries. Socrates, Jesus, and Shakespeare were endowed with a different type of charisma. And yet the word *charisma* is also used to describe the hold that individuals such as Hitler, Stalin, and various cult leaders in recent history have had over their followers. Thus to loosely call all these people charismatic, as we commonly do, obscures the question about the relation of charisma to the cultural context.

11. Weber (1985) *The Protestant Ethic and the Spirit of Capitalism*.

12. Braudy (1986) notes that the charismatic appeal of businessmen in the late nineteenth and early twentieth centuries was crucially advanced by a new class of professionals on the American scene, the journalists who provided the material for the country's new mass-circulation newspapers and magazines. Such journalists almost immediately became critical intermediaries between readers and the world, familiarizing the famous or about-to-be famous to the anonymous masses by describing the former's habits, accomplishments, and effect on others. In an incessant stream of hyperbole, journalists tended to interpret every situation in personal terms, every triumph as resulting from individual will, and every failure as evidence of a character flaw. In so doing, they became instrumental in creating the notion that whatever happens to the corporation is attributable to the virtues or vices of the individual who sits atop it—an idea that, as we have seen, is at the heart of the contemporary conception of the charismatic CEO.

13. In a popular series of articles on the business practices of John D. Rockefeller, the progressive-era journalist Ida Tarbell (1905) did much to dispel the charismatic aura surrounding her subject by presenting judgments such as the following:

Very often people who admit the facts, are willing to see that Mr. Rockefeller has employed force and fraud to secure his ends, justify him by declaring, "It's business." That is, "it's business" has come to be a legitimate excuse for hard dealing, sly tricks, special privileges. It is a common enough thing to hear men arguing that the ordinary laws of morality do not apply in business. Now, if the Standard Oil Company were the only concern in the country guilty of the practices which have given it monopolistic power, this story would never have been written. Were it alone in these methods, public scorn would long ago have made short work of the Standard Oil Company. But it is simply the most conspicuous type of what can be done by these practices. The methods it employs with such acumen, persistency, and secrecy are employed by all sorts of businessmen, from corner grocers up to bankers. If exposed, they are excused on the ground that this is business. If the point is pushed, frequently the defender of the practice falls back on the Christian doctrine of charity, and points our that we are erring mortals and must allow for each other's weaknesses!—an excuse which, if carried to its legitimate conclusion, would leave our businessmen weeping on one another's shoulders over human frailty, while they picked one another's pockets. One of the most depressing features of the ethical side of the matter is that instead of such methods arousing contempt they are more or less openly admired. And this is logical. Canonize "business success," and men who make a success like that of the Standard Oil Trust become national heroes! The history of its organization is studied as a practical lesson in money-making. It is the most startling feature of the case to one who would like to feel that it is possible to be a commercial people and yet a race of gentlemen. Of course such practices exclude men by all the codes from the rank of gentlemen, just as such practices would exclude men from the sporting world or athletic field. There is no gaming table in the world where loaded dice are tolerated, no athletic field where men must not start fair. Yet Mr. Rockefeller has systematically played with loaded dice, and it is doubtful if there has ever been a time since 1872 when he has run a race with a competitor and started fair. Business played in this way loses all its sportsmanlike qualities. It is fit only for tricksters."

14. Jencks (1979) *Who Gets Ahead?*; Mills (1956) *The Power Elite*; and Parkin (1971) *Class Inequality and Political Order*.

15. If managerial capitalism shifted the orientation of the CEO from charismatic to rational authority, investor capitalism returned charismatic orientation to the fore. In this process, the analysts and business journalists who mediate the relationship between the firm and its investors changed the nature of charisma in business organizations. In particular, especially in the largest organizations, analysts and the business media now participate in both the creation

of charisma and the diffusion of its authority throughout the organization. They accomplish this through the mass media's substitution of symbolic social relationships for actual ones within the corporation. The CEO of a large pharmaceutical company informed me, for example, that "what the media writes about me is the most important [sic] in my employees' perception of me. They feel that they get to know me personally through those profiles. You would be amazed at how every line and sentence is dissected and discussed among employees."

16. Madsen and Snow (1991) *The Charismatic Bond*, 12.

17. Although, in the last two decades, the new "leadership" literature has suggested that organizations led by charismatic CEOs are more effective than others, little evidence suggests that this is so. Meanwhile, the argument for more rational organizations was precisely that they were more efficient. We seem to have thrown over a half-century's work on organizations out the window for no demonstrably valid reason.

18. Chandler (1977) *The Visible Hand*.

19. Doereinger and Piore (1971) *Internal Labor Markets and Manpower Analysis*.

20. For another example of such an orderly internal succession process, see Reginald Jones's account (quoted in chapter 3) of the process that eventually led to the selection of Jack Welch as his successor as CEO of General Electric.

21. Paltrow (1991) "American Express Tries to Head Off More Surprises"; and Sandler (1990) "American Express Dismantles Its Eighties' Superstore."

22. Lorsch (1996) "American Express (A)."

23. Morris and Marvick (1953) "Authoritarianism and Political Behavior."

24. During the tenures of its current CEO, C. Michael Armstrong, and his predecessor John Walter, AT&T has spun off divisions such as NCR and Lucent, acquired new lines of business in cable television and cellular services, attempted to integrate these new businesses, and, when integration has failed, embarked on a strategy of spinning them off again. See Elstrom (2001) "How the 'Turnaround CEO' Failed to Deliver."

25. Simmel (1902) *The Sociology of Georg Simmel*, 402–8.

26. Jeffrey Pfeffer (1981) has suggested as much in arguing that many actions that CEOs take are taken precisely *because* the range of more "plausible" actions is constrained.

27. Madsen and Snow (1991) *The Charismatic Bond*, 19–23.

28. The type of reflected charisma that the Stanley Works directors found in John Trani by virtue of his association with Jack Welch was also a factor in Xerox's selection of Rick Thoman as CEO in May 1999. Thoman, a former executive at IBM, had been a long-time direct report to that firm's much-

respected CEO, Louis Gerstner. The Xerox directors were aware of the turn-around success that had followed Lou Gerstner at his stints not only at IBM but also at R. J. Reynolds and American Express. Because Xerox was in the midst of an attempted turnaround itself, the directors believed that Thoman would be able to fix Xerox's problems the way Gerstner had fixed IBM's.

29. Mauer (1997) "Optimism Over New CEO Boosts Stanley Works' Stk Again."

30. It has never actually been clear what Trani meant by the phrase "Coca-Cola of hardware." Yet Stanley Works today remains a traditional manufacturer trapped in a cyclical industry, with no obvious way out.

31. Goffman (1967) *Interaction Ritual*.

32. The résumé Dunlap had presented to Sunbeam (and to Scott Paper before that) turned out to have concealed not just his dismissal as president of Nitec Paper Corporation (where he was accused of producing fictitious profits by means of off-the-books expenses, overstated inventory, and nonexistent sales) in 1976 but also his firing, six months before he joined Nitec, by another company that had accused him of behavior damaging to its business, after only seven weeks on the job. As a result of Dunlap's alleged conduct at Sunbeam, where he served from July 1996 until June 1998, the company was forced to re-state financial results for six quarters ending March 31, 1998. Sunbeam filed for bankruptcy protection early in 2001, while Dunlap was targeted in separate law-suits brought by shareholders and the SEC. Meanwhile, two of the Big Four ex-ecutive search firms were implicated in Dunlap's successful misrepresentation of his past, as neither Korn/Ferry (which handled Sunbeam's CEO search in 1996) nor Spencer Stuart (employed by Scott Paper in the 1994 search that led to Dunlap's hiring there) had detected the falsifications in his résumé. See Norris (2001) "The Incomplete Résumé"; Greene (2002) "Former Sunbeam Chief Plans To Settle Class-Action Lawsuit"; and Lublin (2001) "Search Firms Have Red Faces In Dunlap Flap." For an account of Dunlap's sociopathic management style (from which I have quoted in chapter 3), see Byrne (1999) *Chainsaw*.

33. The decision as to whether to move or not is akin to the problem that economist Robert Frank (1985) refers to as choosing one's pond, as candidates consider whether it is better to be a big fish in a small pond or vice versa. While the research often suggests that the former is preferable to the latter in terms of monetary rewards, most CEOs regard status as so important that they are willing to make the jump to the larger pond when given the opportunity. One factor in their decisions is that CEO employment contracts now cushion the economic downside of such gambles considerably. The same cannot be said, however, for the reputational consequences of failure.

Chapter Seven: Open Positions, Closed Shops

1. Colvin (2001b) "The Great CEO Pay Heist."

2. Institute for Policy Studies (2000) *Executive Excess 2000: Seventh Annual CEO Compensation Survey.*

3. A 2000 study by the research firm Sanford Bernstein found that companies will have to spend 13 percent of their earnings to pay for existing stock option grants. The figure is close to 50 percent for high-technology companies. See Fox (2001) "The Amazing Stock Option Sleight of Hand," 88.

4. Perry and Zenner (2000) "CEO Compensation in the 1990s."

5. Robert Merton and Myron Scholes shared the 1997 Nobel Prize in Economics for their work on the Black-Scholes formula for pricing options.

6. For example, in 1993, the Financial Accounting Standards Board (FASB), which sets the legally recognized standards for financial accounting and reporting, was confident enough in the accuracy of Black-Scholes for estimating the value of a stock option to propose that the cost of options be included in a company's earnings statements. In response, corporate lobbyists descended on Washington to make the claim that expensing stock options would result in a decrease in the number of options that firms would be willing to grant. Congress and the SEC ended up killing the FASB proposal (Edwards [2002] "Enron Collapse"). In the winter of 2001–02, it appeared possible that one upshot of the Enron scandal would be Federal legislation requiring companies to book stock options as expenses, although corporate opposition to such measures remained as fierce as ever.

7. While many people argue that the amount that a CEO is paid is negligible compared to the total wealth of the firm, one also needs to consider that if the CEO's pay is out of line, it is likely that the senior executives who are immediately around him are also being overpaid (see table 7.1).

8. Green (2001), 638.

9. Frank and Cook (1995) *The Winner-Take-All Society,* 640.

10. Bok (1993) *The Cost of Talent,* 225.

11. See chapter 2 for further discussion of how the work of Bok and Graef Crystal illuminates the link between the peculiar conditions of the external CEO labor market and the ratcheting up of CEO pay.

12. Jensen (1986) "Agency Costs of Free Cash Flow, Corporate Finance, and Takeovers"; Lazear (1995) *Personnel Economics;* Murphy (1986) "Top Executives Are Worth Every Nickel They Get"; Rosen (1981) "The Economics of Superstars"; Rosen (1986) "Prizes and Incentives in Elimination Tournaments"; and Rosen (1996) "The Winner-Take-All Society."

13. See chapter 2 for a review of the scholarly literature on the link between the CEO and corporate performance.

14. Michaels, Handfield-Jones, and Axelrod (2001) *The War for Talent*.

15. Pfeffer (1994) *Competitive Advantage*.

16. While the combination of the chairman and CEO positions is not necessarily in the best interests of the firm, it remains, of course, the dominant convention in U.S. governance practices. Yet even if the board would like to bestow the chairmanship on a new CEO, it would seem to make sense to wait for a reasonable period to see how the incoming CEO performs. CEOs advocate on behalf of the structures that they perceive to be best for themselves, not necessarily those that are best for the firm. The governance design outcomes most commonly seen reflect the power that charismatic candidates exercise over boards that are bent on hiring a corporate savior at any cost.

17. Bell (1996) *The Cultural Contradictions of Capitalism*, 77.

18. Weber (1985) *The Protestant Ethic and the Spirit of Capitalism*, 540.

19. Bell (1996) *The Cultural Contradictions of Capitalism*, 78. While Bell distinguishes between the "Protestant ethic" and the "Puritan temper" as codes of value, I use the two terms interchangeably.

20. The facts, again, are well known, but some of them are still worth repeating here. Since the 1970s, the top 1 percent of households have doubled their share of the national wealth. In 1997, the top 1 percent of Americans had more wealth than the entire bottom 95 percent. As the wealth gap between the top 10 percent and bottom 10 percent of Americans has increased, the middle class has been the biggest loser over the last quarter-century. Middle-class wealth and earnings are falling as a share of total wealth and earnings in the United States, despite an economy that has dramatically increased per capita GDP. Simply put, the American middle class upon which our whole economic, political, and social system is founded is receding rapidly. The average worker, adjusting for inflation, is now making less than the average worker did during the Nixon administration. Anderson and Cavanaugh (1999) "A Decade of Executive Excess", 144.

21. As quoted in Bok (1993) *The Cost of Talent*, 249.

22. "A company that bets its future on its people must remove that lower 10 percent, and keep removing it every year—always raising the bar of performance and increasing the quality of its leadership," Jack Welch announced to his shareholders early in 2001 (Burrough [2001], 608), later reiterating this assertion in his address to Harvard Business School's graduating class of that year. This approach reflects a Darwinian view that to improve an organization the weak, rather than be brought up to a higher level of skill and achievement, must be left to perish. It is a low-end tool that should have died out with other

statistically discriminating practices, since many of those affected tend to be women, minorities, and other groups that are underrepresented in managerial positions.

23. Temin (1998) "The Stability of the American Business Elite," 34.

24. Friedman and Selden (1975) *Capitalism and Freedom*.

25. Sørensen and Tuma (1981) "Labor Market Structures and Job Mobility."

26. Abbott (1988) *The System of Professions*.

27. Just as the notion of social closure in external CEO selection as an intentionally discriminatory process is simplistic and misleading, so too are human-capital explanations that would maintain, for example, that legitimated candidates are qualitatively different from those that are excluded by the external CEO selection process. The latter view is unpersuasive, given the difficulty in separating the two groups along any meaningful set of characteristics and the poor quality of available information about candidates' capabilities. The process of allocating people to the position of CEO is not a black box whose inner workings can be understood only by the application of an abstruse concept such as "human capital." One can ignore the sociological dimensions within which such allocations take place only at the cost of significant misspecification and error in recounting the process.

28. As an example of explicitly religious faith in the self-regulating power of markets, consider former Enron CEO Kenneth Lay's declaration in the midst of the recent California power crisis: "I believe in God and I believe in free markets." Dolbee (2001) "Prophet or Profit?"

29. I know of one firm that has had three CEOs in the space of five years. After three CEO firings during this period, the board, in each case, almost immediately embarked on the search for the next chief executive, believing that it would find someone else to rescue the company despite its having chosen so badly before.

30. Popper (1962) *The Open Society and Its Enemies*, vol. I, 126 (italics original).

31. Ibid., 135.

32. The structure of contemporary MBA education is a particularly potent means of socializing students, inducing them to internalize certain ideas, values, and norms, and diffusing these ideas, values, and norms throughout the organizations that these individuals later join. As the anthropologist and business school professor John Van Mannen (1983) has noted, the inculcation of a particular set of ideas and attitudes is particularly powerful in fulltime MBA programs, which are often characterized by intense educational and social experiences. To paraphrase his findings, Van Mannen says that the internalization of ideas in these programs is especially thorough because of the elimina-

tion of the barriers ordinarily separating social and educational life, and the total absorption of the students in this milieu, so that life within the setting of the program becomes reality itself. In fulltime MBA programs such as those at Harvard Business School or MIT's Sloan School of Management (which Van Mannen analyzes using Erving Goffman's concept of the "total institution"), all aspects of student life are conducted in the same building or buildings and under the same single administrative authority, with students having limited contact with anyone or anything outside of the institution. Most of the educational experience is undergone in the immediate company of a large group of socially similar others, all of whom are treated alike and required to read and discuss hundreds of the same case studies. In such a setting, great importance is placed on students' acquiring the ability to socialize with their peers in ways that allow for the building of trust, the free and easy exchange of information, and so forth. Not surprisingly, such an environment becomes a highly effective medium for transmitting the traditions, beliefs, attitudes, and behaviors that characterize the business elite.

The intense educational and social experiences described above then carry over from the business school environment to the world of business itself, where they form the bases of important professional networks that sustain and reinforce the values and ideas absorbed in business school by those who have directly obtained a professional business degree. Many of the graduates of fulltime MBA programs go on to take high-status positions in organizations as managers and executives, roles in which they are highly visible. Individuals hoping to have their stature reinforced by a resemblance to these high-status individuals then often copy their beliefs, attitudes, and behaviors.

33. In response to the increasing demands made on students in MBA programs, there has been a recent tendency to shorten cases. In the editing process, the sections of a case dealing with the organizational, industry, and macroeconomic context are often the first to be compressed.

34. Cohen, March, and Carnegie Commission on Higher Education (1974) *Leadership and Ambiguity*.

35. Michael Porter and Linda Hill, both of the Harvard Business School, are now separately suggesting that we need to abandon our traditional conceptions of leadership and equip students and managers with new frameworks, theories, and approaches to this topic. Porter has undertaken a new research project that, in part, seeks to integrate competitive strategy and leadership frameworks. His goal is to highlight that leaders are only one component—albeit a sometimes critical one—of a complex organizational system leading to sustainable competitive advantage, and to bring to the fore the impact of industry structure and competitive dynamics on firm performance. A new initiative of Hill's

departs even more significantly from conventional leadership perspectives. Her work increasingly suggests that leadership is actually a collective property rather than an individual one. That is, leadership behaviors—setting direction, creative problem-solving, and risk-taking—are a consequence of particular organizational structures, such as decentralized decision-making and organizing tasks around teams, and not simply the province of individuals. While such a concept of leadership runs counter to the ethos of American individualism, Hill has begun to accumulate an impressive body of case studies indicating that the most effective organizations are those in which leadership behaviors are diffused throughout the organization, not confined to a few "elect" individuals.

36. Eccles and Nohria with Berkley (1993) *Beyond the Hype*.

37. Barber (1980) *The Pulse of Politics*.

38. See chapter 3 on the role of the contemporary business press in the rise of the charismatic CEO.

39. The neglect of social structure, culture, and social institutions in economics today is surprising, given the history of the discipline. Indeed, the great original thinkers in the field—Adam Smith, David Ricardo, and Alfred Marshall, for example—were motivated by the idea of creating social institutions to better the lot of society. The Austrian school of economists, especially von Hayek and Schumpeter, cared deeply about institutions and the nature of the interrelationships between economics and social structure. Commons and Veblen, both leading American economists in the early twentieth century, brought culture and society to the forefront of their analyses, arguing that these were the motors of economic action, not peripheral to it. All of these individuals described the disruptive role of technology in society, the role of political institutions in shaping the relationships between capital and labor, the importance of status in determining consumption patterns, and the tendency of capitalists to find ways to short-circuit competition through a variety of macro-closure mechanisms (e.g., cartels, trade barriers, and price-fixing agreements).

These economic thinkers also repeatedly warned against the application of abstract economic theorizing at the expense of empirical data, and about treating the market as a process distinct from the larger society. These now-unfashionable heretics have largely been forgotten by contemporary economists but are carefully read by those outside of the economics profession. Among those who have learned from them is the political theorist Francis Fukuyama, who has pointed out the critical role of a culture of trust as both a source of social cohesion and a lubricant in the marketplace (see Fukuyama [1995] *Trust)*. Another is the sociologist Diego Gambetta, who has argued that when capitalist markets are superimposed on societies in which state institutions (such as courts, the police, and the enforcement of property rights) are weak, we are likely to see the rise of mafias—which is exactly what has happened in Russia (see Gambetta [1993] *The Sicilian Mafia*). The concept of social capital as a means of both enabling and constraining market opportunities while also providing the foundations of a civil society is a product of sociology. Yet sociologists are rarely brought into debates about economic policy, in America or abroad. Meanwhile, even though a few intrepid explorers within economics (especially in the emerging fields of behavioral economics and institutional economics) are venturing across the boundaries separating their discipline from others, most economists ignore such fields as psychology, sociology, anthropology, and history. The result is a surprising amount of economic research that seems to ignore the infinite variety of human traits, the historical and environmental factors that help shape them, and the values that underlie them.

40. For almost a quarter-century now, neoclassical assumptions about the market have pervaded, colored, and organized our understanding of all market phenomena, and neoclassical economic explanations of the world—cloaked in mathematical formulas all but impenetrable to outsiders—have been elevated to the highest status. In the meantime, we have lost the ability to think critically about what is, at its core, a social rather than a natural science. The implications of this loss became especially evident in the last decade of the twentieth century, when at the hour of capitalism's greatest victory—the fall of the Soviet empire—the West could offer Russia nothing better than the free-market nostrums that have taken such a fearsome toll on that long-suffering nation. History now seems to be repeating itself in the case of Argentina. An exploration of how neoclassical economics has come to wield the authority that it does—despite its manifest failure to understand and explain much observable economic reality—might begin by considering the increasing power and prestige of the natural sciences over the last century, and the strategies with which various disciplines in the social sciences and even the humanities have responded to this development.

Appendix: Research Design, Methods, and Sample

1. I took two steps to make sure that my reliance on the two largest search firms for data on CEO searches offered a representative sampling of the broader large-company CEO labor market. First, I compared the firm characteristics of the 100 cases I had collected against a random sample of 100 firms from an 850-firm sample of large corporations. I did not find any statistically significant difference between these two sets of firms along the characteristics of sales, num-

ber of employees, sales-growth rates, percentage of outsider board members, and total shareholder return. I also provided the search firms I was studying with a list of 100 firms from my sample that I knew had experienced CEO turnover in the previous five years but were not clients of either of these firms. I asked search consultants at both firms to identify the firms that had conducted the searches for these companies. Again, using the criteria of sales, employees, sales growth, percentage of outsider board members, and total shareholder return, I compared these firms against the 100 cases I had collected. Again, I found no statistical differences between these two groups.

2. I also present ran a simple logit model that considers the choice of insider versus outsider selection conditional on the existing CEO departing. The results are similar.

3. The presence of multi-colinearity means that while the regression estimates retain all their desirable properties, the variances of the regressor estimates of the parameters of co-linear variables are quite large. These high variances arise because in the presence of multi-colinearity the regression-estimating procedure is not given enough independent variation in a variable to calculate with confidence the effect it has on the dependent variables. Having high variances means that the parameter estimates are not precise and hypothesis testing is not powerful because diverse hypotheses about the parameter values between centrality as measured by interlocks, and centrality as measured by Bonacich power, cannot be rejected.

REFERENCES

Abbott, Andrew Delano. 1988. *The System of Professions: An Essay on the Division of Expert Labor.* Chicago: University of Chicago Press.

Akerlof, George A. 1970. "The Market for 'Lemons': Qualitative Uncertainty and the Market Mechanism." *Quarterly Journal of Economics* 84: 488–500.

Amihud, Yakov, and Baruch Lev. 1981. "Risk Reduction as a Managerial Motive for Conglomerate Mergers." *Bell Journal of Economics* 12: 605–17.

Anderson, Sarah, and John Cavanaugh. 1999. "A Decade of Executive Excess: The 1990s." Sixth Annual Executive Compensation Survey (September).

Andrade, Gregor, Mark Mitchell, and Erik Stafford. 2001. "New Evidence and Perspectives on Mergers." *Journal of Economic Perspectives* 15 (no. 2): 103–20.

Anonymous. 1998. "Finance and Economics: Fall Guy." *The Economist* (November 7): 76–77.

Baker, George P., and George David Smith. 1998. *The New Financial Capitalists: Kohlberg Kravis Roberts and the Creation of Corporate Value.* Cambridge: Cambridge University Press.

Baker, Wayne. 1984. "The Social Structure of a National Securities Market." *American Journal of Sociology* 89: 775–811.

Barber, James David. 1980. *The Pulse of Politics: Electing Presidents in the Media Age.* New York: W.W. Norton.

Baron, James N., Frank R. Dobbin, and P. Deveraux Jennings. 1986. "War and Peace: The Evolution of Modern Personnel Administration in U.S. Industry." *American Journal of Sociology* 92: 350–83.

Beckett, Paul, and Anita Raghavan. 1999. "Former Citigroup President Dimon Gets $30 Million Separation Package." *Wall Street Journal* (April 3): C1

Bell, Daniel. 1996. *The Cultural Contradictions of Capitalism.* New York: Basic Books.

Berger, Peter L., and Thomas Luckmann. 1967. *The Social Construction of Reality.* New York: Doubleday.

Berle, Adolf A., and G. Means. 1932. *The Modern Corporation and Private Property*. New York: MacMillan.

Bertrand, Marianne, and Sendhil Mullainathan. 2000. "Do CEOs Set Their Own Pay? The Ones without Principals Do." NBER Working Paper No. W7604.

Birger, Jon. 2000. "Glowing Numbers." *Money* (November): 112–19.

Blalock, Hubert M., Jr. 1967. *Toward a Theory of Minority Group Relations*. New York: John Wiley.

Blau, Peter, and Otis D. Duncan. 1967. *The American Occupational Structure*. New York: Wiley.

Bleakley, Fred R., Peter Pae, and Michael Siconolfi. 1993. "Robinson Quits at American Express; As Board Support Unravels, Chairman Resigns Post; Succesor to Be Named." *Wall Street Journal* (February 1): A3.

Blossfeld, Hans-Peter, and Gotz Rohwer. 1995. *Techniques of Event-History Modeling: New Approach to Causal Analysis*. Mahwah, N.J.: Erlbaum.

Bok, Derek Curtis. 1993. *The Cost of Talent: How Executives and Professionals Are Paid and How It Affects America*. New York: Free Press.

Bonacich, Edna. 1973. "A Theory of Middleman Minorities." *American Sociological Review* 38 (no. 5): 583–94.

Bonacich, Phillip. 1987. "Power and Centrality: A Family of Measures." *American Journal of Sociology* 92: 1170-82.

Borkovich, Kenneth A., Robert Parrino, and Teresa Trapani. 1996. "Outside Directors and CEO Selection." Working paper, University of Texas, Austin.

Boyle, Matthew. 2001. "The Dirty Half-Dozen: America's Worst Boards." *Fortune* 143 (May 14): 249–51.

Brandeis, Louis Dembitz, Alfred Lief, and United States Supreme Court. 1930. *The Social and Economic Views of Mr. Justice Brandeis*. New York: Vanguard Press.

Brandeis, Louis Dembitz, and Ernest Poole. 1914. *Business—A Profession*. Boston: Small Maynard & Company.

Brandeis, Louis Dembitz, Osmond Kessler Fraenkel, and Clarence M. Lewis. 1965. *The Curse of Bigness: Miscellaneous Papers of Louis D. Brandeis*. Port Washington, N.Y.: Kennikat Press.

Braudy, Leo. 1986. *The Frenzy of Renown: Fame and Its History*. New York: Oxford University Press.

Brooks, David. 2000. *Bobos in Paradise: The New Upper Class and How They Got There*. New York: Simon & Schuster.

Brown, Roger. 1986. *Social Psychology: The Second Edition*. New York: The Free Press.

Brown, Warren, and Frank Swoboda. 1992. "Stempel Steps Down As Chairman of GM." *Washington Post* (October 27): A1.

Brunswick, Roger, and Gary E. Hayes. 2000. "Dimon in the Rough." *USBanker* 110: 93–94.

Burrough, Bryan, and John Helyar. 1990. *Barbarians at the Gate: The Fall of RJR Nabisco*. New York: Harper & Row.

Burrough, D.J. 2001. "More Firms Rank Employees: Workers at Bottom of Scale Left Vulnerable to Layoffs." Dow Jones Newswire (May 20).

Burrows, Peter, and Peter Elstrom. 1999. "The Boss." *Business Week* (August 2): 76.

Burt, R. 1992. *Structural Holes: The Social Structure of Competition*. Cambridge: Harvard University Press.

BusinessWire. 1993. "Golub Elected Chief Executive of American Express Company; Robinson to Continue as Chairman, Will Also Head Shearson Lehman." (January 25).

Byrne, John. 1986. *The Headhunters*. New York: Macmillan.

———. 1993. "Requiem for Yesterday's CEO; Old-style Execs Who Can't Adapt Are Losing Their Hold." *Business Week* (February 15): 32.

———. 1998. "I Had a Pal in My Mom." *Business Week* (June 8): 110.

———. 1999. *Chainsaw: The Notorious Career of Al Dunlap in the Era of Profit-at-any-Price*. New York: HarperBusiness.

Cahill, Joseph. 1999. "CEO McCoy Quits a Flagging Bank One; Credit-Card Bet Faltered; Stock Price Jumps 11%; Istock is Acting Chief." *The Wall Street Journal* (December 22): A3.

Carroll, Glenn, and Michael T. Hannan. 2000. *The Demography of Corporations and Industries*. Princeton, N.J.: Princeton University Press.

Catalyst. 1998. "The 1998 Catalyst Census of Women Board Directors of the Fortune 500." Catalyst.

Challenger, Gray, and Christmas. 2001. *Annual CEO Turnover Report*.

Chandler, Alfred D. 1977. *The Visible Hand: The Managerial Revolution in American Business*. Cambridge: Harvard University Press.

———. 1962. *Strategy and Structure: Chapters in the History of the Industrial Enterprise*. Cambridge: MIT Press.

Child, John. 1972. "Organizational Structure, Environment and Performance: The Role of Strategic Choice." *Sociology* 6: 1–22.

Cohen, Michael D., James G. March, and Carnegie Commission on Higher Education. 1974. *Leadership and Ambiguity: The American College President*. New York: McGraw-Hill.

Colvin, Geoffrey. 1999. "We Hate to Say We Told You So, But . . . Well, We Don't Actually Hate It—And We Did Tell You." *Fortune* (www.fortune.com/indexw.jhtml?channel=artcol.jhtml&doc_id=29123).

———. 2001a. "Changing of the Guard." *Fortune* (January 8): 84–99.

Colvin, Geoffrey. 2001b. "The Great CEO Pay Heist." *Fortune* (June 25): 64.

Core, John E., Robert W. Holthausen, and David L. Larcker. 1997. "Corporate Governance, CEO Compensation, and Firm Performance." Working paper, University of Pennsylvania, Wharton School.

Coughlin, Richard J. 1976. *Double Identity: The Chinese in Modern Thailand.* Westport, Conn.: Greenwood Press.

Cramer, Richard Ben. 1992. *What It Takes: The Way to the White House.* New York: Random House.

Crystal, Graef S. 1992. *In Search of Excess: The Overcompensation of American Executives.* New York: Norton.

Davis, Gerald F. 1991. "Agents without Principles? The Spread of the Poison Pill through the Intercorporate Network." *Administrative Science Quarterly* 36: 583–613.

Davis, Gerald, and Henrich Greve. 1997. "Corporate Elite Networks and Governance Changes in the 1980s." *American Journal of Sociology* 103: 1–37.

Davis, Michael. 2000. "No Ordinary Jeff; Skilling Will Take Reins at Enron; Lay's Successor Praised for His Skills and Vision." *Houston Chronicle* (December 14): 1.

Desai, Rashmi H. 1963. *Indian Immigrants in Britain.* New York: Oxford University Press, issued under the auspices of the Institute of Race Relations, London.

Dobryzynski, Judith H. 1996. "AT&T's Romancing of John Walter." *New York Times* (October 24): D1.

Doereinger, P., and M. J. Piore. 1971. *Internal Labor Markets and Manpower Analysis.* New York: M.E. Sharpe & Company.

Dolbee, Sandi. 2001. "Prophet or Profit? Energy Chief, Religious Leaders Dispute God's Role in Utility Price Spiral." *San Diego Union-Tribune* (February 2): E1.

Donlon, J. P. 2000. "Why John Chambers Is the CEO of the Future." *Chief Executive Magazine* (July): 157–64.

Douglas, Mary. 1986. *How Institutions Think.* Syracuse, N.Y.: Syracuse University Press.

Dowd, Ann Reilly. 2001. "Seven Ways to Attract Analysts and Investors." *Corporate Board Member* 4 (no. 1): 26–34.

Dumaine, Brian. 1993. "What's So Hot about Outsiders?" *Fortune* (November 29): 63.

Dumont, Louis. 1980. *Homo Hierarchicus: The Caste System and Its Implications.* Chicago: University of Chicago Press.

Durkheim, Emile, and Marcel Mauss. 1963. *Primitive Classification.* Chicago: University of Chicago Press.

Eccles, Robert G., and Dwight B. Crane. 1988. *Doing Deals: Investment Banks at Work*. Boston: Harvard Business School Press.

Eccles, Robert G., N. Nohria, and J. Berkley. 1993. *Beyond the Hype*. Boston: Harvard Business School Press.

Edwards, Robert. 2002. "Enron Collapse." *Morning Edition*. National Public Radio, January 22.

Elstrom, Peter. 2001. "How the 'Turnaround CEO' Failed to Deliver." *Business Week* (July 23): 36.

Engen, John. 2000. "Hiring a Celebrity CEO." *Corporate Board Member* 3 (no. 4): 38–48.

Fama, Eugene F., and Michael C. Jensen. 1983. "Separation of Ownership and Control." *Journal of Law and Economics* 26: 301–25.

Feldman, Amy. 2000. "Has Bank One Found its Savior?" *Money* (July): 62–64.

Festinger, Leon. 1954. "A Theory of Social Comparison Processes." *Human Relations* 7: 117–40.

Fitch, Jessica Madore. 2000. "Dimon Dose a Shot in Arm for Bank One; CEO's Promise of 'Strong Medicine' Gives Stock a Boost." *Chicago Sun-Times* (July 20): 55.

Fligstein, Neil. 1990. *The Transformation of Corporate Control*. Cambridge: Harvard University Press.

Fox, Justin. 2001. "The Amazing Stock Option Sleight of Hand." *Fortune* (June 25): 86–91.

Frank, Robert H. 1985. *Choosing the Right Pond: Human Behavior and the Quest for Status*. New York: Oxford University Press.

Frank, Robert H., and Philip J. Cook. 1995. *The Winner-Take-All Society: How More and More Americans Compete for Ever Fewer and Bigger Prizes, Encouraging Economic Waste, Income Inequality, and an Impoverished Cultural Life*. New York: Free Press.

Friedman, Benjamin M. 1995. "Economic Implications of Changing Share Ownership." NBER Working Paper.

Friedman, Milton, and Richard T. Selden. 1975. *Capitalism and Freedom: Problems and Prospects; Proceedings of a Conference in Honor of Milton Friedman*. Charlottesville: University Press of Virginia.

Fromson, Brett D. 1990. "The Big Owners Roar." *Fortune* (July 30) : 66–78.

Fukuyama, Francis. 1992. *The End of History and the Last Man*. New York : Free Press.

———. 1995. *Trust: Social Virtues and the Creation of Prosperity*. New York: Free Press.

Galaskiewicz, Joseph, and Stanley Wasserman. 1990. "Mimetic and Normative

Processes within an Organizational Field: An Empirical Test." *Administrative Science Quarterly* 34: 454–80.

Gambetta, Diego. 1993. *The Sicilian Mafia: The Business of Private Protection.* Cambridge: Harvard University Press.

Geertz, Clifford. 1973. *The Interpretation of Cultures.* New York: Basic Books.

Ghemawat, Pankaj. 2000. "Egon Zehnder International: Managing Professionals in an Executive Search Firm." Case study, Harvard Business School.

Glassman, Ronald M., and William H. Swatos. 1986. *Charisma, History, and Social Structure.* New York: Greenwood.

Goblot, Edmond. 1925. *La Barrière et le Nieveau.* Paris: Presses Universitaires de Frances.

Goffman, Erving. 1963a. *Behavior in Public Places: Notes on the Social Organization of Gathering.* New York: Free Press.

———. 1963b. *The Presentation of Self in Everyday Life.* Garden City, N.Y.: Doubleday.

———. 1967. *Interaction Ritual: Essays on Face-to-Face Behavior.* Garden City. N.Y.: Anchor Books.

Goode, William Josiah. 1978. *The Celebration of Heroes: Prestige as a Social Control System.* Berkeley: University of California Press.

Granovetter, Mark, and Charles Tilly. 1988. "Inequality and Labor Processes." Pp. 175–221 in Neil Smelser, ed., *Handbook of Sociology.* Newbury Park, Calif.: Sage.

Granovetter, Mark. 1974. *Getting a Job: A Study of Contacts and Careers.* Cambridge: Harvard University Press.

———. 1985. "Economic Action and Social Structure: The Problem of Embeddedness." *American Journal of Sociology* 91: 481–510.

Green, Sandy E. 2001. "Rhetoric and the Institutionalization of Takeover Defenses in the S&P 1500 from 1975 to 1998." Dissertation, Harvard Business School.

Greene, Kelly. 2002. "Former Sunbeam Chief Plans To Settle Class-Action Lawsuit; Dunlap Will Pay $15 Million to Shareholders." *Asian Wall Street Journal* (January 16): 10.

Greene, William H. 1993. *Econometric Analysis.* Saddle River, N.J.: Prentice-Hall.

Grover, Stephen. 1980. "Outsider Chief at International Paper Vows to Develop Inside Succession Line." *Wall Street Journal* (January 21): 12.

Groysberg, Boris. 2001. "Can They Take It with Them? The Portability of Star Knowledge Workers' Performance: Myth or Reality?" Ph.D. dissertation, Harvard Business School.

Hambrick, Donald, and Eric M. Jackson. 1999. "Outside Directors with a Stake: The Linchpin in Improving Governance." Working paper, Columbia University Graduate School of Business.

Hambrick, Donald, and Sidney Finkelstein. 1987. "Managerial Discretion: A Bridge between Polar Views of Organizational Outcomes." *Research in Organizational Behavior* 9: 369–406.

Hannan, M. T., and J. Freeman. 1989. *Organizational Ecology.* Cambridge: Harvard University Press.

Hansen, Morten. 1996. "Searching for and Transferring Knowledge through the Intra-Company Network: Implications for Fast Product Innovation." Ph.D. dissertation, Stanford University.

Hart, Myra, and Hugo Utyerhoven. 1996. "Banc One—1993." Case study, Harvard Business School.

Harvard Business School. 1982. *Reginald Jones—General Electric, Management Succession.* HBS Video Cases. Boston: Harvard Business School. Running time 12:20.

Haunschild, P. R. 1993. "Interorganizational Imitation: The Impact of Interlocks on Corporate Acquisition Activity." *Administrative Science Quarterly* 38: 564–92.

Hintz, John. 2000. "Boy Wonder: CEO Jamie Dimon's Street Smarts Could Step Up Banc [*sic*] One Securities' Game. And That Would Change the Rules for Everyone." *Bank Investment Marketing* (June 1): 45.

Hopkins, Jan, John Defterios, and Steve Young. 1997. "New AT&T Presidential Search Begins." Cable News Network, *CNNfn: Biz Buzz,* July 17.

Hudson, Mike, Robert Parrino, and L. Stark. 1997. "The Effectiveness of Internal Monitoring Mechanisms: Evidence from CEO Turnover from 1971–1994." Manuscript, University of Texas, Austin.

Hull, C. Bryson. 2001. "Enron's CEO Fires from the Lip." Reuters New Agency (April 18).

Institute for Policy Studies. 2000. *Executive Excess 2000: Seventh Annual CEO Compensation Survey.*

Institutional Investment Report. 1998. "Conference Board Report."

Janowitz, Morris, and Dwaine Marvick. 1953. "Authoritarianism and Political Behavior." *Public Opinion Quarterly* 17: 185–201.

Jencks, Christopher. 1979. *Who Gets Ahead? The Determinants of Economic Success in America.* New York: Basic Books.

Jensen, Michael C. 1986. "Agency Costs of Free Cash Flow, Corporate Finance, and Takeovers." *American Economic Review* 48: 323–29.

———. 1993. "The Modern Industrial Revolution, Exit, and the Failure of Internal Control Systems." *Journal of Finance* 48: 831–80.

Jensen, Michael, and Kevin Murphy. 1990a. "CEO Incentives—It's Not How Much You Pay, But How." *Harvard Business Review* 16: 138–53.

———. 1990b. "Performance Pay and Top Management Incentives." *Journal of Political Economy* 98: 225–64.

Jones, Del, Eric Randall, and John Hillkirk. 1993. "Kodak Snaps Up Chief from Motorola; Fisher Arose in Culture of Conflict." *USA Today* (October 28): 01B.

Kahn, Jeremy. 2001. "Accounting in Wonderland." *Fortune* (March 19): 134–37.

Kanter, Rosabeth M. 1973. *Communes: Creating and Managing the Collective Life*. Cambridge: Harvard University Press.

Kennedy, Peter. 1992. *A Guide to Econometrics*. Cambridge: MIT Press.

Kerwin, Kathleen with Keith Naughton. 1999. "Remaking Ford: In His Quest to Make Ford a More Consumer-Oriented Powerhouse, Nasser Is Off to a Fast Start." *Business Week* (October 11): 132–40.

Keynes, John Maynard. 1973. *The General Theory of Employment, Interest, and Money*. New York: Harcourt Brace (originally published 1936).

Khurana, Rakesh. 1998. "The Changing of the Guard: Causes, Process, and Consequences of CEO Succession." Ph.D. dissertation, Harvard University.

Khurana, R., and N. Nohria 1996. "Substance and Symbol: The Effects of CEO Turnover in Large Industrial Organizations." Working paper, Harvard Business School.

Kotter, John P. 1988. *The Leadership Factor*. New York: Free Press.

———. 1990. *A Force for Change: How Leadership Differs from Management*. New York: Free Press.

Laing, Jonathan R. 2000. "Fixer-Upper: Can Jamie Dimon Restore Bank One's Lost Luster?" *Barron's* (July 3): 21–24.

Lawrence, P., and J. Lorsch. 1967. *Organization and Environment*. Boston: Harvard Business School Press.

Lazear, Edward P. 1995. *Personnel Economics*. Cambridge, Mass.: MIT Press.

Logue, Dennis E., and Philippe A. Naert. 1970. "A Theory of Conglomerate Mergers: Comment and Extension." *Quarterly Journal of Economics* 84: 663–667.

Loomis, Carol J. 2000. "Dimon Finds His 'Fat Pitch'; One Bank that Needs Saving." *Fortune* (April 17): 64–66.

Lorsch, Jay W. 1996. "American Express (A)." Boston: Harvard Business School. Harvard Business School Case Study 494093.

Lorsch, Jay W., and Elizabeth MacIver. 1989. *Pawns and Potentates: The Reality of America's Corporate Boards*. Boston: Harvard Business School Press.

Lowenstein, Roger. 2000. "Alone At The Top." *The New York Times Magazine* (August 27): 32.

Lublin, Joann S. "Search Firms Have Red Faces In Dunlap Flap." *Wall Street Journal* (July 17): B1.

Madsen, Douglas, and Peter G. Snow. 1991. *The Charismatic Bond: Political Behavior in Time of Crisis*. Cambridge: Harvard University Press.

Mahajani, Usha. 1960. *The Role of Indian Minorities in Burma and Malaya*. Bombay: Vora.

March, J. C., and James G. March. 1977. "Almost Random Careers: The Wisconsin School Superintendency, 1940–1972." *Administrative Science Quarterly* 22: 377–409.

———. 1978. "Performance Matching in Social Matches." *Administrative Science Quarterly* 23: 434–53.

Marsden, Peter V. 1983. "Restricted Access in Networks and Models of Power." *American Journal of Sociology* 88: 686–717.

Margolies, Susan. 1978. "International Paper Says DuPont's Gee Will Become Firm's President on April 1." *Wall Street Journal* (January 16): 16.

Martin, Justin. 2000. *Greenspan: The Man Behind Money*. Cambridge, Mass.: Perseus.

Mathisen, Tyler. 2001. "What I Look for in a TV Guest." *Corporate Board Member* 4:31.

Mauer, Jennifer Fron. 1997. "Optimism Over New CEO Boosts Stanley Works' Stock Again." Dow Jones New Service, January 3.

McGuire, Patrick, Mark Granovetter, and Michael Schwartz. 1991. "Thomas Edison and the Social Construction of the Early Electricity Industry in America." Pp. 231–46 in *Explorations in Economic Sociology*, Richard Swedberg, ed. New York: Russell Sage Foundation.

McLaughlin, Judith Block, and David Riesman. 1990. *Choosing a College President: Opportunities and Constraints*. Princeton, N.J.: Carnegie Foundation for the Advancement of Teaching.

McLaughlin, Judith Block. 1985. "From Secrecy to Sunshine: An Overview of Presidential Search Practice." *Research in Higher Education* 22: 195–208.

———. 1996. *Leadership Transitions: The New College President*. San Francisco: Jossey-Bass.

Mehta, Stephanie N. 2001. "Cisco Fractures Its Own Fairy Tale." *Fortune* (May 14): 104.

Merrick, Amy. 2000. "Bank One Decides to Trim Its Board; Chairman Says Company Needs a Smaller, More Nimble Panel; Many Industries Are Also Cutting Back." *Wall Street Journal, Europe* (August 25).

Merton, Robert K. 1957. *Social Theory and Social Structure: The Self-Fulfilling Prophecy*. Glencoe, Ill.: Free Press.

Metz, Tim. 1979. "International Paper's Profit Outlook Is Rosy but Some Analysts Are Ambivalent on Stock." *Wall Street Journal* (February 12): 29.

Meyer, John W., and Brian Rowan. 1977. "Institutionalized Organizations: Formal Structure as Myth and Ceremony." *American Journal of Sociology* 83: 340–63.

Michaels, Ed, Helen Handfield-Jones, and Beth Axelrod. 2001. *The War for Talent*. Boston: Harvard Business School Press.

Mills, C. Wright. 1956. *The Power Elite*. New York: Oxford University Press.

Mintz, B., and M. Schwartz. 1981. *The Power Structure of American Business*. Chicago: University of Chicago Press.

Mitchell, Mark L., and J. Harold Mulherin. 1996. "The Impact of Industry Shocks on Takeover and Restructuring Activity." *Journal of Financial Economics* 41: 193–229.

Mizruchi, Mark S. 1982. *The American Corporate Network 1904–1974*. Beverly Hills: Sage.

———. 1992. *The Structure of Corporate Political Action: Interfirm Relations and Their Consequences*. Cambridge: Harvard University Press.

———. 1996. "What Do Interlocks do? An Analysis, Critique, and Assessment of Research on Interlocking Directorates." *Annual Review of Sociology* 22: 271–98.

Mizruchi, Mark, and David Bunting. 1981. "Influence in Corporate Networks: An Examination of Four Measures." *Administrative Science Quarterly* 26: 475-89.

Mizruchi, Mark, Peter Mariolis, Michael Schwartz, and Beth Mintz. 1986. "Techniques for Disaggregating Centrality Scores in Social Networks." *Sociological Methodology* 16: 26–48.

Mukul, Pandya. 1997. "Behind the Shuffle at AT&T." *Business News New Jersey* (July 21): 4.

Murphy, Kevin. 1986. "Top Executives Are Worth Every Nickel They Get." *Harvard Business Review* 8: 125–33.

Murphy, Kevin J. 1998. "Executive Compensation." Working paper, Marshall School of Business, University of Southern California; PDF available at www.ssrn.com.

Nohria, Nitin. 1992. "Information and Search in the Creation of New Business Ventures: The Case of the 128 Venture Group." Pp. 240–61 in *Networks and Organizations*, Nitin Nohria and Robert G. Eccles, eds. Boston: Harvard Business School Publishing.

Nohria, Nitin, and Sandy Green. 2002. "Chrysler: Lee Iacocca's Legacy." Harvard Business School Case Study 9-493-017.

Norris, Floyd. 2001. "The Incomplete Résumé: A Special Report; An Executive's Missing Years: Papering Over Past Problems." *New York Times* (July 16): A1.

O'Reilly, Charles A., Brian G. Main, and Graef S. Crystal. 1988. "CEO Compensation as Tournament and Social Comparison." *Administrative Science Quarterly* 33: 257–74.

O'Reilly, Charles A., and Jeffrey Pfeffer. 2000. *Hidden Value: How Great Companies Achieve Extraordinary Results with Ordinary People*. Boston: Harvard Business School Press.

Ocasio, William. 1999. "Institutionalized Action and Corporate Governance: The Reliance on Rules of CEO Succession." *Administrative Science Quarterly* 44: 384–416.

Paltrow, Scott J. 1991. "American Express Tries to Head Off More Surprises." *Los Angeles Times* (July 7): Business 1.

Parkin, Frank. 1971. *Class Inequality and Political Order: Social Stratification in Capitalist and Communist Societies*. New York: Praeger.

———. 1974. *The Social Analysis of Class Structure*. London: Tavistock.

Perry, Todd, and Mark Zenner. 2000. "CEO Compensation in the 1990s: Shareholder Alignment or Shareholder Expropriation?" SSRN Working Paper. University of North Carolina.

Pfeffer, Jeffrey. 1981. "Management as Symbolic Action: The Creation and Maintenance of Organizational Paradigms." *Research in Organizational Behavior* 3: 1–52.

———. *Competitive Advantage through People: Unleashing the Power of the Work Force*. Boston: Harvard Business School Press.

———. 1998. *The Human Equation: Building Profits by Putting People First*. Boston: Harvard Business School Press.

Pfeffer, Jeffrey., and G. Salancik. 1978. *The External Control of Organizations*. New York: Harper & Row.

Podolny, Joel M. 1993. "A Status-Based Model of Market Competition." *American Journal of Sociology* 98 (no. 4): 829–72.

———. 1994. "Market Uncertainty and the Social Character of Economic Exchange." *Administrative Science Quarterly* 39: 458–83.

Polanyi, Karl. 1957. *The Great Transformation*. New York: Rinehart.

Popper, Karl. 1962, 1966. *The Open Society and Its Enemies*. Volume I: *The Spell of Plato*. Princeton, N.J.: Princeton University Press.

Popper, Margaret. 2001. "Bank One Shares May Be Floating on Thin Air." *Business Week* (April 10); see http://www.businessweek.com/bwdaily/dnflash/apr2001/nf20010410_503.htm.

Porter, Michael E. 1990. *The Competitive Advantage of Nations*. New York: Free Press.

Poterba, James. 1997. "The Rate of Return to Corporate Capital and Factor Shares." NBER Working Paper.

Powell, Walter W., and Paul J. Dimaggio. 1983. *The New Institutionalism of Organizational Analysis*. Chicago: University of Chicago Press.

PR Newswire. 1993a. "IBM Chairman John F. Akers Announces CEO Search" (January 26).

————. 1993b. "Westinghouse Chairman Paul Lego to Retire" (January 27).

————. 2000. "Lucent Technologies' Board of Directors Names Henry Schacht Chairman and CEO" (October 23).

Pratt, John W., and Richard J. Zeckhauser. 1991. "The Agency Relationship." Pp. 1–35 in *Principals and Agents: The Structure of Business*, John W. Pratt and Richard J. Zeckhauser, eds. Boston: Harvard Business School Press.

Raghavan, Anita. 1999. "Deals & Deal Makers: Jamie Dimon, in Life After Citigroup, Bides His Time as He Looks for 'The Job'." *Wall Street Journal* (November 12): C1.

Raghavan, Anita, and Paul Beckett. 1999. "Companies Want Dimon To Become 'Mr. dot.com'." *Wall Street Journal Europe* (November 12): 17.

Raghavan, Anita, and Jonathon Sapsford. 2000. "Jamie Dimon Takes Top Spot At Bank One." *Asian Wall Street Journal* (March 29): 13.

Reidy, Chris. 2000. "Gillette Ousts CEO Hawley after 18 Months." *Boston Globe* (October 20): D1.

Reinganum, Mark. 1985. "The Effect of Executive Succession on Stockholder Wealth." *Administrative Science Quarterly* 30: 46–60.

Riesman, David. 1956. *The Lonely Crowd: A Study of the Changing American Character*. Garden City, N.Y.: Doubleday.

Roethlisberger, Fritz Jules. 1947. *Management and the Worker; An Account of a Research Program Conducted by the Western Electric Company, Hawthorne Works, Chicago*. Cambridge: Harvard University Press.

Rosen, Sherwin. 1981. "The Economics of Superstars." *The American Economic Review* 71: 845–58.

————. 1982. "Contracts and the Market for Executives." Pp.181–212 in *Contract Economics*, Lars Wein and Hans Wijkander, eds. New York: Blackwell.

————. 1986. "Prizes and Incentives in Elimination Tournaments." *American Economic Review* 76: 701–15.

————. 1996. "The Winner-Take-All Society." *Journal of Economic Literature* 34: 133–35.

Russell Reynolds Associates. 1994. "Reflections." New York: Russell Reynolds Associates.

————. 2001. "CEO Turnover in a Global Economy, International Survey of Institutional Investors." New York: Russell Reynolds Associates.

Sandler, Linda. 1990. "American Express Dismantles Its Eighties' Superstore." *Wall Street Journal* (January 9): C1.

Santoli, Michael. 2001. "The Whole Truth." *Barron's* (May 28): 23.

Scism, Leslie, Anita Raghavan, and Michael Siconolfi. 1997. "Lost Trust: The Boss's Daughter and Right-Hand Man Clash—and She's Gone; At Smith Barney, Dimon Asked if Bibliowicz Went Around Him to Weill; A Tiff Over No-Load Funds." *Wall Street Journal* (July 3): A1.

Scott, W. Richard. 1995. *Institutions and Organizations*. Thousand Oaks, Calif.: Sage.

Sellers, Patricia. 2000. "What Really Happened at Coke." *Fortune* (January 10): 114

Serwer, Andrew. 2000. "There's Something About Cisco." *Fortune* (May 15): 114.

———. 2001. "My 'Dear John' Letter." *Fortune* (May 14): 114.

Shiller, Robert J. 2000. *Irrational Exuberance*. Princeton, N.J.: Princeton University Press.

Shils, Edward. 1982. "Charisma, Order, and Status." Pp. 199–213 in *The Constitution of Society*, Edward Shils, ed. Chicago: University of Chicago Press.

Shivdasani, Anil, and David Yermack. 1998. "CEO Involvement in the Selection of New Board Members: An Empirical Analysis." Working paper, New York University, Center for Law and Business.

Silverman, Gary, and Leah Nathans Spiro. 1999. "Is This Marriage Working? The Citigroup Merger Is Going Reasonably Well. But There Are Signs of Tension between Weill and Reed." *Business Week* (June 7): 126.

Simmel, Georg. 1902. *The Sociology of Georg Simmel*. Toronto: Free Press.

———. 1955. *The Web of Group Affiliations*. Glencoe, Ill.: Free Press.

Smelser, Neil J., and Richard Swedberg. 1994. *The Handbook of Economic Sociology*. Princeton, N.J.: Princeton University Press.

Smith, Abbie. 1990. "Corporate Ownership and Performance: The Case of Management Buyouts." *Journal of Financial Economies*: 147–64.

Sørensen, Aage B. 1983a. "Processes of Allocation to Open and Closed Positions." *Zeitschrift fur Soziologie* 12: 203–24.

———. 1983b. "Sociological Research on the Labor Market." *Work and Occupations* 10: 261–87.

———. 1998. "Theoretical Mechanisms and the Empirical Study of Social Processes." Pp. 238–86 in *Social Mechanisms*, Peter Hedstrom and Richard Swedberg, eds. Cambridge: Cambridge University Press.

Sørensen, Aage B., and Nancy B. Tuma. 1981. "Labor Market Structures and Job Mobility." *Social Stratification and Mobility* 1: 67–94.

Stearns, Linda Brewster, and Mark Mizruchi. 1993. "Corporate Financing: Economic and Social Aspects." Pp. 603–18 in *Explorations in Economic Sociology*, Richard Swedberg, ed. New York: Russell Sage Foundation.

Strauss, Anselm, and Juliet Corbin. 1990. *Basics of Qualitative Reserach: Grounded Theory Procedures and Techniques*. Thousand Oaks, Calif.: Sage.

Strauss, Cheryl. 2000. "There's No Magic: If a Corporate Savior's Arrival Boosts a Stock Price, Sell." *Barron's* (August 28): 23.

Stuart, Toby, Ha Hoang, and Ralph Hybels. 1999. "Interorganizational Endorsements and the Performance of Entrepreneurial Ventures." *Administrative Science Quarterly* 43: 668–98.

Swedberg, Richard. 1994. "Markets as Social Structures." Pp. 255–82 in *The Handbook of Economic Sociology*, Neil Smelser and Richard Swedberg, eds. Princeton, N.J.: Princeton University Press.

Tarbell, Ida. 1905. "John D. Rockefeller: A Character Study." *McClure's Magazine* (July): 226–49.

Tedlow, Richard S. 2002. *Giants of Enterprise: Seven Business Innovators and the Empires They Built*. New York: HarperBusiness.

Tedlow, Richard S., and Richard R. John. 1986. *Managing Big Business: Essays from the Business History Review*. Boston: Harvard Business School Press.

Temin, Peter. 1997. "The American Business Elite in Historical Perspective." Working paper, National Bureau of Economic Research, Cambridge, Mass.

———. 1998. "The Stability of the American Business Elite." Working paper, National Bureau of Economic Research, Cambridge, Mass.

Thurow, Lester C. 1992. *Head to Head: The Coming Economic Battle among Japan, Europe, and America*. New York: Morrow.

Tilly, Charles. 1998. *Durable Inequality*. Berkeley: University of California Press.

Tuma, Nancy B., and Michael T. Hannan. 1984. *Social Dynamics: Models and Methods*. Orlando, Fla.: Academic Press.

Useem, Michael. 1984. *The Inner Circle*. New York: Oxford University Press.

———. 1993. *Executive Defense: Shareholder Power and Corporate Reorganization*. Cambridge: Harvard University Press.

Van Mannen, John. 1983. "Golden Passports: Managerial Socialization and Graduate Education." *The Review of Higher Education* 6: 435–55.

Vancil, Richard M. 1987. *Passing the Baton: Managing the Process of CEO Succession*. Boston: Harvard Business School Press.

Veblen, Thorstein. 1973. *The Theory of the Leisure Class*, with an introduction by John Kenneth Galbraith. Boston: Houghton Mifflin.

Wahl, Melissa. 2000a. "Bank One Gains Wall Street Credibility with Citigroup Veteran as CEO." *Knight-Ridder Tribune Business News* (March 28).

————. 2000b. "Bank One's Problems Go Deeper than Ailing Credit-Card Division." *Knight-Ridder Tribune Business News* (January 15).

Walsh, Mary Williams. 2001. "Luring the Best in an Unsettled Time." *New York Times* (January 30): 1.

Warren, Robert Penn. 1946. *All the King's Men*. New York: Harcourt Brace.

Wasserman, Noam, Bharat Anand, and Nitin Nohria. 2001. "When Does Leadership Matter? The Contingent Opportunities View of CEO Leadership." Working paper, Harvard Business School.

Watkins, Michael, Carin Knoop, and Cate Reavis. 2000. "The Coca-Cola Company (A): The Rise and Fall of M. Douglas Ivester." Harvard Business School Case Study 9-800-355.

Weber, Max. 1947. *Economy and Society*. Berkeley: University of California Press.

————. 1985. *The Protestant Ethic and the Spirit of Capitalism*. London: Unwin.

Weber, Max, Guenther Roth, and Claus Wittich. 1978. *Economy and Society: An Outline of Interpretive Sociology*. Berkeley: University of California Press.

Weber, Joseph. 2000. "The Mess at Bank One." *Business Week* (May 1): 162–67.

Weiss, Gary. 2000. "Jamie Dimon: The Wrong Man for the Bank One Job?" *Business Week* (April 18): 24.

Weston, J. F. 1970a. "Diversification and Merger Trends." *Business Economics* 5: 50–57.

————. 1970b. "The Nature and Significance of Conglomerate Firms." *St. John's Law Review* 44: 66–80.

Wetlaufer, Suzy. 1999. "Driving Change: An Interview with Ford Motor Company's Jacques Nasser." *Harvard Business Review* (March-April): 78–88.

White, Harrison. 2002. *Markets from Networks: Socioeconomic Models of Production*. Princeton, N.J.: Princeton University Press.

Whyte, William Foote. 1951. "Small Groups and Large Organizations." In *Social Psychology at the Crossroads*, John H. Rohrer and Muzafer Sherif, eds. New York: Harper.

Whyte, William Hollingsworth. 1956. *The Organization Man*. New York: Simon and Schuster.

Williamson, Oliver. 1975. *Markets and Hierarchies*. New York: Free Press.

————. 1981. "The Economics of Organization: The Transaction Cost Approach." *American Journal of Sociology* 87: 548–77.

Woodward, Bob. 2000. *Maestro: Greenspan's Fed and the American Boom*. New York: Simon & Schuster.

Worrell, D., W. Davidson, and J. L. Glascock. 1993. "Stockholder Reactions to Departures and Appointments of Key Executives Attributable to Firings." *Academy of Management Journal* 36: 387–401.

Yoshino, Michael, Carin Knoop, and Cate Reavis. 1998. "Egon Zehnder International: Implementing Practice Groups." Harvard Business School Case Study 9-398-052.

Young, Shawn. 2001. "Lucent Could Cut Jobs, Take Big Charge." *Wall Street Journal* (January 24): B8.

Zelizer, Viviana. 1978. "Human Values and the Market: The Case of Life Insurance and Death in 19th-Century America." *American Journal of Sociology* 84: 591–610.

———. 1981. "The Price and Value of Children." *American Journal of Sociology* 86: 1036–56.

———. 1983. *Morals and Markets: The Development of Life Insurance in the United States*. New York: Transachon Publishers.

Zelleke, Andy. 2001. "The British "Non-executive" Chairman: Corporate Governance or Co-leadership." Ph.D. dissertation, Harvard University.

Zuckerman, Ezra. 1999. "The Categorical Imperative: Securities Analysts and the Legitimacy Discount." *American Journal of Sociology* 104: 198–1437.